PENGUIN BOOKS
BITTER CHOCOLATE

Pinki Virani, forty-one, set a new trend in the genre of faction in India with her best-selling *Aruna's Story*. This book was translated into several Indian languages. Her next work, *Once Was Bombay* was among the first to deal with an Indian city as a socio-political entity—instead of romanticizing it— in story-telling format.

Pinki Virani took an American Masters in Journalism through a scholarship from the Aga Khan foundation, which was followed by an internship at the *Sunday Times* in London. She returned to India and a career in Journalism, eighteen years ago, during which she has risen from reporter to editor. She is the first woman editor of an eveninger in the country, *Mid-Day*.

Married to senior journalist Shankar Aiyar, she lives in Mumbaii.

PINKI VIRANI

bitter chocolate

Child Sexual Abuse in India

PENGUIN BOOKS

PENGUIN BOOKS
Published by the Penguin Group
Penguin Books India Pvt. Ltd, 11 Community Centre, Panchsheel Park,
New Delhi 110 017, India
Penguin Group (USA) Inc., 375 Hudson Street, New York, New York
10014, USA
Penguin Group (Canada), 90 Eglinton Avenue East, Suite 700, Toronto,
Ontario, M4P 2Y3, Canada (a division of Pearson Penguin Canada Inc.)
Penguin Books Ltd, 80 Strand, London WC2R 0RL, England
Penguin Ireland, 25 St Stephen's Green, Dublin 2, Ireland (a division of
Penguin Books Ltd)
Penguin Group (Australia), 250 Camberwell Road, Camberwell, Victoria
3124, Australia (a division of Pearson Australia Group Pty Ltd)
Penguin Group (NZ), 67 Apollo Drive, Rosedale, North Shore 0632,
New Zealand (a division of Pearson New Zealand Ltd)
Penguin Group (South Africa) (Pty) Ltd, 24 Sturdee Avenue, Rosebank,
Johannesburg 2196, South Africa

Penguin Books Ltd, Registered Offices: 80 Strand, London WC2R 0RL,
England

First published by Penguin Books India 2000

Copyright © Pinki Virani 2000

All rights reserved

22 21

ISBN 9780140298970

Typeset in Sabon Roman by SÜRYA, New Delhi
Printed at Anubha Printers, Noida

contents

• acknowledgement

When your publisher tells you it is India and her subcontinent's first book on the subject, what can you leave out? More important, how much can you compress? When is basic information too basic and additional information an overload, even if it is a 'first-time'? This is where commissioning editor Raj Kamini Mahadevan comes in; an important fort of an Author's battle is conquered through the bloodless blue pencil of skilled editing, thanks amma Mahadevan. And thank you Big D—David Davidar, Chief Executive Officer, Penguin Books—for funding this research and investigation.

Research was initially facilitated by Child Relief and You and R. Lakshmi in their documentation department who inundated me with tons of reference material in those few weeks. I decided against doing a booklet after that point; but columnist Ashok Banker and the husband-wife journalist-team Nikhil Wagle and Meena Karnik insisted I follow through with detailed investigation to write a book as simply as possible on such a subject. Journalist Sheela Raval provided her perspective; Veena Lakhumalani at the British Council in Calcutta and the Mumbaii British Council and Library assisted in enormous measure; that repository of 'stree shakti' in the form of books at what is perhaps India's only by-women-for-women library, Vacha, continuously challenged and provoked my thought processes. Those special officers in the Mumbaii Police unofficially networked with their counterparts in the emerging metros of India to get this book—apart from cases histories which churn the stomach and sicken the soul—a definitive idea of the statistical prevalence of Child Sexual Abuse in our country. And police officer Dr Kiran Bedi, who so spontaneously suggested that I speak to the women prisoners in Tihar jail when I met and told her about the connection between Child Sexual Abuse and women growing up to be convicts. I thought a lot about Dr Bedi's offer when I returned home, I visualized how effectively I could do it and how this could turn out to be a pilot project in India. So tempting. Then I realized I would re-victimize the women by talking to them about their sexual abuse in childhood, after which I would simply walk out of the jail leaving them with awful memories— which they might be revealing for the first time in their lives—and with no friend or counselling facility to comfort them. But thank you Dr Bedi. And thank you all, truly.

Of course I am grateful to each and everyone mentioned in this book for their input including the mental health professionals—specially Anita Ratnam—and the adult and child psychiatrists—specially Dr Shekhar Seshadri—who have unstintingly given of their time and patience. As I am to those who must remain unnamed because some identities and places have been changed for their protection. Except for the founder of the gay movement in India Ashok Row Kavi, I must also protect the identities of the homosexuals and lesbians who forwarded my e-mails to each other, introduced me to their friends through their gay colleagues all over the country and allowed a 'straight' like me an insight into their private pain as adults who were once children.

And how do I slot those wonderful people who helped me simply because? Some said it was the subject matter of the book, others helped as random acts of kindness like the editor Gayatri Devi Vasudev and film-maker-playwright Chetan Shah. None of them—far too many to mention—expected anything in return, all of them wished me well. They gave me solid advice along with phone numbers; they ensured that I got invited to relevant seminars; they checked out specialists in their cities and promptly e-mailed, faxed and phoned with the information; they couriered me books and mailed me xeroxes; they fed my mind and sometimes they even wound up feeding me on my investigative travels, beginning with the comfortingly hot 'chaay, burun pau, maskaa' at the Majlis office. Bless you for encouraging me so selflessly. I guess you were God's way of reminding me that even though such enormous evil exists, the world still turns on the axis of its good people.

N.B.: Mumbaii has been spelt with two i's for a reason in this book. Numerologically—if you believe in these things—a single 'i' spells disaster. The two 'i's' work to some advantage; though the most beneficial was the original 'Bombay'; my earlier book *Once Was Bombay* has the details. But more to the point: the present spelling leads to a mispronunciation of the city's name; international television channels refer to the city as 'Mumbaay' when it should be pronounced in its authentic Marathi way, Mumbaii. Like Hawaii. Chennai gets pronounced correctly because of its two n's. I also consider the spelling as Mumbaii to not be incorrect: after the name change it has yet to be decided how my city's name is to be spelt in English; in Marathi and Hindi it has always been written as Mumbaii, the long 'e' or the deerg. Typical, that those who clamoured short-sightedly for this unnecessary name-change should orphan this crucial international element of the issue.

Dear Reader,

You have looked at the cover of this book, you have looked at its back cover and the question you might want to ask of me is this:

Have you been sexually abused in your childhood?

I shall be as direct:

Yes.

I could tell you, at this point, about the mostly mystical marrying of an Author with her, or his, subject matter. I could then explain how it is me who has wound up doing this book instead of someone else. I would not be lying as I lay out my procession of thought before you to consider. My first book, *Aruna's Story*, is about the politics of rape and the rape of women; Penguin publisher David Davidar read my newspaper article on the nurse Aruna Shanbaug's fiftieth birthday while she lay in a semi-coma, a quarter of a century after she had been raped, and asked me to develop it into a book. My second book, *Once Was Bombay*, is about the communal politics in what was once India's premier city and the gang rape of it by politicians. This book is about the rape of an entire childhood, of scores of innocently unsuspecting children in the upper and middle-class homes of India.

But I would also be truthful when I say this: I have no compulsion to tell the world about the sexual abuse in my childhood.

I refuse to be a victim.

This, I have attempted in all spheres of my life; each time one falls down one must simply pick up oneself after weeping a bit, brush away the tears and dirt and move on.

That's the spirit.

The flesh, though, responds to its body's nervous system: the nervous system and its intricate, treacherous circuitry.

Which begins sending out signals the moment a man, or a woman, sexually abuses a child.

I had, and still have, to deal with my—I hate the use of the personal pronoun in this context—abuser. And it is only now, after the detailing for this book, that I realize—and recollect—why I have so many marks on my legs, between the knees and calves, where they could be seen when I wore dresses and skirts. Instead of going to a beauty parlour where hot wax could be poured over my legs and the hair yanked out by their root, I declared it to be a detestable process and instead would shave my legs. I began doing this early in age, as prominently as possible at home, and as I would shave I would cut my legs. Strips of skin would shave off too, one gash went rather neatly almost to the bone; blood, lots of it, on the floor. When I would be forced to wax instead, I would develop red skin rashes and allergies on my legs so that I could keep shaving. As I shaved, I nicked, wounded, profusely scarred. I was hurting myself because my pain was not being validated, that I could not bear to have that man around me.

In 1999, too, I childishly thought my spirit and will would be victorious again.

For my second book *Once Was Bombay*, it was decided that if I could literally rise to the idea, the presentation would be a previously untried one in faction (facts written in story-telling style). A blend of short stories and novellas which would be connected and yet be able to stand alone as individual pieces of oral history. David Davidar added that he was very keen that one of these novellas deal with the life of a middle-class man, born and brought up in what was then Bombay, preferably Muslim, who was attacked by the rioters after the demolition of the Babri Masjid in Ayodhya. The key element in this novella, he felt, would be the slow but obvious 'falling down' of the area in which this man lived: symbolic of what was happening to the middle class and their city.

'What about your father?' he asked.

'Can't write about me,' I protested.

'It is not about you,' replied David Davidar, quite brutally I thought. 'It is about your father, the changing times and city through his eyes.'

My father. Who has known about my sexual abuser and never once told this man off. My father. Who actually holds this man the way his mother did: in thrall.

But this was not about me, it was about my father and his feelings.

I spent several hours and days with my father, questioning and cross-questioning him. I went to his shop and sat there for what appeared like forever to understand his actions and reactions. We must have made for some sight in the middle of Mumbaii's Bhendi Bazaar: the shopkeeper and his daughter.

Most times I did not like what I heard about myself and how he saw me, often I resented his problematic patriarchy and his world view. But something else was emerging, as a writer this was an exciting realization.

August 1999. Here I am reading the reviews of *Once Was Bombay*. The reviews are polarized, like my city and my country. The book holds steady on the national bestseller lists. The letters I receive, the phone calls, most of the reviews, refer to the section called Mazagon, Bombay-10, as being written 'brilliantly', 'humanely', 'effectively, through the eyes of the middle-class businessman'. I close my eyes and send up a prayer, thank you God for not allowing the child in me who feels betrayed to surface, thank you for bringing out only the hard-core journalist in me. I have succeeded in seeing, compassionately understanding, and reporting on how my father sees life. And me, as part of his environment and upbringing and beliefs. I realize I have performed convincingly in a perverse way as well: an old friend read the novella and said I had been very harsh on myself.

Just two days before I sat down to write the section called Mazagon, Bombay-10, there was complete emotional chaos; I am not sure whether it was connected or a terrible coincidence. The nervous system and its intricate, treacherous circuitry, who can tell? To me it was a volcanic explosion from within and I could feel the lava bubbling up in me, spewing out and coursing down hotly over my body.

Eventually, there was ash and calm.

Resolution. Of some sort; I can, since, see my father differently. I have known of him as that silent young boy yanked out of school and sent to work in an ink-smeared, cauldron-like manual printing press while the elders of his family drank, and destroyed what might have been my father's better future. I have always appreciated that my father, who despite the awful failings of his family and the enormous disadvantages his father heaped upon him, rose above it all to ensure with his wife that their daughters got an education which professionally qualified them for a far secure future than he could have ever imagined for himself. I can now go beyond gratitude.

'I am okay now,' I told my friend Anita who is passionately involved in the book trade; we were talking about how a comprehensive book on Child Sexual Abuse in India was needed. 'So it won't be me doing that book, that's for sure. Besides, what has been done to other kids is so bad, I have been lucky in comparison.'

She said three words, she said them calmly, 'Do not minimize.'

Now I have one more truth to tell you, dear reader: I wish I was not the one doing this book.

It has cost me, it has cost me the earth.

I cannot remember when my sexual abuse began; I cannot recall, no matter how hard I try, whether my recollection of the first time it happened is actually the first time it happened. Was it happening before and for some reason I have blocked it out? I know this is not important, but it destroys me each time I have had to deal with it while doing this book: where was everybody when it was happening; damn them, shouldn't somebody from the family have been there to stop it?

Damn it, so much power abused, so much trust betrayed, where are the parents of these children? The politics of domination, the vulnerability of a woman, the girl's very gender being a liability to herself as a human being: damn, damn, damn, a young woman can never really say what she wants to, wear what she wants to, go where she pleases; she cannot feel complete freedom because she is always, always in sexual threat. And these little boys who are being sexually abused by the males in their own homes; why are protectors turning predators?

The man who sexually abused me in my childhood now lives in an upmarket area of South Mumbaii, he and his wife have a child and they lead an upmarket life. I feel worried as I write this—would I be hurting his daughter with this disclosure? My stomach clenches; I hope not. And his wife whom I like as a determined woman? I hope to God not.

An acquaintance who heard from the literary grapevine that I was doing this book, phoned to cross-check. She presumed that the book was all, and only, about me. 'Oh,' she trilled, 'it must have happened in your Dongri days. Well you must feel all right since you have left it, and him, behind you.'

'Dongri may be downmarket and undoubtedly children are being sexually abused in Dongri as they are anywhere else, but it did not happen during my Dongri days. Incidentally, the man lives in your neighbourhood now, just a few buildings away.'

The acquaintance has not phoned since; we do this a lot, we like to think that people who sexually abuse children cannot possibly be People Like Us. And if they are rich and famous, we simply close our eyes to their reported perversities. We think they 'do it only once'; sexual abusers are multiple abusers, the same child often, other children at the same time or subsequently. Like the singer Michael Jackson. We also thought nothing of the film-maker Woody Allen taking pictures of his stepdaughter in the nude and having sexual intercourse with her. The children of single mothers are constantly being hit upon by sexual assaulters, most of these perpetrators are the single mother's man-friends or subsequent husbands, when not the elderly neighbourhood uncle. This is being proved again and again with cases all over the world as also in India.

I recall the time I was joint editor of *Stardust*, learning production and being helpful with rewrites and interviews until Nari Hira, Magna Publishing chief, could give the green signal on the city magazine we subsequently launched. I edited a story of a big star sexually molesting a sixteen-year-old on his sets in full view of the unit and the girl's mother. During an intimate scene he said loudly, 'Naariyal phod du kya?' ('Should I go ahead and perform the "auspicious" ceremony?') The widowed mother of this girl was hysterical with rage and frustration, she went on record with her quotes. The story created some commotion though most refused to believe it, the girl and her mother were hounded out of the Hindi film industry, the male star went on as before.

My research has led me to the works of internationally-renowned authors, and others, who have been sexually abused as children. Oprah Winfrey. Maya Angelou who was sexually abused by her mother's partner. 'Mr Freeman lived with us, or we lived with him (I never knew quite which)' she writes in *I Know Why The Caged Bird Sings*; Maya first felt something which was 'too soft to be a hand' and was raped by 'a mush-hard thing'. Freeman was acquitted by the court because Maya could not find the words as he stood glowering at her, he was murdered a few hours after leaving the court; the child in Maya simply stopped talking as a result, well until she was a young adult.

The singer Billie Holiday in her autobiography *Lady Sings the Blues* reveals that she was raped when she was ten by a forty-five-year-old man. Quentin Bill's biography of his famous aunt, the writer Virginia Woolf, says that she was sexually abused from the age of six in her nursery by her stepbrother Gerald Duckworth and then by his brother George Duckworth from 1888 to 1904, well until she was in her twenties, even as they sexually abused her sister, Vanessa, as well. Centuries of denial and the public's disinclination to speak about the problem except in the most lurid of cases was overcome in America when the former Miss America of 1958, Marilyn Van Derbur Atler, publicly announced in 1989 that she had been sexually abused by her millionaire and socialite father from the time she was five, and right through until the age of eighteen. This led to literally thousands of adults who had been sexually abused in their childhood speaking out too. (It being America, this also lead to the False Memory Syndrome with therapists actively planting the idea which encouraged adults to think they had been sexually abused in childhood by their parents. As an American newspaper headlined it: 'You fed them. You clothed them. Now they are back to say you raped them!')

This is a personally important one: Latino rock guitarist Carlos Santana. His guitar has been my strength; *Black magic woman* to me is about strings being stretched to their limits to still produce that most magical of all God's creations: music. Music can do a lot, it can even make you strong in your broken places; Carlos Santana said this too on American television in the early part of 2000, 'Music mends.' I wonder why record companies have not understood this. In India there are ragas for all moods and times, from dawn to midnight. Why are there no cassettes of non-film lullabies? 'Music mends,' says Carlos Santana, if only the music mandarins could understand this.

Carlos Santana had been sexually abused when he was eleven years old for a relentless two years. Now fifty-two, he had kept it his deepest and darkest secret for almost forty years. 'Now,' he said on American television, 'I am free from feeling guilt, shame, judgement, fear.'

There are other names too. Edgar Allen Poe, Edith Wharton, Ingmar Bergman, Alfred Hitchcock. Two Indian authors have also briefly touched upon their own experiences in their fiction. I do not mean Raj Kamal Jha or Arundhati Roy.

The latter, who has written of brother-sister incest with

almost tempting tenderness was asked by Anna M.M. Vetticad in the 26 July 1999 issue of *India Today* how discriminating she was in her choice of issues. Replies the Booker Award winner, 'I am not shopping for causes. When my essay on the Narmada came out, I got a call saying, "That was a brilliant piece you wrote. Now I would like you to do one for me on child abuse." And I am like, "For or against?" It is so ridiculous, the very idea that people think it is a mechanical business, writing well. It comes from thinking.' Anna M.M. Vetticad says, 'So when you are asked to write on child abuse . . .' Arundhati Roy cuts in with, 'Will you write about child abuse? Will you write the chairman's speech at the underwear manufacturing company? This is an external view of it. Exactly the same way as every publisher in the world is asking me, "Will you write another book? Will you sign another contract before you have written a book?" Of course not.'

Point taken Ms Roy. But the next time you are asked a question on Child Sexual Abuse, please do us—the affected—a favour. Please don't say anything. The way you—specially you—say it, the pseudo-intellectualization hurts. 'For or against'?

This made me wonder though, suppose someone does want to write a book from the other point of view—that of the perpetrator's—what are the facts they would work with?

What is a perpetrator like, does he only come from a paternally dysfunctional family like mine? Even then, can he have a reason for doing what he does?

I have been closely scrutinizing books, studies, surfing the internet, sending e-mails to mental health care professionals in countries where a substantial volume of work has been done on Child Sexual Abuse. I have also spoken with psychiatrists and counsellors in India and a few perpetrators myself. I cannot find a single thread which binds them all; which is why I have to underscore that this has everything to do with 'sexualized sex', otherwise called lust. Sexualized adults lust for little children and sexually assault them. Lust leads.

Patriarchy, power, penetration—these are all the factors that assist greatly in allowing a child to be sexually, and physically, abused; in a few cases they are reasons. However, they cannot be used as psychodynamic catch-alls which explain everything and nothing. The crux of it is that hectic adult activity described as sex, too much of it; in both, practice and the mind; and to the exclusion of a lot else which really should be what differentiates humans from animals. We do not want to admit this, for it would prove us as succumbing to the most basic of our instincts. To do so would mean accepting that we do not want to rise above it. We would much rather fuck: indiscriminately, repetitively.

Sex, being led by sex. So much easier than working on one's intellect or real self-worth where one's thinking, and consequent actions, are refined to the point where they become like burnished gold, lustrous and elegant. Lots of sex, that much easier than self-limitation. Aleksandr Solzhenitsyn, author and winner of the Nobel, in a recent essay on the abuse of the world's environment, says, 'It is difficult to bring ourselves to sacrifice and self-denial because in political, public and private life we have long since dropped the golden key of self-restraint to the ocean floor. But self-limitation is the fundamental and wisest aim of a man who has obtained his freedom. It is also the surest path towards its attainment. If we do not learn to limit firmly our desires and demands, to subordinate our interests to moral criteria, we, humankind, will simply be torn apart as the worst aspects of human nature bare their teeth. It has been pointed by various thinkers many times: if a personality is not directed at values higher than the self, corruption and decay inevitably take hold. We can only experience true spiritual satisfaction not in seizing, but in refusing to seize. In other words: self-limitation.'

Solzhenitsyn could well be talking about a human being's internal environment. Where the instant gratification of senses, at the expense of real internal feelings of self-worth, can only lead to deep unhappiness. For instance, the sexual revolution; has it really benefited women? The sexual revolution has made it acceptable for a man to live with a woman for years without marrying her, he need not marry her even when she has his child. When sexually bored with her, he can dump her and her child and move on to the next woman. Ergo, the women's sexual revolution has only benefited men. The woman is left holding her child, and fending off other men who try and sexually assault her and her children.

Alfred Kinsey said this in 1948: 'It is clear in general that adult sexual involvement with children is a manifestation of the peak level of sexual activity, particularly in males'. What is 'peak' level? At what age would such a level peak? It would appear that adults who want to sexually abuse children can peak, suddenly and quickly, as soon as there is a child at arm's length. Young aunts and uncles to geriatric grandfathers included.

The perpetrator is really no different from such uncles and grandfathers. They do not necessarily have to—though this is also a pattern—put themselves where accessibility to children is a major factor. As examples, but not speaking generally: a physical training or swimming instructor, a worker, say in a non-government organization, who is in a position of authority over children. Speaking specifically: perpetrators are first in the child's home and among its known family and friends' circle.

I always thought that cruelty, too, subsumes a certain concept; this thought process also underlies the working of our police and courts to provide justice. I am wrong, and I suppose so is anyone else who thinks on these lines when it comes to children. I discovered this with a sense of shock when I was trying to understand why parents, fathers and grandfathers specifically, physically and sexually abuse the children of the family. I looked at the British literature around the abused child, at checklists provided for professional child-workers in cases of battered children and applied these lists to the perpetrators. Not one case fits neatly, no pronounced pattern emerges.

Except one. Parents who have been beaten by their parents are disposed to beat their, and other, children. Similarly, there are very clearly adult male perpetrators who have been sexually abused as children themselves even if not by their own parents; so now they are the perpetuators, doing it to other children. Which does not make it right at all, even if the psychiatrists choose to see this as, 'An effort to preserve his masculine image, thus limiting himself from overcoming the sexual trauma of his past. His anger and his sex drive have become intertwined.' No human being has the right to sexually abuse a child or rape an adult, be it a woman or a man. After all there are enough adults—male and female—who have been sexually abused in childhood and who would never, ever, sexually abuse a child in turn; many of these make for excellent parents too. Perhaps even better than those parents who have never been sexually abused in childhood, though it is far too high a price to pay for perfect parenting.

Among adults who sexually abuse children are also some homosexuals—who think of it as sexual initiation for the boys they bodily and emotionally assault. And some among them are lesbians—who see it likewise for the girls. This is as immoral and depraved as anyone else who sexually violates children.

These heterosexuals, homosexuals and lesbians do not generally come from dysfunctional homes. They look perfectly normal and sane, which they are; they are not sadists nor perverts who experience greater sexual thrills only when children protest. They can be good providers themselves, and make for functional fathers in the case of heterosexual men. They are not necessarily alcoholics or users of narcotics. They have not had bad experiences like abandonments, they have not been brought up with harsh discipline by their parents or beaten up by them, they do not have rigid or obsessive personalities themselves, they are of average intelligence and have no physical problems, they deal with everyday conflict situations and stress with relative ease, their own marriages are all right, they get enough sex in their relationships, they have no excessive dependency needs and there are no 'ghosts' around like powerful and destructive parents or grandparents. In the case of heterosexuals, their families have the usual amount of eye contact and touching, they talk to each other without being cold or rough, they do things together with the family and even if their family members do not particularly love each other, they are not bonded in hate. They are not necessarily from joint families; there are a reasonable number of neighbours, friends and relatives, the perpetrator and his family is not a socially isolated one. There is also no long-term poverty in the homes of most of these perpetrators, family members are decently employed as is the perpetrator.

So: why do they do it? Why do these perpetrators stick fingers, penises, tongues, bananas, candles and pencils into any and every orifice of a child? Why do adult males fondle budding breasts and play with tiny testicles?

Quietly cross-questions Deepika D'Souza, director of the Mumbaii-based India Centre for Human Rights and Law which is working towards strengthening its child rights wing: 'Why do so many men pee in public? Because as far as such men are concerned the road is there, to be pissed upon. Because they can. Because there is nobody to stop them. I would think they sexually abuse children for the same lack of concrete reason.'

Doctors can find themselves as despairing when questioned why adults set upon children sexually. Mulls Calcutta psychiatrist Dr Sujit Ghosh, who also works with the subject of male sexuality, 'The myth of penetration and manliness is quite firmly grounded. The pressure of being a virile male stud is just as much. And penetration does seem the most reconfirming ritual to it. But I would not rule out lust.'

Dr Rajesh Parikh is the country's first neuro-psychiatrist: he examines the neurological basis for psychiatric disorders and also the psychological manifestations of neurological disorders. In other words, he connects brain to behaviour to thought to feeling and consequent action. Dr Parikh is currently part of the core committee of the Asian Union Against Depression, a World Health Organisation affiliate, which is organizing intensive ways and means of collecting data from general practitioners from all over Asia on smiling depression. Smiling depression is that other word for masked depression where people have difficulties with sleep and appetite, they do not feel like meeting other people, they might have headaches often, they might feel weak all the time, their bodies might hurt, they frequently complain of getting tired very easily. Women in our country—not excluding the subcontinent—suffer a great deal from smiling depression. The data for this project will be collected through specially formulated questionnaires distributed to general practitioners all over Asia, including India, and will take a few years to compile. Severe depression is one of the most common long-term effects of adult females and males who have been sexually abused in childhood in the West; it could well take the form of smiling depression in Asia too as Eastern (including Indian) cultures do not have the vocabulary which encourages the verbalization of feelings.

At this Author's request Dr Rajesh Parikh has agreed to put in appropriate questions and their co-relates in the Indian, and its neighbouring countries', set of questionnaires asking whether the patient, male or female, had been sexually abused in childhood. In the unlikely event of any other organization conducting such an extensive survey, Dr Rajesh Parikh's project would be the first of its kind as authenticated documentation on both, smiling depression and Child Sexual Abuse as one of its causes in India, Nepal, Bangladesh, Sri Lanka, Bhutan and Pakistan.

Dr Rajesh Parikh says, 'For reasons we do not completely know chemical reactions get triggered off in the brain by traumatic events, Child Sexual Abuse is particularly traumatic. The adult who has been sexually abused in childhood can also have a neuro-physiological change in the brain when recalling the trauma. These chemical reactions can give rise to depression, mania, post-traumatic stress disorders and a host of other effects which doctors working in the field of Child Sexual Abuse would need to probe for.'

He is asked about the neurological basis for psychiatric disorders and the psychological manifestations of neurological disorders with specific reference to perpetrators of Child Sexual Abuse in India. Dr Rajesh Parikh replies ruefully, 'As a neuro-psychiatrist I would really like to believe that all these men are disturbed. I would like to think that all of them have personality disorders, that they are deviants or that they have low self-esteem. But this would not be right on my part because it is simply not true for all cases. Most adult males who sexually abuse children are . . .' Dr Parikh searches for the word, 'They are . . .'

Bastards?

Dr Rajesh Parikh nods in agreement, 'I do not approve of the usage of strong language but yes, grown-up men who sexually molest children are . . .'

Bastards?

'Definitely.'

Dr Shekhar Seshadri's is a well-known name in the field of the Indian child's mental health, particularly in connection with Child Sexual Abuse. Working from Asia's premier institute, the National Institute of Mental Health and Neuro Science (Nimhans) in Bangalore as his base, he is the first doctor in the country, and the Indian subcontinent, to work on the subject of Child Sexual Abuse. He has conducted several studies and workshops all over India apart from one-to-one counselling with both child and adult victims of Child Sexual Abuse. Ask him about perpetrators and he replies, 'There are those who have been sexually abused themselves as children although this should not be used as the reason for perpetuation. There are a few who are genuinely mentally ill. There are the paedophiles and it would be a mistake to think that all paedophiles are mentally sick. There are those who have been misinformed that sex with a virgin or a child is the treatment for sexually transmitted diseases, Aids or impotence. And then there are the . . .'

He pauses, looking for a word which would describe such men.

Bastards?

'There is a reason why I would hesitate to use that word. It should not be seen as a categorization for someone to either keep perpetrating or stop himself from coming for psychiatric help so that he can desist.'

These bastards would form an overwhelming percentage of the males who sexually abuse children?

'Yes, these otherwise "normal" types who lead seemingly casual lives would form the largest chunk of adults who sexually abuse little bodies and minds. And most of them do it for no other reason than sex. That is really the basic thing. All the other stuff may, or may not, be present like power and domination, sexuality and its abuse, gender and patriarchy, class and caste. In my experience, the other issues do come up but sex takes the prominent form. This sex element is the least discoursed phenomenon because it is the least understood.'

It is expected that when a man is plainly a bastard he will be honest about it and do everything for the wrong reasons. But perpetrators do not fit into any pattern; this is perhaps the most difficult thing to prove in court when he is a doting grandfather, an elderly gent, an ancient elder who prays with his wife and plays with his grandchildren. To the presiding judge this accusation is then an aberration, the alleged act a cooked up one since such behaviour would be inconsistent with the man's general behaviour. The benefit of the doubt is given to the perpetrator because he has his good reputation and social standing which must be protected at all cost. Including against the interests of the child; for this child there is nothing more damaging than the bastard's inconsistency.

Child Sexual Abuse happens because the system of silence around the act perpetuates it. Child Sexual Abuse happens because this system of silence encourages some more men to want it to happen; and so the political, societal, cultural and religious attitudes which serve to underestimate the child, specially the female child, creates a climate in which abuse can thrive.

They do the same thing to women. They tell her to not get raped, she must stay out of the rapist's way. In other words, they try and prevent sexual assault by focussing on altering the behaviour of the victim. Women are expected to learn kung fu, just in case, or not walk through parks alone, generally make themselves as less accessible to sexual assault as is humanly possible. The same thing is applicable to children. Points out the sociologist Swift, 'This results in not the prevention of sexual assault but the prevention of sexual assault on cautious women and children, and those proficient in the physical martial arts. The attacker continues to victimise the young, the weak, the vulnerable or the uninformed. Sexual assault is not prevented by this approach, but rather displaced.'

Swift wrote that in 1979; in 1987 sociologist Leventhal pointed out, 'The ultimate goal of any program to prevent sexual abuse is to teach behaviours so that when an adult makes a sexual advance towards a child, the child will act in an appropriate manner by saying no and telling a responsible adult what happened. Yet none of the evaluative efforts has examined the direct outcome. Instead, a change in knowledge, which is really an intermediate measure, has been examined without any evidence that such a change is linked to changes in behaviour.'

And yet prevention programmes are relevant even if they have to be seen as a small—albeit important—part of a more comprehensive approach to protecting children from sexual abuse and its consequences. Child-centred programmes are necessary and effective when dealing with strangers because the rules for dealing with strangers require less interpretation than those with family members: do not enter into a conversation, do not go too close, get away as soon as possible.

But points out Bill Gillham in his *Protecting Children From Sexual Abuse*: 'Expecting children to protect themselves from people they know is quite another matter. Children are, on the whole, remarkably compliant: they trust easily (And who would want them to be fearful, mistrustful and suspicious?). Yet it is this known category of implicitly trusted (or at least unsuspected) adults which often constitutes the largest category of risk.' He adds, 'The cynic who observed that sex is five per cent motivation and ninety-five per cent opportunity might have had Child Sexual Abuse in mind.'

I know this thought will automatically come up: yes, yes, basic information on this is a good idea for our children; what are the schools and teachers doing about it? What is the media doing? Schools and teachers play a very important role in the awareness of Child Sexual Abuse; but parents play the most important role. They have given birth to that child, it is the child's right to be appropriately informed and correctly educated by its parents. When it comes to their children, why do parents think mostly of their rights and rarely of their responsibilities?

What can the media do vis-à-vis Child Sexual Abuse in India? The media cannot stop Child Sexual Abuse in Indian homes, only those adults who live in it can. The media can report on this most evil of social crimes, be a mirror to society, as also perform the additional role of information dissemination and subject-awareness. The print media already does this, as do magazines and television programmes for the not cerebrally challenged: like Prannoy Roy and his New Delhi Television's news capsules on Star which report on Child Sexual Abuse cases as they emerge and Raghav Behl's Television 18 which produces real-life court decisions as the tautly shot *Bhanwar* for Sony which spot-lit the infamous non-resident Indian Mehra case. But given the magnitude of the problem and its in-built secrecy in upper and middle-class homes, television needs to do much more to take awareness on Child Sexual Abuse right into living and bedrooms. There needs to be a sustained focus.

In Western countries, information dissemination on Child Sexual Abuse is woven into print comics and television cartoons (at one point, Superman was assisting a sexually assaulted child) and popular television serials for both children and adults (*Santa Barbara* dealt with the subject over several episodes by making it a story track). Youth channels could prove invaluable here, considering there are teenagers in thousands who have been sexually abused in childhood. And it would certainly help both, India and its teenagers, if these music channels could start treating their young audience like the aware human beings they are instead of androids refusing to grow out of an age of compulsive revelry. On an average, the veejays and channels behave like hysterically gay parrots who find themselves baffled during a break.

United Television which produced the very watchable *Hip Hip Hurray* with its talented young actors for Zee could think of doing episodes on Child Sexual Abuse when the serial re-emerges in a new avatar. The writer Dinesh Raheja could consider a story track for his interestingly conceived *Just Mohabbat* airing on Sony. Both these are television programmes aimed at youngsters; programmes for adults could well have similar, and sustainable, tracks too. This is possible and with a great degree of sensitivity, notwithstanding what some producers feel on the subject of Child Sexual Abuse.

Like twenty-four-year-old Ekta Kapoor, daughter of

actor Jeetendra. She gives an interview to the *Indian Express* to announce her going public with her television company as also producing a Hindi film to be directed by David Dhawan (he of conveyor belt number one fame). When—can?—Bollywood ever produce a film which enjoys the personhood of children, the way Mani Ratnam and his audience did in his *Anjali* or Santosh Sivan in *Halo*? The 'mainstream' Hindi film industry continues to treat children like an extension of their parents on the silver screen; either they are being kidnapped for ransom, held over boiling cauldrons of an evil-bubbling liquid, watching their father being shot dead or their mother being propositioned by the villain so that they grow to avenge the horror; or they are just being senseless brats.

Ekta Kapoor thinks she was a 'spoilt rich brat'; she must feel she has sufficiently grown out of at least two of those three self-proclaimed vices since. For she expounds, 'Frankly, I think Indian plots on television are more superior to those on international television.' She points to what she describes as 'progressive ideas' and proclaims that American television rarely handles 'adult themes' like those shown on *Sailaab* and *Hasratein* with any sensitivity. Then this young producer mocks, 'They (American television) have not got over themes such as incest and child abuse.'

Kapoor has produced what she refers to as a 'mega-successful family comedy' comprising a harried father virtually run over by his wife and a surfeit of women in his household including his five daughters; there is also a photograph on a wall of a woman, presumably dead, who comes alive every now and then to also harangue the man. Her other creative offering has a middle-aged widow, at most times tremulously unwell, getting her daughter married into a 'good family' in the same city without checking at all on the bridegroom or his credentials. It is left to the daughter—otherwise sharp and voluble—to discover on her wedding night that her husband is very obviously mentally deficient; her character is not given the option of talking to the boy before marriage either. She must now live with, and like, this retard or else her widowed mother will collapse with a shattered heart. A 'progressive' idea?

Consider advertising films: little girls, invariably to the exclusion of other kinds of dresses, in spaghetti straps and other suggestive clothing, complete with curls bobbing about their carefully painted faces; Lolitaesque mode. ('My daddy's the strongest!' My mummy? Oh she is washing the toilet, frying puris in the latest and best oil which will not give my daddy a heart attack, or she is out at work where she gets so exhausted and filthy that she needs the strongest tea and the best germicidal soap when she gets home.) The little boys in these ads then, how can they not be men-in-the-making? Reconfirming this at the end of every second advertisement on television is a male voice-over, that deep but fruitily friendly paternal voice of authority suggesting you buy the product. Women's voices at the end; sure, they are there so that you do not think advertising is a man's world, as they are for sanitary napkins, lipsticks, nail polishes but not necessarily shampoos.

Says Dr Anjali Monteiro, head, unit for media and communications, Tata Institute of Social Sciences, 'Any representation in any medium, be it advertising or cinema, that legitimizes and normalizes violence to children, sexual or otherwise, should be questioned. In advertising one obvious change over the past decade is greater visibility of children in more advertising, as also a greater number of ads being targeted at children. One also sees a greater degree of objectification at work. Not only are children more visible, but they are also being represented as attractive objects and at times—particularly in the case of female children—as objects of desire. There are examples where these representations can be grossly and overtly sexual, for example the Mexx print ad where a little boy is shown at the bedside of a woman with his pants down. Most of the time these representations are a little more subtle and hence the more insidious. A little girl in an off-the-shoulder black velvet dress and ringlets, dancing in Bollywood film heroine style, frontally, for the camera, may even appear cute to some viewers. But this objectified representation of the little girl mimicking an adult object of desire is to me objectionable. While its links with Child Sexual Abuse may not be direct, it normalizes a particular way of looking at young girls, a way of seeing that it shares in common with pornography, namely, the girl as an object of gaze for the voyeur and not as a person. Such modes of representation also begin to set the benchmark for the way little girls dress in everyday life, so much so that one sees young girls today wearing more and more inappropriate clothes. Which their conservative parents are quite happy about; partly also because these girls are pre-pubescent and hence—the parents incorrectly think—not at that dangerous age where they have to worry!'

If advertising is only about getting people to buy products, not changing society for the better, it stands to logic that the hidden persuaders have no right to subvert the existing norms of society to their detriment either. So: can we expect the Indian advertising fraternity to internalize certain norms so that they reject or resist representations that are voyeuristic of children?

'No,' booms the guru of advertising Alyque Padamsee. 'Expect nothing from advertising which you do not see in society.' Padmashree Padamsee, as is evident, remains steadfastly loyal to the trade he has stamped. Thus, it is unexpected that he blushes when it is pointed out that his own work in creative advertising does not reflect such a thinking. One never saw little boys being taken to the market by their mummies when Lalitaji took Ravi to the bazaar to buy her bhaajis and Surf and even publicly remonstrated him to behave himself. There was also that time when men were drooling over Karen Lunel's body and the morality brigade fuming over her little green bikini; but Padamsee had tapped right into a working woman's important yearning: her almost always unmet desire to have an uninterrupted bath when she can privately soap away her worries, soothe her fears in a shower with the sensuous thrum of water on her skin.

Padamsee is uncharacteristically modest but refreshingly honest, 'I hit lucky. Maybe it was subconscious but I did not deliberately plan gender-sensitive advertising. Yes, I think it was subconscious because as a child I always had strong women around me, especially a strong mother.' Alyque Padamsee's office is on the top floor of the building named after his mother, Kulsum Terrace. She lived here too, the fiery and gritty Kulsum, who sat at the crucial curve of the enormous horseshoe-shaped dining table set in the high-ceilinged courtyard-like room as antiseptic sunshine filtered in through the skylights. Kulsum, subconsciously or otherwise, also taught her son a lesson or two in effective parenting. By Alyque Padamsee's own admission, 'I make a far better parent than partner.'

The father in him made a public service advertising film, thirty seconds, titled *A Father Is A Girl's Best Friend*. The opening visual is a tied girl-doll. A male hand unravels the bandage from her eyes, 'A father is a girl's best friend by opening her eyes to education.' The hand unties her hands, 'By freeing her from the drudgery of housework.' The hand unties her feet, 'By helping her find her feet.' Not surprisingly this public service ad has not been shown enough, those being the days of undiluted Doordarshan. But what is to stop public service advertising around children and Child Sexual Abuse today, specially with the profusion of channels? Nothing, except the Indian advertising fraternity itself which will probably see no staggering profit, of the monetary sort, in it.

The 'new', 'improved' millennial male in Indian advertising, however, does make money. And so we must see advertising with this kind of man taking time off from the board meeting to eat a soggy sandwich with his spaghetti-strapped daughter. The millennial male has yet to grow into Father Courage, though, to share soiled nappy change time with the exhausted mother.

But will the mother—in real life—let him?

Will the woman relinquish some aspect of those mystical powers attributed to motherhood?

And will a mother ever tell her son about menstruation? Why must he learn from outside what happens to his mother and sister, and what will happen to his wife, every month?

Why does a mother not explain to her son about other people's daughters; isn't she one herself?

Why is a mother, in turn, rude to a daughter-in-law? Why should the man be the crux of the lives of either?

If a father does not do it, why does a mother not give her son condoms and tell him about Aids?

Why does a mother not get off her pedestal—upon which her husband and son have dumped her so that they can glorify her from afar—to put them in their place?

Why does a woman not draw the line with her man even when she has a home to her name, money in the bank and a good job?

Why do mothers and fathers keep telling their daughters how to behave, why isn't it already high time they told their sons?

Film-maker, actress and human rights supporter Suhasini in Chennai is trying; she is clear that one half of human experience need not be off limits to the other half of the population. She intends succeeding despite the contrary messages from the relatives and friends around her son. Says she, 'It has been very important for me as a mother to not mystify my son simply because of his gender. I have found it difficult but imperative that I explain to my son that he see his "maleness" as a complete paradigm, inclusive of humanity and femininity. But I find my task made all that more difficult by relatives and friends who insist on feeding the "male" element in my son instead of addressing him as a child.'

Needed in India, urgently, a million more mothers like Suhasini.

Otherwise the 'male' will keep doing his thing. The 'male' who refers to his girlfriend as 'baby', when he is particularly frisky he refers to her vagina as 'pussy', he buys her teddy bears and likes to look at pictures of her in frilly knickers. And oh, how he trips on Britney Spears as she wears school-girlish clothing but knots it below her breasts, her hair is tied girlie-like but her tongue curls right from under as she apologetically croons-moans, 'Oh baby baby, how was I supposed to know.' Cold, calculating Britney Spears—no surprise that her latest interview is all about 'still being a virgin'—continuously feeding the ultimate warped male fantasy of fucking a child.

Don't believe it? Surf the internet, there are sexualized Bambis here with honey trap-like vaginas and other Walt Disney creations with huge digital penises. And the paedophiles having the time of their lives with the digitally altered bodies of children, specially little boys.

Later in this book is information on how India—specifically Goa, Mumbaii and Kovalam in Kerala—are turning into the international paedophile's delight. There are also details on children running away from their own homes in which they are being sexually assaulted. Some of these are being subsequently kidnapped from the strange streets they find themselves on and whisked away into brothels for little boys and girls: in India and abroad.

A missing child. From a 'good' home, a 'fine' family. No apparent reason to run away.

But these stories can be as much about children running away as grown-ups not looking and seeing, about adults who prefer to sugar-coat rather than confront reality.

These are not 'nice' things to say, I suppose. Perhaps this will be the reason this book will be badly received by those very parents who need to know such things. I would worry about this if I was not a journalist who wants, and chooses, to stand by the country's future generations. We can all sense this—assuming politics, and parents, do not ruin it—something special is on the brink for India and its future citizens. We are at its cusp now, where Generation Next—our kids—are talking about real freedom, the kind that comes from within, and self-determination; all of which is energising for India. Child Sexual Abuse represses children; the repression of children is unlikely to create a flourishing society, economically, emotionally, equally or spiritually. This is my attempt at protecting the emergence of another wounded generation.

But I am steeling myself for any kind of backlash—the unbridled power we accord to patriarchy in India comes with its own manipulative mechanism.

And I am taking enormous courage for this book from my husband Shankar Aiyar, my fellow journalist, my good friend—he hugged me tight when I first told him. My fingernails cut into my palm in shame as I told him. But I felt no guilt, I have never seen what was done to me as my fault. He was at Cambridge when I had my little, late-at-night emotional crisis in 1999. I phoned a psychiatrist friend who could not correctly help me; my mistake, he believes in strong medication, besides Child Sexual Abuse is a subject which his mind just switches off from, so appalling does he find it.

I disconnected and dialled my husband at Cambridge: international phone calls and e-mails can go a much longer way than the original inventors ever thought. Shankar continues to hold me tight, he never lets me go: the best friend a woman can have is her husband if he is a good—real—man. Let me not give you an incorrect impression: we have had our upheavals, far too many of them; we did not even have that sparkling swirl a courtship should, since professional and financial questions quickly hung heavy over our joint future. We still, to this day, have to work very hard on our emotional partnership; this might also be because there is no third person in our house. Not that having a child cements marriages anymore, if we go by the numbers coming unglued. Meanwhile, relatives and acquaintances—who clearly see their own children as bonded labour or slaves for a lifetime—want to know who will 'look after' us in our old age since we do not have children.

It is because of my husband, and without his knowledge, that I have been through two intense, and terribly expensive, psychiatric sessions. One of the long-term effects of Child Sexual Abuse is fertility control. What I needed to understand from both these psychiatrists—one man, one woman—were two things: was my childhood abuse stopping me from wanting a child; was I solely, and slyly, responsible for the decision my husband and I had taken not to have children? I am so relieved to write that our decision has been ours, and most important, it has been of our free will.

Shankar now says he could have told me that and at no cost, that he is 'almost grateful' for 'one of our better joint decisions'.

I too knew it, the background I come from has helped me acquire a handy crap-cutter which I have carefully built into my system; I use this on myself and my environment. I knew it anyway since before I met my husband, I was planning on being a surrogate mother for a friend. But the research on this book gave rise to my own demons and they needed to be first fed, before they could be fully and finally slaughtered. Both psychiatrists have given me diagnoses independent of each other: fertility control is not among the after-effects of the sexual abuse in my childhood. I displayed short-term effects and still have some long-term effects of Child Sexual Abuse. There are other points which make me cringe with embarrassment on earlier behaviour: some destructive friendships and relationships, other stuff.

Once, after a blazing row over our professional lives (the only time I seriously thought a journalist being married to a journalist is not a good idea), I bitterly ruminated that having a baby would have been better, it would have served Aiyar right! He would have had to earn vast quantities of money for the child's future and possibly be chained to a hated job as a result; I would have had to do nothing at all save slave over the child, smug in my motherhood—even if secretly unsatisfied—I could have shut myself off from all other worries of the world. I could have actively practised learned helplessness. As Martin Seligman explained in 1975, when he developed the theory of learned helplessness: experiences which are perceived to be inescapable seem to sap human motivation to the point that desire to initiate action, solve problems and overcome obstacles declines. Further, the ability to perceive success is undermined and messages that are indicators of success tend to be missed. A point of helplessness and depression is reached.

Not the best reason to have a child, fortunately for us, I snapped out of it. Learned helplessness, though, is what happens to children who are sexually abused over a period of time and receive no external assistance at all. Learned helplessness is also what happens to educated and intelligent young men and women after social and family pressure has been successfully exerted on them to produce babies. Hidebound by tradition, they blindly have these babies. Is tradition a good reason to bring a child into existence?

It is with all young couples in mind that I write this book. And I must thank the sexually victimized children who spoke to me, even if I did not go beyond their comfortable questioning. That I could be responsible for their secondary victimization made me feel wary; but it is clearly something which does not bother most legal practitioners who tear the child to shreds in court. I have also considerably pared down the case studies which, when put down on paper, can easily read like child pornography. It takes very little to titillate a certain kind of person. Almost all the investigation and research for this book has, therefore, been condensed into a reader-friendly but near-academic presentation. Perhaps I err on the side of caution. But I have been petrified that I could do worse—turn the child's plight into some kind of distant but delicious horror which does not, or cannot, happen in any reader's home.

If, as a reader of this book, you have been sexually abused in childhood, please know this first—it was not your fault. Some of you may nevertheless feel unsettled while reading sections of this book. It is all right to feel this way, Child Sexual Abuse is unsettling; anyone who is not unsettled by the subject would be the one with the problem. If you are a reader who has been sexually abused in childhood, never disclosed it to anybody and are now grieving as you look at this book, it is all right. It is all right to grieve, in doing so you honour your pain. But you must, thereafter, move on.

Which is why I separately address those who might be feeling re-victimized. If you are, I say this to you: please skip more than the first half of the book and go straight to the section where an exit cycle has been explained. In the earlier section there is a reference to the survivor's cycle. A survivor of Child Sexual Abuse is one who has lived through an appalling experience in which her, and his, inner integrity has been sought to be destroyed. There has been a violation of such enormous proportions that it is only to be expected that the survivor's automatic response will be protection. But please do not find this protection in remaining in the survivor's cycle. Adults who were sexually abused in childhood are not just 'survivors', they have another far more complete adult identity as whole individuals; to introduce yourself as a 'survivor' of Child Sexual Abuse is to trap yourself in that vicious circle. So: read the exit cycle. My best wishes on its execution and your future life as a complete adult.

This book is for adults. But it is about children. Our children, and the child in each of us. The real child, and the child that is crying loudly inside the adult. Please help protect this child.

• **PINKI VIRANI**
Mumbaii
27 July 2000

notebook one

•

Vaishali   **Three months**   **Mumbaii**

Vaishali's aayee is changing her diaper when the phone rings in the hall. She calls out to Uday, the boy-servant whom they have brought from their village to assist her in housework after she delivered Vaishali.

'Uday, answer the phone.'

Vaishali's aayee hears Uday moving from the kitchen to the hall, Uday is being of help even if he is slightly moody at times. Actually, she had wanted a girl from the village but her mother-in-law had said there were unmarried men in the house, her husband's two brothers; and her mother-in-law felt the girl might try to act fresh with her sons. Seventeen-year-old Uday it was, vetted by her mother-in-law.

'It is your mother,' says Uday from the door of her bedroom.

'Tell her I will call her back.'

Uday disappears and reappears. 'She says it is important.'

Vaishali's aayee puts the blue powder-puff she has just picked up back into its plastic container and loosely caps it. She quickly sets bolsters around Vaishali on the bed and tells Uday to keep an eye on her.

Vaishali's aayee goes into the hall and picks up the receiver.

'What is so important, aayee?'

'We are fixing your brother's marriage.'

'Oh, this is good news, who is the girl?'

Vaishali's aayee sits down on the sofa-cum-bed in the hall to listen to the details of her brother's future bride, her family, the auspicious dates—these are right now because the next six months are inauspicious—the dowry they are willing to give this computer engineer boy, all the preparations which have to be quickly done, the people who have to be invited; the girl's side will pay the expenses, of course, for the hall and dinner . . .

There is a slight sound from the bedroom, Vaishali's mother cocks her ear, no sound after that.

'Uday,' she calls out, 'is Vaishali sleeping?'

'Yes,' he answers from the bedroom itself, 'she is.'

Vaishali's aayee continues the phone conversation and hangs up when the door bell rings.

'Enough for now about your son's marriage,' she tells her mother, 'you have spoken of nothing else for the past twenty-five minutes, you have not even asked about Vaishali. Now I have to go, we will talk later.'

Vaishali's aayee answers the door, it is her second brother-in-law, home for lunch as always, and he heads straight for the bedroom to look at Vaishali. Everyone in their house dotes on the three-month-old infant.

Vaishali's chacha goes towards her bed where she sleeps diaperless, her podgy little legs crooked outwards at the knees. Uday is sitting at the edge of the bed, he gets up and goes back into the kitchen. Vaishali's chacha bends over to nibble-nudge her on her toes with his mouth. He frowns. He sniffs. He stops mid-stoop and runs his eyes over Vaishali. He straightens up.

'Did you leave her alone?' he demands of Vaishali's aayee.

Vaishali's aayee gets frightened, she says, 'Yes, yes, just for a few minutes to talk on the phone. But what is wrong?'

'You damn women, always talking-talking!'

Vaishali's chacha bends over her again and softly begins sniffing in a systematic way, in her vagina area. Vaishali's aayee protests, 'Chee, what are you doing?'

'Shut up,' he tells her, 'just shut up, you cannot even keep an eye on your own infant! Wait till my brothers come home, then you will understand what you have done.'

Vaishali's chacha gently sets his dialling finger on Vaishali's vagina area and moves it. His finger encounters a sticky spot. He rubs the stickiness between his two fingers and then sniffs at it.

'Take her for a bath,' he orders Vaishali's aayee.

'But I gave her a bath in the morning. She will catch cold.'

'Just do it.'

Vaishali's chacha goes to the kitchen and Vaishali's aayee takes her to the bathroom.

By the time Vaishali is back in bed, re-bathed, powdered, re-diapered, breast-fed, swaddled and content, Vaishali's chacha has slapped Uday and sacked him.

Vaishali's aayee gets her slap in the night.

• what is child sexual abuse?

Is what happened to Vaishali—even though she does not know it, and hopefully never will—Child Sexual Abuse?

Yes. It is.

A tuition master reprimands his girl-student by touching her—non-accidentally and clearly more than once—on the side of her breasts instead of her arm. Child Sexual Abuse?

Yes. Definitely.

The family doctor shows the child pornographic pictures.

Yes.

A grandfather never shows his penis to his granddaughter or touches her vagina. He makes her sit on his lap and strokes her thigh. Sometimes the granddaughter feels something hard as she sits on his lap and he strokes her. But because they love each other so much, she lets him. Yet, the feeling of discomfort lingers.

Yes.

Child Sexual Abuse includes:

- an adult exposing his, or her, genitals to a child or persuading the child to do the same
- an adult touching a child's genitals or making the child touch the adult's genitalia
- an adult involving a child in pornography which includes showing a child pornographic material
- an adult having oral, vaginal or anal intercourse with a child
- any verbal or other sexual suggestion made to a child by an adult
- an adult persuading children to engage in sexual activity among themselves
- an adult inserting foreign objects into a child's body for his, or her, own sexual gratification

A comprehensive, albeit wordily academic, definition of Child Sexual Abuse would be the one provided by Driver and Droisen in 1989: 'Any sexual behaviour directed at a person under sixteen years of age without that person's informed consent. Sexual behaviour may involve touching parts of the child or requesting the child touch oneself, itself or others; ogling the child in a sexual manner, taking pornographic photographs, or requiring the child look at parts of the body, sexual acts or other material in a way which is arousing to oneself; and verbal comments or suggestions to the child which are intended to threaten the child sexually or otherwise to provide sexual gratification for oneself. It must be defined by every circumstance in which it occurs: in families, in state-run and private institutions, on the street, in classrooms, in pornography, advertising and films.'

To be noted, carefully: the definition encompasses both adult males and adult females since Child Sexual Abuse is a crime committed by women as well even if their numbers are miniscule when compared with men-perpetrators.

Also to be noted: the use of the phrase 'informed' in the first sentence itself of the definition by Driver and Droisen. It is a phrase that has been carefully applied. For what would constitute sexual 'consent' in an under-sixteen-year-old child? What are the criteria for deciding that the information the child has makes him/her suitably informed? Which is why, the world over and in India too—after extensive surveys, studies and professional opinion on the intelligence and emotional quotient of teenagers—it is generally prescribed that all those sixteen years of age and below are to be considered as incapable of informed consent. These children, even if teenagers at sixteen, have not formed certain defences inside themselves, like older people. They, therefore, need special protection. The phrase 'informed consent', then, takes on a very important connotation in a definition which encompasses almost every walk of life for the child.

There are large sections on the internet as there are pockets in the real world—unfortunately, they exist in India as well—who appear to delight in the sexualization of a child; they revel in its early eroticization, completely ignoring the very adult—and mostly perverted—reasons for this being the case. These people tend to comprise sexualized adults, as also religious fanatics who see women purely as procreative objects, paedophiles and one stream from among the homosexuals and lesbians who cite 'sexually active' children as their reasons for ignoring that important lakshman rekha of a child's age.

This book follows the sixteen years of age and below stipulation in addressing Child Sexual Abuse. (To be noted: teenagers are considered legally 'juvenile' till the age of eighteen; crimes by them are dealt with by the juvenile board.) Accordingly, cases which have come to light of other girls, and the few boys, in their late teens—seventeen, eighteen and nineteen—being sexually abused by the male members of their families have not been included. However, this does not intend to invalidate what those teenagers go through specially since age is no guarantee against emotional wounding; least of all a calendar which moves from sixteen to seventeen with more rapidity than a human being's maturity.

What would be the immediate signs that the child is being sexually abused? There will be sudden physical and behavioural changes in the child, some of which could be the following. Please remember that the signs may not necessarily show up as a cluster:

- bed-wetting (this is not to be confused with sleep disorder bed-wetting)
- continuous loose motions or passing stools in bed
- hysterical reactions
- temper tantrums, aggressive behaviour
- depression, anxiety, withdrawal
- deep sense of isolation

- avoiding certain adults
- not concentrating at school or failing in exams
- attempting to physically hurt itself
- constant rubbing of body part against objects
- use of sexual words
- the child becoming focussed on its own genitals
- sexual exploration and abuse of other children
- constant throat and urinary infections
- irritation in the throat, anal and genital area
- recurrent abdominal pain
- sexually transmitted diseases
- running away from home
- masturbation
- substance abuse
- inability to eat certain foods that resemble the male organ or semen
- precocious sexual behaviour
- promiscuity, prostitution-like behaviour
- genital, urethral or anal trauma
- pregnancy
- committing suicide (This is being added after two cases last year, in 1999: in September an eleven-year-old middle-class Mumbaii girl killed herself after being sexually molested by her father; and in July a thirteen-year-old girl was raped by her stepfather in Lucknow, her mother got him arrested immediately but the girl committed suicide in September.)

Or there might be none of the above signs.

Instead, the child might very suddenly get hysterical. At least from the point of view of the parents who clearly are not in touch with their child's internal tuning it would appear to be hysterical. For the child, this outburst would represent an eruption of what it has been trying to quell

9

since a while. As a family in Delhi discovered. Their child suddenly begins to get frightened of the family dog. She insists the family dog is going to eat her up. It takes a long time for the parents to realize that their daughter is being sexually abused by her mother's brother whenever he visits, under their very nose since the last few years.

Or the child might not even get hysterical, it might not say anything at all. It might slowly, and quietly, begin playing telling games with its toys; and how many parents care to monitor what the child is doing with its toys? Child counsellors often allow, and encourage, their little patients to tell them 'stories' through toys during therapy. These ordinary looking toys which appear to be scattered around among cushions and colourful books are specially placed there to assist the child in talking about what has happened. Well into a few unsuccessful sessions, the child might pick up a toy tiger and stuff it under a cushion. 'Lock it up in that jail,' the child will tell the doctor, 'otherwise it will eat you up.' Later, much later, the counsellor will keep near the child an anatomically correct doll: a male doll with reasonably defined genitals; some counsellors view this as obscene and feel it frightens the child, others see it as enabling children to bring their experiences from the abstract to the concrete. Even if the counsellor has introduced the male doll into the proceedings with great caution and sensitivity, the child might get frightened. Or it might ignore it for the longest time. And then, without warning, pick it up, point towards the penis and say, 'Naughty tiger, hurts me.' Several conversations will follow, perhaps running even into weeks, about the naughty tiger and hurt without the child disclosing the perpetrator's name. That a toy will, and can, be such an important means of communication with a child; do the parents ever realize this?

And some children might bury it so completely that

when it resurfaces in their late teens and early adulthood it is almost unrecognizable as Child Sexual Abuse.

A twenty-two-year-old girl participating in a sex-and-gender workshop has fits when they begin to discuss Child Sexual Abuse.

A twenty-year-old medical student refuses to go to college, she is extremely fearful about it. The clinical diagnosis is anxiety neurosis with panic. During therapy she reveals that she had been raped by her uncle when she was eleven years old and threatened with dire consequences if she ever told anybody. The uncle continued to be a frequent visitor to her house, interacting freely with her father and brother who were always happy to see him. This made her wonder about her father and brother too, and she became reserved in all her interactions with them.

When she finished with her all-girls school to join medical college she developed panic attacks when speaking with male classmates. She hated her male classmates so much that no amount of therapy helped, she had to drop out of college altogether.

The uncle continues to visit their home.

•   **home as hell**

All right.

Granted that Child Sexual Abuse is an evil practice.

Also agreed that Child Sexual Abuse is about a ruthless combination of sexual abuse, of emotional abuse and of physical abuse.

But why now, all this and so much of it too, when these are acts restricted to perverts?

And why an entire book on Child Sexual Abuse in India when it is perpetrated only by the lower classes upon

11

their unfortunate children?

Because there is this misconception among several in the so-called upper classes that what happens among People Like Them, specially People Like That (Plat), does not touch, and therefore should not concern, People Like Us (Plus). Those people do not come in contact with our children and us? Really? Where do you suppose—if you incorrectly insist that Child Sexual Abusers come only from People Like Them and That—drivers hired for cars and other vehicles, bus conductors, cooks, peons in schools and offices, mailmen, delivery boys, watchmen, come from?

Because you need to know, especially if you are a concerned parent, that the People Like Them are not as much the People Like That as they are the People Like Us. The former do not have constant physical access to our children as the latter do.

Because right now in Varanasi, there is a mother on the run; she is being hounded by her husband and his family for confronting him with sexually abusing his school going, thirteen-year-old daughter for over a year. She is a middle-class housewife.

Because in Mumbaii a young mother is moving every single court so that she can keep her little girl away from the grandfather; he has stuck his finger into her so often, and with so much affection, that the baby's hymen has been torn. The mother is upper class and several judges will not believe her for this reason. Her husband believed her until his father reminded him that he was part of the family business. The husband chose his own survival over that of his wife and daughter. The husband's mother, the child's grandmother that is, knew what her elderly husband had been doing to their granddaughter, she did nothing to stop it.

Because in a Delhi court a child has been cross-questioned by an army of lawyers hired by her bureaucrat-father. 'Which finger did your papa put into you? This one, or this one?' Papa took his little girl to a hotel room where he was joined by female and male colleagues. They switched on blue films, they had orgies. Papa made his little girl drink alcohol and they all, aunties and uncles, did things together. But papa was particular, nobody could touch his little girl whom he loved so much except him. So while the aunties and uncles watched, only papa did things to her. The lawyer asks her in court, 'What colour drink did your papa give you? White or brown?' The child says white. 'Yesterday you said brown, today you are saying white? Papa did not give you anything to drink, did he? You little liar!'

Because a woman had to run all the way from America to India to physically separate her daughter from her non-resident Indian father who had been systematically abusing the girl all these years. She, and her parents, approached a court in India for both divorce and custody over the daughter. The court said it found her accusations against her husband 'eerie', therefore unbelievable.

Because a fifteen-year-old, a student in one of Chennai's best colleges, has taken to being a high-class call-girl on weekends. This is how she deals with the 'guilt' of not being able to sexually ward off her mother's second husband, an industrialist.

Because a young wife holds her breath as her husband bathes their little daughter in their Mumbaii flat; the wife has been sexually abused as a child by the family cook in their Andhra Pradesh village.

Because a four-year-old is being abused by her father in Calcutta and her mother is hesitant to take any concrete steps against this since they are well known and this would create a public scandal. The parents have a history of marital disharmony, the Child Sexual Abuse might well be carrying on even as this book is being read. 'We are absolutely helpless to do anything as there are no guidelines, acts or social service networks that professionals could resort to in such instances of suspicion,' says psychiatrist Dr Sujit Ghosh. 'The existing legal framework, too, is completely unrealistic apart from being user-unfriendly when it comes to intervening on, and even preventing, Child Sexual Abuse.'

Because on 26 January 2000, a ragpicker found six-year-old Sunny's sexually assaulted body in a dumping ground at a Mumbaii suburb. His friends later said Sunny never disclosed his name but he did often speak of an uncle who gave him chocolates. Sunny's grandmother said he told her too about the chocolates but she never paid attention because they were busy with the preparations for Sunny's chacha's wedding.

Because Dr Sharda Chand of the Dufferin Hospital in Lucknow, the only approved centre in Lucknow for the medico-legal examination of rape victims, says that the youngest victim of child-rape that the hospital has recently seen is a six-month-old girl. 'The child was in a mess, badly mutilated and bleeding profusely. It took our team all their skill to sew up her internal organs.' February 2000, say other doctors sardonically at the same hospital, was their leanest month, only eleven cases compared with twenty which they get of rapes, half the victims being below thirteen years of age.

Because Syeeda Hameed, member of the National Commission for Women, says in her inaugural address at 'Recognising Violence Against Children in the Private Sphere' that, 'It can be a myth that home is the safest place for children.' She adds that around forty children had deposed before the National Commission for Women in

1999, narrating tales of sexual abuse at home.

Because at the same seminar super-cop Kiran Bedi says that 56 per cent of sexual violation cases against children take place within the home of the victim or the offender. She adds, 'The victim cuts across all categories of class, caste, religion and educational background; the offender belongs to no particular age group.'

Because an eleven-year-old girl has been raped by 'Sirji', her class teacher, in his home. He took her from her home in the central Mumbaii area of Wadala to his home in the distant suburb of Ghatkopar, with the help of his sister who phoned the girl's parents and said she would be safe.

Because in the Mumbaii suburb of Malad, a physical training teacher of a municipal-run school has sexually molested several girls. The thirty-five-year-old instructor denies it in spite of a few of the girls complaining to their parents after one girl was hounded out of the school by him when she refused to oblige and take off her clothes on the school's terrace. The teacher denies it because he knows that the time the legal system takes will ensure he is exonerated. The girls by then will have finished school, be married, perhaps have had children, why would they want to come to court as victims?

Because a nine-year-old child artiste from the Tamil and Telugu film industry has been severely injured in her vagina by her fifty-year-old neighbour, a well-employed family man in Hyderabad. Her mother, a small-time actress, has died of the shock. The child, along with her twenty-year-old physically impaired sister who can only drag her body around, is now in Hyderabad's only shelter for girls, Ankuram. They are from two different fathers, neither wants them; their maternal relatives say they cannot help either. Their mother's boyfriend, a junior artiste in the film industry, moved into their house with his friends and liquor bottles and began contracting work in the films for the nine-year-old. Then they were shifted to Ankuram by the Juvenile Rights Forum and Childline.

Because Childline is registering far too many phone calls from children in sexual and physical agony. Childline—brainchild of a Mumbaii wonder-woman who shuns the spotlight, thirty-four-year-old Jeroo Billimoria—is a centrally-funded phone line for children in distress; they can dial 1098—dus nau aath, ten nine eight—to try and get help. Ten nine eight is available in Mumbaii, Calcutta, Chennai, Delhi, Hyderabad, Nagpur, Patna, Bhopal, Coimbatore. It is to be connected in Ahmedabad, Varanasi, Bhubaneshwar, Jaipur and Goa. In the existing cities it has registered, till 1999, 780 calls from children needing protection from sexual and physical abuse. In Delhi alone, from October 1998 to December 1999, it has registered 315 phone calls from children being sexually and physically abused. Other Indian metros are no different. Childline city co-ordinator Neelam Kawalramani gives a Mumbaii example. A child servant, in a doctor's home, has welts and marks and as much as a tiny body can take. 'They promised the child's parents in the village that they would educate it in the city. When I asked the doctor's wife why she had not done it, she replied, "Oh the child did not want to study",' says Kawalramani who shifted the child out of the doctor's house and initiated proceedings against the couple. Has the child also been sexually abused? Is a child who has gone through this much going to just come right out and say it? And what future pattern of behaviour is being set for the doctor's two children as they watch this?

Because international data on Child Sexual Abuse is suggesting that a large number of female criminals take to crime because they had been sexually abused in childhood. Child Sexual Abuse cuts across all cultures in the world and even reduces it to a 'sameness'; there is thus an urgent need for the recognition of the problem so that measures are put in place to prevent little girls from being sexually abused and growing into criminals.

Because little boys who have been sexually abused also grow up to be criminals but with a twist. Three teenagers have been arrested in a Mumbaii suburb on 30 December 1999, for sodomizing two young boys, ages seven and five, before killing them. The teenagers have said they did it because they were sexually abused as children by their elders.

Because formal education or being a public figure does not have much to do with stopping Child Sexual Abuse. A well-known male lawyer in Delhi, who speaks effectively on human rights, is also well known for continuously sexually abusing his two nieces until they were old enough to put a stop to it themselves.

Because mere empowerment, too, does not seem enough to stop it. In Pharala, the Nawanshahri area of Punjab, a sarpanchni—woman sarpanch—is refusing to come to the aid of an eight-and-a-half-year-old girl who has been raped by her chacha, father's younger brother. The sarpanchni, has in fact, aligned with the chacha's sisters and beat up the mother for daring to lodge a complaint. She says, 'If you don't obey the panchayat and the village's important men, people will start boycotting you.' The village has declared the girl unmarriageable even as she screams in pain at the Nawanshahr Civil Hospital, the child cannot urinate or defecate without severe trauma. The only support her mother has is a widowed mother who came to comfort them when she heard the child screaming in pain at the hospital. The girl's vagina and other wounds have not healed even after forty days, the mother plans on taking the child to Ludhiana for an Aids test.

Because there are more than enough surveys today which are being collated to prove that Child Sexual Abuse (CSA) is on the rise in our country. And it is as rampant in high-class and middle-class homes as 'lower' ones.

•   **what the numbers reveal**

Numbers? What kind of statistics should anyone want as proof that the enemy is within—that the highest number of Child Sexual Abuse takes place within the four walls of a supposedly secure home? What numbers would constitute 'more' or 'too much' so that the so-called society in India finally agrees that Child Sexual Abuse is today's crisis?

Meanwhile the perpetrator is emboldened—that father, the uncle, cousin, grandfather, male relative and friend of the parents—and he does it yet again. He has free and easy access to the child's body in the child's own home and he knows that even if the child hesitantly voices her—and increasingly his—trauma, the truth will be denied. 'Hush,' the child will be told, 'little children should not talk like this!' Child Sexual Abuse, thus, for the perpetrator is about malevolence, and the mastery of it.

But yes, there are numbers available today. Statistics which make for damning disclosures about what is really happening to children among Indian families, more so in upper-income Indian homes. It can no longer be our best kept, and darkest, secret.

The police agree with this. Off-the-record, that is. 'It is an invisible crime,' they say. 'A denied social syndrome and we can do nothing. We can only deal with evidence.' And so they can only move when a child is brought in, torn from stem-to-stern, a ruptured anus, a tiny vagina in shreds. By that time it is late, far too late. The child is stitched up and sent back home sixty days later. To live with blood, pain, school, homework. And the perpetrator who mocks from the sidelines as he is sprung on bail.

The World Health Organization says one out of every ten children in India is being sexually abused at any given point of time.

A Tata Institute of Social Sciences study conducted in 1985 among adults between the ages of twenty and twenty-four proved that one out of three girls had been sexually abused as children, and one out of every ten boys. That is: 30 per cent of the girls had been victims of Child Sexual Abuse, and ten per cent of the boys. 50 per cent of this Child Sexual Abuse happened at home.

A 1996 survey—now considered a landmark in work on Child Sexual Abuse—conducted by Samvada in Bangalore among 348 girl students from eleven schools and colleges, threw up startling data. Conducted scientifically by Anita Ratnam with Lucy Kumar, Dr Arun Kotenkar and Dr Shekhar Seshadri, the first doctor in the country to specifically study Child Sexual Abuse, it found:

- 83 per cent of the girls had been subject to eve-teasing, 13 per cent of these had been vocally and visually sexually harassed when they were less than ten years old
- 47 per cent had been molested, 15 per cent of these when they were less than ten years old: they were used for masturbation, mostly by male relatives
- 15 per cent had been seriously sexually abused as children, 31 per cent of them when they were less than ten years old: they had been raped, forced into oral sex or penetrated with foreign objects and 75 per cent of

the abusers were adult family members
- around 50 per cent of these Child Sexual Abuse cases involved family members and close relatives, they happened at home.

Dr Shekhar Seshadri has recently completed a study on boys, 146 of them between the ages of sixteen and twenty. He has found that 15 per cent of them have been abused as children by uncles, male cousins, family friends and neighbours; this homosexual abuse starts at six years of age. Another 8 per cent of the boys had their first sexual experience with elder women from the age of twelve onwards; with family friends, the neighbouring aunts, female cousins and mother's friends. The boys saw these experiences with older women as pleasurable initiation into the world of sex, it is not a reaction that came up equivocally in connection with the homosexual experiences. Much of this sexual abuse of boy-children happened at home.

Sakshi, the Delhi-based organization which spearheaded work on Child Sexual Abuse in the early 1990s, has a study of 357 school-going girl children. 63 per cent have been victims, around half had abusers from within their homes and close family circles.

Rahi of Delhi has run a survey specifically addressing non-lower-class women. This Child Sexual Abuse survey conducted among 600 English-speaking middle-and upper-class women in Delhi, Mumbaii, Calcutta, Goa and Chennai has women of ages ranging from fifteen to sixty-six.

- 76 per cent of these 600 women had been sexually abused in childhood
- out of these 457, 40 per cent had been sexually abused by at least one family member
- 71 per cent had been sexually abused by relatives and family friends

- 2 per cent of the 457 were sexually abused before they were four years of age
- 17 per cent between four and eight years of age
- 28 per cent between the ages of eight and twelve years
- 35 per cent between twelve and sixteen years

In most cases of the survey of this section of Indian society, the abuser was a part of the victim's everyday life, in the form of a father, brother, male cousin, uncle, male family friend, male neighbour and servant. A majority of the respondents had multiple abusers, once again proof that women internalize the oppressive qualities of their oppressor; those victimized borrowing the worst qualities of their aggressors and using it on themselves. The abuse of the women took place when the respondents were children in Mumbaii (115), Delhi (72), Calcutta (28), Chennai (7), Patna and Nagpur (5), Bangalore and Srinagar (4), Pune, Goa, Allahabad, Jamshedpur, Ahmedabad and Dehradun (3), the others were sexually abused as children while residing from Cochin to Chandigarh. More than 50 per cent of these cases happened at home.

Other organizations in India working on child rights collate the figures at five out of every eight girls and three out of every eight boys. That is 62.5 per cent of girls and 37.5 per cent of boys, from the ages of a few months all the way up to sixteen years of age, are victims of Child Sexual Abuse in India.

The police unofficially peg Child Sexual Abuse in India at 40 per cent of girls and 25 per cent of boys under the age of sixteen, cutting across class and community lines. This does not include physical violence against a child, child rape and child prostitution which the police categorize differently.

Perhaps the answer lies, as always, somewhere in

between. Child Sex Abuse in India would realistically stand at around 50 per cent of girls and 30 per cent of boys under sixteen years of age. However, this book will use the police's figures as final: 40 per cent of girls and 25 per cent of boys below sixteen years of age are victims of Child Sexual Abuse in India.

Given the furtiveness of the perpetrator, the secrecy by society and the silence of those lambs, the sexually sacrificial children, it would be well-nigh impossible to run a confirmation on any kind of statistic. It would also be very difficult, even with the most sophisticated co-relates— without the presence of, say, an exhaustive nationwide survey on kids below sixteen—to indicate whether Child Sexual Abuse is on the increase. The one point that can definitely be made from international data and sociological experience is that Child Sexual Abuse does not increase exponentially if there is an intensive awareness on the subject and immediate intervention by concerned adults in potential situations. In societies outside India, where parents and schools have empowered children on how to avoid or deflect sexual abuse, there is even a small fall in cases.

However, it would be incorrect to say that any reporting on Child Sexual Abuse does not necessarily indicate an increase, and that it merely reflects the situation that more cases are coming forward to be reported. In the Indian context this would be as ludicrous as saying women are not raped any more than they used to be, it is just the reporting of their rape that has increased. Child Sexual Abuse is an Indian family's deepest, and most jointly-held, secret. What is the likelihood of these secrets finding their way out of the family while the child is still in a position to be rescued from the abusers within it? And how is this family to be identified when social, economic and educational status are no barriers to Child Sexual Abuse;

neither are caste or religious background? Thus almost all Child Sexual Abuse cases remain unreported in a country where only 25 per cent of the rapes on adult women reach a police station.

What has reached the police stations in Mumbaii is perhaps the most damning indictment of the entire ostensible 'upper' social structure. Nahida Sheikh and Trupti Panchal have compiled data from a handful of police stations in Mumbaii's inner city areas. This very small survey which works out of information available on police records reveals more than enough. That upper and lower classes behave no differently when it comes to sex. That 68 per cent of Child Sexual Abuse on 'lower' class little girls had been perpetrated by male family members and acquaintances trusted by the victims. More than half this Child Sexual Abuse has taken place at home.

So. They are all the same—these evil perpetrators of Child Sexual Abuse, class no bar. They use their own home, or that of the little child's. Home is clearly where the maximum harm is.

The study also reveals another similar pattern among upper, middle and lower-class homes. The perpetrators tend to coldly calculate the time for the act, when they are free. Normally, they are gainfully employed males. Only 27 per cent of this survey have non-working offenders, the rest have their own business or are employed (peons in offices, carpenters, drivers). Alcohol is used as an excuse when they are caught as is the line, 'She made me do it to her.' Again, just like the middle and upper classes.

There is another set of statistics which need very carefully studying in connection with Child Sexual Abuse—that of child prostitution. The End Child Prostitution in Asian Tourism (Ecpat) estimates this global phenomenon to be a US$ 5 billion industry including trafficking, sex tourism and pornography. In India, it accounts for Rs 11,000 crore of the Rs 40,000 crore commercial sex industry.

A survey by the country's Central Welfare Board has found that:

- there are an estimated 2 million child prostitutes in our country between the ages of five and fifteen years
- 80 per cent of these child prostitutes are to be found in the five major metros
- girls between the ages of ten and fourteen years are the most vulnerable
- 15 per cent of these child prostitutes are below fifteen years of age and 25 per cent between the ages of fifteen and eighteen years
- 5,00,000 children—little boys included—are forced into this trade every single year

Says Keith Oliver, detective in the police force of Great Britain, who recently extensively toured India through the British Councils to speak with concerned citizens and the police. 'It is no secret that places in India like Goa are being used for sex tourism. The internet is being used in a big way by paedophiles the world over to access "easy" places to visit, these people then reach places like Goa for, and only, sex with little children, specially the boys. India should not sit in isolation on this subject, also because your children are being sent to other parts of the world too by pimps for child prostitution.' Perhaps this is where they go, the little girls and boys who vanish forever from our minds after we see their pictures in the papers and on television as 'missing'.

Police and organizations who work with rescued child prostitutes report a not insignificant number of these children having run away from home. One of the key reasons for this is they were being sexually abused in their homes. Sneh Sadan in Mumbaii runs fifteen homes for children who have run away from home, at any given point of time they house 370 children, of which half would be girls. Points out their social worker Sangeeta Punekar, 'These children run away because they feel emotionally neglected or are abused at home, physically and sexually. They do not tell us this immediately but eventually they do disclose if they have been sexually abused. Most of the children doing the disclosing are the girls and they have run away to escape from the sexual abuse of their stepfathers, fathers, paternal and maternal uncles, even their aunts' husbands or aunts' father-in-laws. I watch these parents flying in from parts of India to take their children back home and I really wonder why they had these children in the first place. It seems to me that not too many children in India are being borne out of love.'

• child rape

Sangeeta Punekar's words echo in what organizations working with street children report. An increasing number of similar stories; with children running away from home because of sexual assault. These children have been subjected to varying degrees of sexual abuse, from oral sex to fondling to finger, object and penile penetration. A Star News feature on Delhi's street children had a male child, he could not have been over twelve years of age, sleeping on a railway platform. He had run away from home in Patna where his stepfather, a police official, had been trying to rape him.

Penile penetration is the only kind being considered by the law as child rape currently, objects like candles, bottles and bananas are not; additionally, forcing the penis into a child's mouth slips through the legal cracks and sodomy gets tagged under 'unnatural offences'. (At the time of this book going to press, the Law Commission of India has recommended measures to redefine rape laws to prevent the sexual abuse of children and women; laws can only be changed when Parliament agrees.) But even under the restrictive legal definition of child rape—and the fact that rapes also go unreported—the statistics are horrific.

There is no breakdown available on how many of these child rapes have taken place at home or by male members of the family but the rough pattern would be around 50 per cent, maintain police authorities. Is it this 50 per cent which emboldens the other half towards sexually molesting a child or this extreme form of Child Sexual Abuse outside the house?

It can also happen like this. So suddenly, so devastatingly, in any home. A family in Calcutta orders a crate of mineral water, their nine-year-old daughter opens the door as the maid is otherwise occupied. The deliveryman is a known one, from around the corner. He whisks the child away to the deserted stairwell, rapes her and runs away. He is yet to be caught, he is not likely to be.

Why did the child not even scream? Has he been 'priming' her from before, touching her when he came for previous deliveries? Or did the child not scream because she is used to it in her own home? Has the deliveryman been doing it to other children? Why have they not complained? Or have they, and their parents have told them to keep quiet? Has the deliveryman been doing it to little girls, and boys, in his own neighbourhood? Where has this deliveryman come from, some other city where he did it to another little girl outside her own home? Is he another Uday who has been simply thrown out of one home like little Vaishali's, and landed in another?

Increasingly it is meshing. People Like Them. People Like Us. The nastiness of one spilling over into the other.

And more and more it is happening. Children setting upon other children. Criminally, sexually.

- On 12 February 2000, three pre-teen boys raped a seven-year-old girl in Calcutta; they lured the girl who was watching video in her own home to a secluded place through her nine-year-old male neighbour. They tempted her with chocolate and then gang raped her.
- A seven-year-old girl was similarly lured by her teenaged neighbour in Krishna Nagar, Uttar Pradesh. He raped her in broad daylight, and when asked why, he said, 'I wanted to see what it was like.'
- An eleven-year-old boy from Hyderabad has played 'doctor-doctor' so savagely with his nine-year-old sister that she bled till late evening. Their father is a child specialist.
- In another 'mummy-daddy-get-married' game, a fourteen-year-old boy in Chandigarh has bit his ten-year-old cousin sister's nipples so hard that she needed extensive medical attention.

Are these children getting this message from adults—that it is all right to do something, anything, to a child? Child psychiatrist Dr Shekhar Seshadri nods grimly and says, 'When children set upon children to sexually abuse them, it is very different from the initial, mild and occasional sexual exploration they conduct among themselves at a particular age. The increasing cases of Child Sexual Abuse among children, and upon each other, tend to be for three reasons. Substance abuse like drugs, glue-sniffing, alcohol and the like which reduces restraint. If they have themselves been sexually abused by their elders. Or when they model themselves on adults.'

Meanwhile, the statistics grow. Every child who is raped by an adult turns into a statistic. A life barely lived, already a horrific statistic:

- 3,393 children were raped in 1993; 634 of these were below ten years
- 3,986 children were raped in 1994; 727 of these were below ten years
- 4,067 children were raped in 1995; 747 of these were below ten years
- 4,083 children were raped in 1996; 608 of these were below ten years
- 4,414 children were raped in 1997; 770 of these were below ten years

That is an 8.1 per cent increase in 1997 over 1996, of children sixteen years of age and below.

And it is a 30 per cent increase in five years, from 1993.

Look closely, compute roughly. These statistics also reveal that there is a shocking 26.6 per cent increase of rapes on children below ten years of age within a year, from 1996 to 1997.

Curious about a state-wise breakdown? Madhya Pradesh, Maharashtra, Uttar Pradesh, Andhra Pradesh, Delhi and West Bengal accounted for a staggering 65.8 per cent of the total number of child-rape cases reported in 1997.

Another permutation. Of all the rape victims reported in the country in 1997, children alone account for 28.8 per cent of the all-India share.

Figures for 1998 initially available at the time of this book going to press is 15,031 cases of rape in the country. Of this 56 per cent involve women in the age group of 16 to 30 years; 22.8 per cent are children raped in the age group of 10 to 16 years and children below 10 tote up 4.2 per cent of the total rapes committed in 1998. Children are still accounting for more than a quarter of the country's reported rapes. This, even though the reporting of rape has lessened in the country due to the understaffed, and largely indifferent, police as also a painfully slow, and largely callous, judicial system which does nothing to empower a woman's complaint. A child's rape by an adult goes into the same police station and courts. Or it does not, as is sadly apparent in the figures between 1997, when the rape cases reported were 15,336, and the 1998 figures which register a 2 per cent, 'on paper', decline. This 'on paper' decline, therefore, also does not accurately reflect the real percentage of child rapes.

So: let us work with 1997 statistics—4,414 children raped.

That is: there are twelve children being raped every single day in India.

And then there are those children who are raped but their cases do not get registered as police complaints. The Bundelkhand Mahila Manch speaks of one such case in their area. A ten-year-old girl was invited into the home of her neighbour for 'kanya puja'. The 'master of the house' molested her, then penetrated her. The girl's parents went to the police where they were advised to drop the case since it would be 'very difficult' to get a conviction.

And, yet again, there are cases of children being raped within their own homes—by their extended families as well—and these do not go at all beyond the barred doors of the house. Just as there are cases of little boys being sodomized by uncles and male cooks which have yet to make it in any quantifiable number to any police station in the country. Little boys keep quiet, some of them even think of it as a 'rite of passage' until they grow older and find themselves an emotional mess. Little girls, well, they are little girls and the family's honour, izzat, shaan, is deep within that little vagina. Ergo, they cannot make it to a police station either, otherwise who will marry them then?

Police point out that almost all the cases of girl-child rape making it to police stations are from lower class, lower-middle-class and some middle-middle-class homes. There is virtually a deafening silence from upper-middle and upper-class homes. Since it does not stand to logic that little girls from these two classes are not being raped, and since there is also unofficial evidence that child rapes do transpire in these homes, police surmise that around 25 per cent of child rapes are not being reported in the country. This would include the police—perhaps even erring on the side of caution—unofficially computing child rapes which do not get reported from the other class of homes as well.

So that's 5,517 children being raped annually.

Assume that there is no growth at all in the child rape rate in the country from 1997 to 2000. Again, just to err on the side of caution.

That makes it fifteen children raped in India on any day.

Two questions.

If there are fifteen children being raped every single day in India today, how many more children are being otherwise sexually abused every single day?

If there is a 28.8 per cent increase in child rape, what kind of unreported increase is there in other forms of child sexual abuse?

One answer, in the form of yet another question.

Now do we still want to maintain this conspiracy of silence about what we are allowing to be done to our children?

•   a mother on the run

Think about this conspiracy of silence, even as a woman in Varanasi runs to protect her daughter from further sexual abuse. A brave woman paying a very heavy price for no fault of hers. Ila Pandey from Karvi in the Chitrakoot area of Uttar Pradesh, married to Jagdish Pandey of the dairy department in Karvi. They were married in 1986 and have three daughters, ages eleven, nine and four. In February 1999, her eldest daughter writes a small note to her mother disclosing that her father has been doing 'gandi harkat' with her. 'Gandi harkat'. Dirty acts. Ila confronts her husband, he brutally beats her up.

Ila contacts Vanangana, the local women's organization, for help. They try to intervene but are brushed off by Jagdish Pandey. Ila falls so ill with the stress that her mother who is visiting stays back to take care of her and on 7 March 1999, takes her away to the natal home. Ila manages to take her youngest daughter with her, Jagdish Pandey prevents her from taking her elder two daughters. Vanangana monitors these two daughters in Ila's absence while she reaches Varanasi and contacts the Social Action and Research Centre which works closely with Child Sexual Abuse in the district.

'Jagdish Pandey kept the two girls back saying they had their exams,' says Tulika Srivastava of the Association for Advocacy and Legal Initiative in Lucknow. 'He did sign papers to the effect that he would send the girls after their exams. On repeated requests from Ila for her two older daughters, Jagdish Pandey went to Chandauli and before the family mediator, Prem Shankar Tiwari, promised to send them within three days. But he did not do it, not even in May when their school was shut for the summer vacations.' It is only three months later, on 10 June 1999, that Ila Pandey can return to her husband's home; and with the legal and moral support provided by the two non-government organizations, she collects her two daughters in the absence of their father. She immediately appears before the judicial authorities in Karvi to record her statement that she is taking her children out of their father's custody.

When Jagdish Pandey discovers that his two daughters are no longer in his home, he enters the office of Vanangana, abuses the social workers and threatens them with rape and murder. He files a case of kidnapping against Madhavi Kukreja and Huma Khan, the Vanangana workers, and Manju Soni, a local activist from Karvi. Vanangana lodges a complaint of threat and intimidation against Jagdish Pandey at the police station, this does not deter him and he continues to threaten them, as also his wife and children who have since been moving from place to place. They have been running, hiding, running, Ila and her three daughters.

Star News reaches Karvi and a district official says on-camera, 'These things should remain in the family, it should not be encouraged to come out in the open or more people will be influenced to do such things.' Another man says, 'Well, the wife was sick all the time so what is a man to do?' And a judicial officer of Chitrakoot says, with a smile, on-camera, 'Child Sexual Abuse cases are ugly and disgusting. Such things should not be made public.' Meanwhile, Jagdish Pandey files a criminal writ petition in the Allahabad High Court for the stay of his arrest. Two days later, on 7 July, Ila Pandey intervenes to oppose the stay of his arrest. On 14 July, Jagdish Pandey requests the court that on his behalf, it should attempt reconciliation with his family. On 16 July there is an in-camera hearing with Ila and her eleven-year-old who refuse the offer of reconciliation. The court decrees that the case has to proceed and be decided on merit.

On 25 July the bail application of Jagdish Pandey, filed in the sessions court at Karvi/Chitrakoot, is rejected. Since he has spent forty-eight hours in police custody, he is suspended from his job. This comes into effect only when a group of women demonstrate outside the premises of the dairy department as well as outside the judicial and police premises. Jagdish Pandey's brothers in Karvi continue to threaten the social workers as well as Ila Pandey through her parents. On 5 August, the kidnapping complaints against the social workers are registered as first information reports and the additional chief judicial magistrate's court in Karvi directs that action—arrest and investigation— begin, following an application filed by Jagish Pandey's brothers at the court. The first information report covers the following sections of the Indian Penal Code: 363 (kidnapping or maiming a minor for begging), 366 (kidnapping, abduction or inducing a woman to end her marriage), 380 (theft in dwelling house), 387 (putting a person in fear of death and/or grievous hurt for extortion). All these offences are cognizable and non-bailable. In other words, the women who helped Ila Pandey can be arrested and thrown into jail at any minute.

One man commits incest, his brothers support him. How many women—how many generations of them—pay for it?

Yet the women supporting Ila Pandey and she herself stand firm. In October 1999 they hold a 'jan sunvaai'—a unique public hearing—in Karvi. Ila stands up to speak, as do several other women to narrate their stories of complete helplessness when it comes to physically and sexually protecting their girl children. Women in the audience break down as other women speak and weep, haltingly.

More than one hundred men present set up a chant saying such matters should be settled within 'the four walls of a home'. They whistle, they scream, they raise slogans. A politically-aligned student body—which has since insisted in other parts of the country that Valentine's Day be banned ('because it makes girls cheap') and women must not be allowed to wear jeans on the campus ('because it distracts us')—takes out a procession opposing the public hearing and raises slogans against Vanangana, 'Vanangana hatao, parivar bachao' ('throw out Vanangana to protect your family').

What kind of students are these who think that a family can be protected by ignoring the horrors within a home? What kind of homes are these students themselves coming from?

Grass-roots workers activist Bhanwari Bai stands up. She has come all the way from Rajasthan to narrate what has happened to Sonia in Ajmer. Sonia is all of sixteen, she has been married a few months in Ajmer and her father-in-law rapes her. In the presence of her husband and mother-in-law, who do nothing to discourage him.

The men in the hall boo and laugh. They distribute pamphlets demanding that the administration arrest these women activists as they are 'polluting Chitrakoot, the holy land of Ram' by raising such issues.

What kind of mothers do they have who could not teach them anything better? What kind of fathers have encouraged them? What does it say of the families which comprise such men? And what does this say of the families which such mothers and fathers come from?

●_____

arun

_____

Arun   **Ten years**   **New Delhi**

Arun is being regularly sodomized by his father's brother.

One day he picks up the courage, whips out the knife he has kept under his pillow and silently brandishes it when his uncle touches him. The sexual abuse stops.

Five years later.

Arun is fifteen, and asleep. He wakes up with a start, he has heard muffled laughter, he feels body heat near him. His eyes adjust to the lack of light, his uncle is standing over him, exposing himself. The boy's fingers go to his chest, he feels something sticky on it, and then more of it. His uncle muffles his laughter.

The boy gets up and goes to the bathroom. He pours water on himself. He scrubs himself with soap.

He goes back to bed.

The next morning he starts washing his hands.

Ten times a day.

Fifty times a day.

Seventy times a day.

Furtively.

He washes his hands ninety times a day when he thinks no one is looking.

One hundred and twenty-five times a day and night. Two hundred.

His fingers are red, the skin around his nails is peeling.

His parents take him to a well-known, and expensive, psychiatrist in Delhi.

There are several sessions, the psychiatrist prescribes 'downers' so that he does not wash his hands that often. Eventually, the boy tells the psychiatrist that he has been sexually abused by his uncle. The psychiatrist prescribes a new set of pills. The boy is now very drowsy and completely disoriented but terribly disturbed. He tells the psychiatrist this. The pills are changed once again.

The boy cannot attend to his studies anymore as a result of the pills. A male friend visits with books and notes and the boy breaks down. He tells his friend about what is happening to him right then. His parents will not believe him, his psychiatrist will not believe him, his uncle maintains his innocence. The friend makes a few inquiries and is told about Ifsha, an organization counselling cases of Child Sexual Abuse.

Ifsha tries to help Arun, minus all the pills; decent progress is made in Arun's condition through intensive counselling.

But then one day, Arun simply drops out of counselling.

And that is that; there is no end to Arun's story because no one, perhaps not even Arun, can know how it will turn out to be.

•   boy versus girl victims

Arun's reaction to Child Sexual Abuse in the form of his horror and disgust is not that of a 'sissy' or a 'chukka'. It is, under the circumstances, not abnormal.

There is no difference at all in how little girls and boys react, and how they subsequently feel when they are victims of Child Sexual Abuse. Perhaps the one, and only, difference would be that little girls are as traumatized when men and women sexually abuse them, boys see this activity with older women—unless they are related—as all right. Boys with early homosexual inclinations also tend not to see it as sexual abuse by adult males.

The sexual abuse of boy-children tends to lessen, if not completely stop, as they approach puberty and acquire the physical strength to ward off their attackers. Lack of body-strength is one of the reasons why girl-children continue to remain vulnerable to sexual abuse even into adulthood. Everything else about Child Sexual Abuse remains the same for both genders. Especially the bewilderment—which is the real world? Does reality belong to the daytime with its smiling grandfather and affectionate uncle? Or is it part of the night with its furtive shadows, groping hands and thrusting penises?

This profound confusion causes internal conflict and this very conflict leads to additional empowerment of the abuser. And guilt—a very high degree of it—in both boys and girls as they grow up, mentally and physically torturing themselves over the 'shame' of their abuse. Was It My Fault? It Was Not My Fault. It Was My Fault. Was It?

Boys and girl-children also have identical short-term and long-term effects of Child Sexual Abuse. And the nature and extent of these effects are equally dependent on variables like the child's age at the onset of abuse, the child's relationship to the offender, the duration and frequency of abuse, the use of force, penetration or invasion with an object by the abuser and family power dynamics. There is no set gender, age, mode or duration under which Child Sexual Abuse can be quantified and categorized.

There are some children who are far more resilient than others in coping with the effects of their sexual abuse. A study of such resilient children showed some or all of the following to be present:

- there was early detection of their sexual abuse and quick intervention
- following this intervention, the proceedings were not protracted or recurrent

- they were from otherwise well-grounded and non-dysfunctional families
- the children are of above average intelligence

For the less resilient children it could be generally said:

- children are prone to maximum abuse from the ages of four to sixteen, specially between six and twelve
- longer duration is associated with greater impact even if it is non-contact abuse like exhibitionism and verbal sexual invitations
- the use of force or threat of force is associated with greater impact
- those children sexually abused by their parents, stepfathers, grandparents, brothers, sisters, immediate uncles and aunts and first cousins—meaning, closest family and in the ostensibly safe environs of home—are likely to be more affected; girls and boys sexually abused by their fathers and mothers are the most affected; boys sexually abused by their mothers are devastated
- those children who have suffered contact abuse like penetration with penis, finger, tongue or object have very high impact; excessive fondling leads to the child being badly affected
- disorders develop if emotional support—by friends and specially by parents or family—is denied to the child after disclosure even of non-contact abuse
- those who have 'enjoyed' it as children feel a very high degree of guilt for doing so, most so if they are young girls

This guilt for 'enjoying' it in an incorrect situation—even when the child cannot be held responsible in any way for the situation—can have long-standing consequences.

Thirteen-year-old Katayun was the youngest among a large happy household filled with siblings in Jamshedpur. Her married sister and husband visited them from Canada one year, as they did every alternate year. Katayun's sister's husband commented on how 'well' she had grown and began watching her body movements as she blushed under his unrelenting scrutiny. He managed to romanticize his intentions and after kissing her moved quickly to molesting her young body. He would masturbate into Katayun's soft, fair palms while digitally stimulating her clitoris into an orgasm.

Her sister and brother-in-law left for Canada, Katayun continued with her life. She went to college, went to work and fell in love with a man. Her family saw that he was not right at all for the soft-spoken, gentle Katayun. But she was adamant, they married, they have a son. The man is domineering and loud, Katayun chooses not to see it. He completely swamps her personality, she chooses not to recognize this either. Instead, she is—as she has always been throughout their relationship—servile. She also actively encourages her son to be exactly like her husband. Just as Katayun has geared her very existence about the nuances of her husband's moods, her son has developed a state of frozen watchfulness. The son's main purpose in life is to please his father, he jumps into every conversation his father has with visitors, his sentences are not appropriate for his age but his father beams with pride, 'My only child you see, no other children to talk to so he learns from our conversations with our friends. That is why he is so mature.' In turn, the son praises his father fully and his father encourages him to disparage Katayun's friends to their face as he laughs loudly.

Katayun does nothing, she does not even acknowledge that her husband and son sap her of any sensibilities she might like to hold on to. She is overprotective of her son even though she loathes his behaviour on the days she cares to notice that she actually despises her husband. She just goes on punishing herself for 'enjoying' it when she was a child.

Boy-children are sexually exploited routinely at home and among known people—mostly males—for the same reasons as girl-children. The perpetrator knows he can get away with his cold and calculated acts because of the furtiveness which exists in families. Threats and blackmail, fear of the abuser, is one cause for a boy or girl's silence in disclosing Child Sexual Abuse. There is the other, more powerful, one—children instinctively know that their disclosure will lead to denial and discomfort on the part of adults. And so the sexual abuse continues and the boy-children are traumatized as much as the little girls by their own kith and kin.

The boy-children also give in to the abuse, without a murmur, for a combination of the same reasons as girl-children:

- child abuse is still sanctioned; indeed, held in high regard in our society as long as it is defined as child rearing; 'for your own good' as the child is told when it is slapped hard or when a school teacher is allowed to whack a cane on its palms
- children are taught that a feeling of duty invariably produces love
- children are told that parents deserve respect simply because they are parents, children don't deserve respect for the same reason
- children are told that parents and elders are always right
- children are taught to be hypocrites, liars and hiders of

truths, for example 'the way you behave is more important than the way you really are'

- children are not taught to be autonomous, they are expected to be obedient to adults
- children are not encouraged to question adult actions, such behaviour is seen as rebellious
- children are perceived as 'belonging' to adults and family members
- children's duties are emphasized rather than their rights
- childhood itself is not valued by adults, it is seen merely as a phase of training to enter the adult world and any 'discipline' as part of this training is deemed normal and justifiable
- children do not realize that the abuser is violating a relationship of trust with them because the abuser is known to them
- the abuse is happening at home and children absorb that happening at home as being safe and consequently all right
- children do not realize what is happening is sexual and incorrect since the abuser has disguised it as a special privilege or an intimate game
- the abuser has both, access and authority over them since they are not strangers, so the sexual abuse is not commonly preceded by physical violence
- the abuser uses his power and position to silence the child including threats and emotional blackmail
- a few of the children 'enjoy' what is being done to them as part of the sexual awakening of their bodies

As a girl-child said to her counsellor in Lucknow, 'Mainey socha sub key papa aisey hi pyaar kartey hain.' She thought everyone's daddy loved them in this way.

• historical ethics of child abuse

Initiation into sex can often be painful and traumatic, there are several women who do not care for it all that much even if their introduction to sex has been relatively smooth. And there are more than enough men—when they get around to admitting it as they grow into mid-life—that sex is not all that it is cracked up to be; the effort that goes in to the act far outweighs the benefits. In other words, sex seems to be enjoyed most in the imagination of adults.

Can a child, then, be expected to react with anything but revulsion when it is set upon sexually by an adult? A child is somewhat aware of its body parts as being distinct from the time it is toilet-trained; this is the 'su su' and this is the 'ka ka' and 'must not touch like that'. Unless it is a close family person disguising his sexual gratification as affection, the child instinctively recoils when the abuser touches its body.

But the perpetrator sees, and feels, no revulsion at all to what he is doing. In India today, there are thousands of men—and some women—who think that there is nothing wrong with an adult sexually advancing on a child. So, should an adult-child sexual relationship be considered abusive? After all, Child Sexual Abuse has been going on in India, and in the world, ever since the first man got free reign over a child's body and was not ostracized by his own family for it.

Biologically: a little girl's vagina and a little boy's anus—and all other body parts—are too small.

Psychologically: it leads to the premature sexualization of a child.

And this is the most important. Ethically: there is no consent from the child. The child is not capable of informed consent. Suppose there is already premature sexualization due to earlier abuse the child might know what she, or he, is consenting to. But is the child—emotionally, mentally, physically or financially dependent on that adult—really capable of firm refusal? Legally, when it comes to a sexually abusive father, the child is under his guardianship and has no free will to start with.

Ethics, thus, is what society can use as its framework of values and with which it can justify 'interference' in the private life of the perpetrator and his victims.

In the final analysis, it is only the ethical aspect of Child Sexual Abuse that can prevent society from complete mayhem in sexual behaviour.

It was the same ethics, in fact, that made pyschoanalyst Sigmund Freud remark in his 1896 thesis, 'The Aetiology of Hysteria', after talking to several overwrought women that 'at the bottom of every case of hysteria there are one or more occurrences of premature sexual experiences'. The reaction was of such outrage from the men, parents of the women and society elders that Freud, unfortunately and hastily, withdraw his remark and added another—that it was every woman's fantasy to be seduced by her father. This resulted in additional psychiatric literature from other analysts reasserting Freud's new 'fact'. That incest was actually very rare since much of it was hysterical women. That if it happened, it did so because of the daughter instigating it. And then, of course, there were the mothers with their own unresolved complex using their daughters as surrogates to act out their own incest wish for their fathers.

Latter-day analysts have long since, and rightly, rubbished Freud's redone theory, but most do acknowledge one aspect of his work: the theory of the subconscious mind. This helps explain why so many victims of Child

Sexual Abuse are disturbed but the memories of the acts of abuse themselves stay locked away somewhere in their minds.

Research work on CSA could be said to have started even before Freud, in 1860, when French forensic physician Ambroise Tardieu published several papers on battered children, rape and Child Sexual Abuse. He was immediately shouted down by society and his contemporaries. Later, Freud's student, Sandor Ferenczi, confirmed Child Sexual Abuse and pointed out that it lead to severe psychological distress; however, he added, being listened to and comforted helped healing in CSA victims. He died in 1933 and nobody ever accepted his insights on Child Sexual Abuse. Incidentally, in 1946 when the American paediatrician and radiologist John Caffey discovered the physical evidence of child battering by means of x-rays, he was shouted down as people preferred to believe that children had 'bone problems'. No one wanted to see the obvious; that parents could be physically battering children, just as they did emotionally. It was only in 1962 when Henry Kempe's book, *The Battered Child Syndrome* was published that this in-family evil came to be accepted.

The acknowledgement of Child Sexual Abuse has met with far greater resistance the world over. Even when faced with clear physical signs, doctors have refused to identify it as Child Sexual Abuse. In India, doctors still do this, their notations include 'simple injury', 'patient's promiscuity', 'congenital problem of absence of hymen', 'consequence of excessive masturbation'. When a physically or emotionally disturbed child is brought into a doctor's clinic, how many of these doctors can honestly say that they have also looked for signs of Child Sexual Abuse as part of their diagnosis? Agreed that a child's body heals rapidly compared with an adult's, within seventy-two hours many of the minor physical signs are known to disappear; and since enough of Child Sexual Abuse is perpetrated in homes under the guise of affection, there tend to be no marks at all. Yet when doctors have been confronted with signs, have they questioned a burn, a grasp or pinch mark, scratches around the lower body, genitalia, anus, thighs, knees or buttocks? Not one adult who has been sexually abused in childhood in India remembers the doctor going beyond a superficial inquiry; though a lot of adults—including men—do remember being 'felt up' sexually by their ageing male family doctors.

In 1953 Alfred Kinsey and his researchers sampled over one thousand women, one in four reported Child Sexual Abuse and 80 per cent said they were petrified by the encounters. Kinsey and his colleagues minimized the impact and even discounted their accounts by stating, 'It is difficult to understand why a child, except for its cultural conditioning, should be disturbed at having its genitalia touched.' In 1966—right in the middle of the sexual revolution—Noel Lustig blamed the mothers of the victims, 'While rejecting their husbands sexually and generating in them considerable sexual frustration and tension, these mothers have played conspicuous roles in directing the husbands' sexual energies towards the daughters.' Internationally, until the 1970s, emerging accounts of Child Sexual Abuse were dealt with denial, minimization and blaming the victim.

And then the women's liberation movement gained ground—the time had come to deal with Child Sexual Abuse through the women's movement. By the late 1970s and early 1980s a lot of work was being done on the subject in America and England. In India this happened only in the early 1990s as part of the women's movement. An understanding of her rights has also taken women out of their four-walled prison called the kitchen into a work place. These women, specially middle-class women, are increasingly joining the ranks as office-goers. They may be emotionally wobbly, as yet unsure of their role beyond second-salary earners, but they are out there. And they have begun to think of themselves as human beings with feelings and secrets which need to be told, so they have begun talking. And out have started tumbling the family's best-preserved skeletons from the 'khandaani' closets. The women have been talking about violence in their homes, then sexual violence.

Listening intently have been two women—mainstream working women—one a journalist, the other a lawyer, Jasjit Purewal and Naina Kapur. And this is how Sakshi came into being. Sakshi—meaning witness—is the Indian subcontinent's premier organization dealing with Child Sexual Abuse. Sakshi began with recognizing the extreme violence which women face in the name of religion, tradition, culture and family. Closer questioning uncovered links between violence against women and the silence that shrouds sexual violence on both women and their children. Since then Sakshi has been working in the field of sexual violence against women and children. Sakshi has spearheaded the legal movement to comprehensively recognize Child Sexual Abuse in the Indian laws, along with Ifsha, recently set up by Jasjit Purewal as a sister concern. Adds Naina Kapur, 'Kirti Singh of Janvadi Mahila Samiti has joined Sakshi and Ifsha in our effort.'

Around the time Sakshi was formed in Delhi, a doctor specializing in child psychiatry at Bangalore's National Institute for Mental Health and Neuro Science felt the time had come for him to do something about it, there were far too many children coming into his out-patient department as victims of Child Sexual Abuse. Dr Shekhar Seshadri began his work, he spoke with Anita Ratnam—also wanting to do something about the problem—and they formulated a survey (see earlier chapter 'What the numbers reveal'), the results of which were proof of what so many victims knew but people refused to believe.

These days the anti-CSA movement gets a fillip the world over—specially in the Western countries—loudly and in all possible forms of media through a terse statement: 'Do not indulge in Child Sexual Abuse as you might get Aids.' The irony, that such a negative message should be used to tell people not to abuse children. More the irony, that this statement winds up admitting that adults do, indeed, sexually abuse children. They penetrate them through their mouths, vagina and anus; they introduce the virus into the child's bloodstream, then they walk away. To penetrate their women and wives, and another set of children.

What chance does childhood have in such an adult world?

'Where you start looking, the number of enemies childhood can have,' points out Vidya Apte of Terre des Hommes, which works for a child's rights in an increasingly cruel adult world. 'What can it be called,' she asks, 'when they marry off young girls, except Child Sexual Abuse?' A socially sanctioned environment which crushes the girl-child as she grows: that motherhood can be her only mission, that she therefore has to be 'married off' at the soonest possible legal age even if she is not mentally or emotionally ready for it. What kind of mother can such a child herself make? Most research clearly states that men do not have an in-built 'father touch', they have to actively work on it if they genuinely want to be decent fathers. Young men—nor older ones, for that matter—are not expected to be fathers in the complete sense anyway. But young mothers are expected to 'mother' from the time they are born. Most research also proves that 'natural motherhood' is a myth, there is no such thing as 'mother pangs', except for social pressure. A woman feels 'motherly' only from the third or fourth month of her pregnancy and this is a primal feel which continues for the infant's food and physical protection. There is no other in-built manual on child-rearing in a young mother who is otherwise bewildered, exhausted and very alone. What kind of 'complete' mother can she make to another child?

Agreeing is Dr Manisha Gupte of Masum, which works for the betterment of women and children in Pune district, 'I have watched young women getting "possessed" in rural Maharashtra. They just do not know how to talk about their repression and their deep unhappiness, there being no outlet they "get the devi". Once I have watched a girl, married off young, tell her father—through this "devi"—about what had been done to her sexually in her childhood. Another time I have watched a girl of seventeen feel pressurized that her family had not found her a match till then while all her friends had been "settled", she got the "devi" and told her family through it that by next year their daughter would be married. The next year the drought lifted, the family saw it as most auspicious and not only found a match for this daughter who was a bit slow mentally but also pulled out her fourteen-year-old intelligent sister from school and got her married too, so that money could be saved on the joint feast that had to be given to the village.'

In the rural areas child-women can get a 'devi'. In the cities they must be content with smiling depression.

'From childhood women are being primed to expect too much from marriage and motherhood and too little from anything else,' says Prasanna Invally of Susamvaad which is developing 'marriage workshops' in Marathi. 'Boy children are primed to expect everything from their wives in the marriage, and not give too much if anything at all.' The workshops Susamvaad has conducted till now reveal young couples—about to get married—coming in with 'they lived happily ever after' dreams because the partner is being expected to heavily 'adjust'.

A few churches in India run similar, but smaller, programmes for the about-to-be-wed young couples in their parishes with a padre conducting the short talk-cum-course. There is now this famous, but unfortunately unconfirmed, report of a Mumbaii parish where a young lady thought so deeply about what had been explained to her in connection with marriage and motherhood that when the time came to say 'I do', she said 'I don't' and simply went back to work as a single, career woman till she felt she could marry when wanting to get married and not just to have babies, and all of this without being pressurized by her family to do so.

Such cases of individualism are, sadly, rare; the family structure in India does not encourage individualism. Explains Dr Shalini Bharat of the Family Studies unit of the Tata Institute of Social Sciences, 'We have a sacrosanct view of the family in our country, even if it teems with strains within. In such a structure human rights are not regarded as rights in the individual sense. There is a "we", but if you hear an "I" the reaction is knee-jerk even if there is only negativity in this "we-ness". Everyone is supposed to subsume their own individuality in a family, specially the women and definitely the children. Those who want to be an "I", as is the wont of the young males, have to do it outside their family structure and home. This leads to our famous Indian characteristic: the duality-and-denial syndrome. Ghar mein kuch, bahar kuch; like being "vegetarian at home". In such an environment it would be well-nigh impossible to get a family to admit that there is a horror like Child Sexual Abuse happening within the four walls of any house no matter how educated or rich or perhaps more so because the social image of the family has to be guarded. If we acknowledge Child Sexual Abuse in our middle and upper-class homes, we would have to look for reasons for this abuse within. We would then have to admit that these reasons are not as terribly complex as we would like to think. And we cannot have our families being seen as anything less than part of a great and ancient culture, can we now?'

•   **unofficial secrets**

Clearly, a lot of work needs to be done on Child Sexual Abuse in India, much of this urgently. Or else Indians might well come face-to-face with Child Sexual Abuse in the form of an incredulous crisis the way Britons did. It is called the Cleveland case and it completely shocked England. It also took the lid right off Child Sexual Abuse.

Cleveland is not a particularly well-known area even in north-east England where it is situated. When the matter came up in the media, one radio station in London thought that this mass Child Sexual Abuse had taken place in Cleveland, Ohio, America. On 1 January 1987, a consultant paediatrician called Dr Marietta Higgs took up her appointment at the Middlesborough General Hospital in Cleveland. She teamed up with Dr Geoffrey Wyatt who was already in place at the hospital and between them they diagnosed suspected sexual abuse in a total of 165 little girls and boys. Average age: 6.9 years. From January to May 1987, Dr Higgs and Dr Wyatt diagnosed sexual abuse in 121 children from fifty-seven families. Four cases were diagnosed by other doctors. In another two months, by July 1987, the figure was up to 165. Most of these cases were of anal abuse. They were diagnosed by the doctors through physical tests known as reflex and dilatation, or quite simply the buttock separation test which reveals signs of habitual abuse.

Medical opinion promptly got divided on the validity of the reflex and dilatation test. But there was no denying that Britain was confronted with a crisis of vast proportions; and both Britain and the rest of the world were facing a challenge to the stereotypes of abusers and abused. For the people accused were not dangerous nor lunatics but 'respectable' men of all ages and from all classes living in decent homes. Even the children generally showed no obvious signs of Child Sexual Abuse. As a High Court judge observed in the case which came up in front of him of three daughters abused by their father in Cleveland. The little girls were aged from nine months to seven years.

- In the case of each child, the diagnosis of sexual abuse is derived from a clinical examination alone.
- In the case of each child, the evidence having been distilled, the diagnosis is of an external penetration of the anus.
- None of the children has had a deprived upbringing.
- None of the children show any signs of a disturbed child, such as bed-wetting, withdrawal symptoms, overt sexuality or other behavioural problems.
- None of the children of school age has been noted at school as behaving other than normally and averagely.
- None of the children have complained of having been sexually abused in any way. Those that can speak and understand, indeed, have denied it.

- No parent or anyone else has complained of any of the children being sexually abused.
- The respective parents seem on the face of it to be estimable people. They were caring parents of happy families. There is abundant evidence to support that assertion by the respective parents and I, having seen them all give evidence before me in the witness box, agree with that finding.
- The local authority do not point an accusing finger at any particular individual as suspected of interfering sexually with any of these children.
- Lastly, all the children appear to have led entirely normal and protected lives, and all who can express their feelings wish to go home.

But the children had, clearly, been sexually abused.

A realization which struck the judiciary by force, as it did the police, social workers, doctors and other health workers. The 165 girls and boys diagnosed as sexually abused caused a complete collapse of the system not only because of their numbers but the incredulity of it. For many the only reaction was denial, for others it was anger at the doctors who had diagnosed the nature and extent of it. Realizing that Cleveland could happen, again, anywhere, British journalist Beatrix Campbell wrote *Unofficial Secrets: Child Sexual Abuse & The Cleveland Cases.* In this book she examines how the police, social workers and doctors brought their own, often conflicting, perspectives to bear on the problem in Cleveland. She also notes how society at large continues to refuse to believe that 'more children are being buggered than battered'.

A few paragraphs from the book:

Another little girl bounces in to say, 'My dad hurt my bummy and made it bleed.'

Her eight-year-old sister just sits; no, she says, everything at home is lovely, mummy is lovely, daddy is lovely.

Dr Woods examines her. He can put two fingers in her vagina and her rectum dilates up to an inch.

Dr Woods tells her maybe there is something she is forgetting to tell him.

She says, 'Yep.'

It takes Dr Woods eighteen months to bring her to disclosure. She agrees to say who has hurt her only if she writes it on a piece of paper and Dr Woods promises to tear it up.

It says: 'Daddy'.

Dr Woods tears up the paper.

She puts her head on Dr Woods' lap and she cries, and cries.

Dr Woods tells Beatrix Campbell, 'Don't assume for one minute that the children have told you everything. They always keep back the worst things.'

Beatrix Campbell says Cleveland could have happened anywhere. She ends her book by asking society to find solutions to Child Sexual Abuse which go beyond punishing, blaming and denying.

Work in this direction is also needed in India, but first there will have to be acceptance of the very existence of Child Sexual Abuse in all classes of Indian homes. And this acceptance is likely to take a very long time to come because if there is such an acceptance, it would affirm that there are a lot of adults abusing children. And then this would start to say something about Indian society. And its false facade of happy families. And the men in these families. And the kind of women who live with these men.

Uncomfortable questions could be raised: about who we intrinsically are, the way we live, and the way we treat each other. The Ugly Indians.

The enemy is so clearly within.

• women as perpetrators

The enemy within, sadly, can include the woman.

Yes, women do sexually abuse children.

'We do not know about any sizeable number of women who sexually abuse children in the Asian context,' points out Dr Shekhar Seshadri of Nimhans, Asia's largest mental health institution. 'Asian women, and this includes Indian women specially the mothers, are not known to sexually abuse children. The cases which we do have are of those women who had been sexually abused in childhood themselves or that of the woman who sees sexually abusing a child as a way of settling a power issue within herself. The latter is more applicable in cultures where patriarchy prevails, India being no fortunate exception.'

It must be noted that if being sexually abused as a child leads a person to become an abuser, then women, who are most often abused in childhood, would constitute the majority of the abusers. They are not. This, even though women report far more trauma then men do from the sexual abuse in childhood.

International studies peg the women who sexually abuse children as being less than 10 per cent of the total numbers of adults—the remaining 90-plus per cent being men. Every other research worldwide on Child Sexual Abuse completely fits the Indian context. Therefore it would be incorrect to ignore this fact. Even if it be as low as 2 per cent (figures taken from 411 cases of sexual abuse referred to a major children's hospital in Britain between 1980 and 1986). This information, however, must not be misused by an unscrupulous lawyer in a court hearing a Child Sexual Abuse to sow that seed of doubt in the judge's mind that 'the mother could have also done it'.

This would be a dangerous dilution of the men's responsibility.

This under-10 per cent includes older women who sexually advance on young boys; not all boys see it as sexual initiation. And long-term effects of this have started showing up in sexually dysfunctional young males and husbands not getting erections. Says Dr Vijay Nagaswami, individual and marital psychotherapist in Chennai, 'I have been struck in recent times by the more frequent reporting of a less commonly observed pattern of Child Sexual Abuse. More of my male clients than can be explained by chance, report that they have been abused during their childhood—when pre-pubertal and sexually immature—by older women. The abuser is invariably an older relative (usually maiden aunt or cousin), servant maid or familiar neighbours (one case has the lady engaging in sexually perverse activities). The predominant motivation for the abusers seems to be sexual. The pattern of abuse ranged from genital apposition to breast suckling. The primary adult manifestation of such abused male children is inordinate ambivalence in making and honouring commitments in their adult intimate relationships, low self-esteem and interpersonally inappropriate attitudes to sex.'

This under-10 per cent also includes mothers who have been sexually abused as children themselves.

But there is another important fact hidden in here.

The world over fathers who have been sexually abused when they were little boys tend to sexually abuse children, their own and others, as adults.

Mothers subconsciously try very hard not to sexually abuse children, their own or others, even if they have been sexually abused when they were little girls. Instead women, specially mothers, take it out on themselves. They also physically abuse the child with slaps and other forms of beatings. They emotionally neglect them by mentally 'blanking out' their children from time-to-time; this space which the mother puts between her and her offspring is seen by psychiatrists as a desire on the part of the mother not to hurt her children the way she was hurt by her elders.

Affected mothers can also unleash a bizarre range of medical perplexities upon their children; it is called Munchausen Syndrome by Proxy. A German called Baron von Munchausen, born in 1720, was often described as a 'gifted raconteur', that's polite for imaginative liar. In 1951, when Dr Richard Asher was researching a set of bizarre physical behaviour by adults, he chose to call it Munchausen Syndrome. This term came into medical prominence and was called Munchausen Syndrome by Proxy in England in 1977 to describe children whose mothers invent stories of illness about their children and substantiate such stories by fabricating false physical signs. This would include perceiving persistent illness in the child, doctor shopping for several opinions, enforcing invalidism by encouraging the child to believe that it cannot walk or go to school, and fabricating the illness. The extent to which the mother is emotionally disturbed can be understood by looking at some of the ways in which she practises Munchausen Syndrome by Proxy on her baby: she smears her menstrual blood or some from raw meat on the baby's nose and then rushes the child for medical attention, she gives the child laxatives for diarrhoea and then collects medicine from the doctor to stop the diarrhoea which she also administers alternatively with the laxative, she induces vomiting in the child, she uses caustics and dyes to make the child break out in rashes, she warms the thermometer and then tells the doctor the child has fever, she withholds food from the child and she tries to poison the baby. And then at the doctor's she revels in the attention.

Research since has revealed Munchausen Syndrome by Proxy to be noticeably prevalent and it has been listed as a warning sign for the British police in connection with the physical abuse of children. Research has also revealed that such mothers have often had a difficult childhood themselves, usually they have lacked love and respect from their own mothers; many have been abused as children. Not all these mothers have been sexually abused in childhood, but many are, the rest being physically and emotionally abused. The point here is that some mothers who have been sexually abused in childhood do take it out on their children but commonly not in a sexual way.

True, the mother can sexually abuse a child; even if she has not been sexually abused herself in childhood. But cases where a mother who has not been sexually abused herself as a child but has sexually abused her own, or other, children are rare the world over. However, they do exist: young, single mothers (unmarried girls who chose not to get married after getting pregnant); a mother doing exactly to her daughter during the day that sado-masochism which daddy tries on her in the nights; mothers doing it to the child along with their husbands/second husbands/ boyfriends so as to keep the partner; mothers involved in bizarre religious rituals where the body of a child is used as a medium. Most of these children tend to be little girls.

The doctors, counsellors, children, adults, social workers, non-government organizations, homosexuals and lesbians spoken to all over India have not come across a single case of a mother sexually abusing her child if she had been sexually abused herself in childhood.

Should a case come to light of a mother sexually abusing her child even if she has not been abused herself in childhood, what would it suggest of Indian mothers? A closer inspection is very likely to reveal a significant proportion of such mothers colluding and contributing in the sexual abuse of children because they are under the influence of powerful, dominant and sexually, physically and emotionally abusive males.

A case has come to be known of one such mother who has 'participated' by facilitating the Child Sexual Abuse by her partners. In Jaipur, a mother in her mid-forties actively attracted a fifteen-year-old school-going girl into their home and even paid and fed her so that her husband could 'play' with her. The husband had told his wife he was tired of her and intended marrying again; to stop this, she brought a young body into the house.

There is also the mother in Bhopal, a young widow with a son, who encouraged her son to 'drink milk' from her well until he was into his mid-teens. 'I realize that was her release,' says the son, now thirty-five and working in Chandigarh. 'Several mothers feel orgiastic when they breast-feed their newly-born, especially their sons. My mother had natural body urges which she dealt with very silently through this process she initiated.' The son identifies as homosexual, he says he prefers it this way because he cannot 'bring himself to touch another woman's breasts'.

Young women also react similarly when sexually abused in childhood by men, they turn to other women for sustenance. This in itself leads to enormous sexual identity confusion, as listed in the long-term effects of Child Sexual Abuse (see chapter 'The aftermath'). Geeta Kumana who has been valiantly trying to run a phone-line in Mumbaii for lesbians in emotional distress, says, 'There have been calls asking if they have turned lesbian because they were sexually abused in childhood.' This is not to suggest that all women, or men, sexually abused in childhood by men become lesbian, or homosexual; or that all lesbians and homosexuals have been sexually abused in childhood. This is also not to suggest that homosexuals and lesbians who have been sexually abused in childhood—like the forty-five-year-old abused by her aunt when she was five—still don't hurt by it. Just as there are cases of young men taking to homosexuality after being sexually abused by men—and the one, as above, by his mother—there are cases of women turning to lesbianism after being sexually abused by men. There are also cases of young girls turning lesbian after being sexually abused by older women with lesbian or bisexual tendencies.

It is not a part of this book's brief to enter into a 'born this way' or 'nature versus nurture' debate in connection with homosexuality and lesbianism. This is also not about numbers and statistics: this is about children. And even if it was about only one child—it is not, there are enough cases and international studies—this point would have to be made. What is relevant here is that children are being sexually abused by both, opposite-sex and same-sex adults. This is traumatizing them to the point where they are unsure of their own sexual grounding; this also leads to incorrect decisions as they grow into adulthood. Ergo, the real choice is taken away from the child and this is the tragedy: that a decision to be 'gay' is being taken from within an area of darkness and pain, not out of one's free and happy will.

A heterosexual trapped in a gay body can be as emotionally shattering as the other way round. Homosexuals and lesbians running support groups for themselves would do well to remember this when dealing with adolescents and adults who profess marked sexual preferences but who have been sexually abused as children.

For instance Nisha who works in Hyderabad and has everything: the intelligence and looks, wealth, her own flat and car, a good career with a computer company. She has a girlfriend working in a computer company in Bangalore and so they fly across to meet up over weekends. Their sex is 'satisfying', Nisha finds her girlfriend's company 'not boring'. Then why is Nisha not happy? Nisha was sexually abused by her aunt when she was nine, that was her first sexual encounter, there were others after that with other women, elder female cousins and her mother's friend. In her late teens Nisha had a man friend but she found that she 'could not respond to him as sexually as I would have liked to even though I prefer the company of men as more mentally stimulating to that of my women partners'. Nisha went into therapy, she still does not have the answers. Has her sexual identity been formed because of her sexual abuse? Has it been formed by the thought-process set off by the abuse? Or has it really and truly been a process of self-questioning which has led her to think about her affinity for women? Nisha flicks her lighter to a slim cigarette, takes a drag and looks out of the window of her flat at Banjara Hills; she sighs and says, 'Not happy this way.'

Psychiatrists Joseph Beitchman, Kenneth Zucker, Jane Hood, Granville DaCosta, Donna Akman and Erika Cassavia, from the University of Toronto and the Clarke Institute of Psychiatry in Canada, published a much-heralded paper in *Child Abuse & Neglect* (16: 101-118) in 1992. This panel reviewed the long-term effects of Child Sexual Abuse and made this observation on sexual identity: 'Adult women with a history of childhood sexual abuse show greater evidence of sexual disturbance or dysfunction, homosexual experiences in adolescence or adulthood, depression, and are more likely than non-abused women to be re-victimised.' They add, 'There may be a small but significant increased rate of homosexual activity among women who have been sexually abused in childhood.'

Does Nisha's happiness lie in a skilful psychiatrist dialoguing with her in the light of the above finding? Sadly, this will not happen as Nisha will not even initiate such an analysis with a psychiatrist; she has convinced herself she is a lesbian.

Equally disturbing is what is being perpetrated by a very small section of lesbians. Just as oversexed men, older homosexuals and bisexual men set upon male children sexually, there are some over-enthusiastic lesbians following the example of the perpetually penetrating male by sexually setting upon girl children. Farida, now a counsellor for students in an upmarket Delhi school, still recalls with barely-concealed rage the time, not too long ago, when she was a student in a well-known northern hill-station boarding school.

'I was fifteen and easily the most attractive, a lot of younger girls would send me notes, roses and things like that. I would be kind to them but not encourage them because these crushes are common among little girls. For instance, in day schools they go crazy for a brief period over their class teacher if she is pretty and young; without active encouragement this kind of thing fades away. What I really had problems with were two obviously lesbian girls in our dormitory; there tends to be some mutual and brief body-exploration among senior girls in boarding schools before they settle on their sexuality. But this was heavy-duty, almost like penis envy on their part. Even then we all ignored what they did with each other once it was lights out, also they were seniormost and had come in together from two well-known families in Delhi only the year before that. Together, they tried very hard to get my attention, they even began leaving me obscene notes. One night, it was during exam days, I was asleep and awoke to pairs of hands on my breasts and groin. I think they thought I would not kick up a fuss and take their sexual abuse, well, lying down. I swung out of bed and hit them as hard as I could. Then I turned on the lights, dragged them to their respective beds and slapped each one very hard on their face. "Don't you dare," I hissed, "don't you ever dare." This news went around quickly in the school and over the next few days I was told by juniors of how this pair would often try and sexually abuse the younger girls. This lesbian pair had been thrown out of another school for the same reason, their parents used all their clout to get them into ours. What were these pseudo-liberal parents thinking of, why did they not think of the other children?

'Recently a psychiatrist friend told me of a young lady who had been similarly traumatized in junior college by senior students, a lesbian group, in her college hostel. Except that hers was hard-spectrum ragging and she had not been able to fight it, they made her strip and did a few unspeakable things to her as "initiation" on her first night as the juniormost in the college hostel. I read in the papers that in the name of ragging a similar thing happened a few years ago in a Mumbaii college hostel to a fifteen-year-old girl by her seniors and the poor thing committed suicide because no one believed her. I firmly believe that matters have come to this because of the unfortunate situation of boys taking the sexual abuse in their schools and colleges by their senior students and professors. Boys see these encounters with older men in their childhood as inevitable initiation, even if painful. If they had the common sense, and the courage, to resist and fight back right from the beginning, we would not have such debased learned behaviour from lesbians in the name of ragging.'

Is ragging Child Sexual Abuse?

It is abuse.

It is sexual violence.

If the perpetrators are above sixteen years of age—be they women or men—and the victim sixteen and below, it is Child Sexual Abuse.

Both, the victim and her, or his, parents are well within their rights to take police and legal action against the perpetrators even if they are students a few weeks above sixteen.

This fine line being drawn here—sixteen, edge of sixteen, the other side of sixteen, etc—may look like a legal landmine. It is. (Perpetrators below eighteen would be tried under the Juvenile Act; the accused above eighteen would be tried as adults under the Indian Penal Code.) But then it is also that support which as a parent you must give your child, and which your child desperately needs if it has been a victim of Child Sexual Abuse.

There are instances outside of schools too where women appear to have turned as blind as men; that the space around children cannot, and should not, be violated. Children seem to be there as much for their sexual gratification as that of lust-driven men, these women who are unthinkingly aping the worst in males.

An eighteen-year-old girl enters into her first sexual encounter with a twenty-six-year-old bisexual aunty who has moved from Kerala to Tamil Nadu. Their relationship lasts for two years. After the bisexual aunty and her husband move out of town, the girl makes 'my fifteen-year-old maidservant lick my pussy'. Sexual gratification derived through the unthinking abuse of class privilege and power.

A wheelchair-bound woman from Pune is in love with another woman but forcibly married off to a man and they move to Dubai. She decides to 'convert' her young maid 'and slowly I trained her', 'today she is able to give me the orgasm I need'. The same pathetic situation.

Comments Ashwini Sukthankar who has edited a book

63

on lesbian writing. 'I think everyone is—or should be—aware that children are not appropriate objects of sexual desire for adults, be they heterosexual or homosexual.' She adds, 'Most child abusers are, however, heterosexual men—even those that sexually abuse young boys.'

She overlooks that reprehensible group—the bisexual men and women—who with their sexually uncommitted behaviour also negate the serious work done by committed homosexual and lesbians for their cause. Nevertheless, the lady makes a valid point; homophobes to note.

•   **the aftermath**

Every child is vulnerable, dependent, innocent and needy, be it a boy or a girl. And so when it is sexually abused there is almost simultaneously the violation of its physical, emotional and mental state. Dr Shekhar Seshadri describes what happens internally and almost immediately to the child. Says he, quoting from *Recollecting Our Lives*, 'The child goes into what is called the survivor's cycle.'

- First the sexual abuse causes confusion. What is he, or she, doing? What is happening to me, I cannot understand. I do not like it but I do not know how to stop it. Is what he is doing normal and okay? Where can I be safe? I cannot save myself, I cannot do anything right.
- This leads to self-estrangement. I am always wrong. Why can't I be like everyone else? I am not normal. I am not important. No one cares about me. No one cares how I feel. I don't count. I do not want to be me.
- And this leads to the saddest part, the wrong set of survival skills. I have to hide inside myself. I have to

protect myself. I cannot let people see who or how I really am. How can I keep from exposing the real me?

- Now the child feels trapped. I cannot change my life or myself. I can't change anything. I am responsible for who I have become. I am responsible for what happened to me because I did not stop it, I did not tell anyone either. I must keep the secret to survive. It is my fault.
- And all of this leads to a negative sense of self. I do not know who I am. I deserve whatever I get. If they really knew me they would dislike me and be disgusted by me. I am a phoney, I am only about falsehood. I do not deserve better. I am a bad person, everyone is better than me.

The cycle continues, wheels within wheels, spokes of shame being added each time the child recalls the sexual abuse and the sense of powerlessness. The cycle continues; as it almost always and invariably does since Indian parents, if they detect the Child Sexual Abuse quickly enough, which is again rare, concentrate on the child's physical aspect and their family's social standing post the abuse. The child's emotional and mental violation is overlooked; that child within, with its feelings all locked up, grows up physically and displays some of the 'sleeper effects' of Child Sexual Abuse, some of which could emerge with dramatic impact as long-term aspects of Child Sexual Abuse.

Thus, the long-term effects of Child Sexual Abuse can be devastating.

- Mental health problems: anxiety, fear, depression as also masked depression, isolation, suicide, self-injury, poor self-esteem, alcohol or cigarette or drug abuse, self-annihilation.
- Traumatic sexualization: in which a child's sexuality—including both, sexual feelings and sexual attitudes—is

shaped in a developmentally inappropriate and interpersonally dysfunctional fashion. Such as prostitution, aversion to sexual contact, confusion about sexual identity, confusion of sex with love and care-getting or care-giving, aggressive sexual behaviour, promiscuity, difficulty in arousal and orgasm, inappropriate sexualization of parenting, re-victimization.

- Child-rearing difficulties: repeat cycle of abuse in same or differently non-sexual format, over-protectiveness, fertility control.
- Stigmatization: the negative connotations—for example, badness, shame and guilt—that are communicated to the child about the experiences and that then become incorporated into the child's self-image.
- Social dysfunction: delinquency, criminal behaviour, acts of violence to self or others, victim role.
- Feeling of powerlessness: the process in which the child's will, desires, and sense of efficacy are continually contravened. Leading from the inability to stop the abuse, the child grows to feel anxious, inefficient and develops a tendency to run away from problems. Other long-term effects include nightmares, phobias, eating and sleeping disorders, disassociation, employment problems, vulnerability to subsequent victimization and becoming a sexual abuser too.
- Feeling of betrayal: children discover that someone on whom they are vitally dependent has caused them harm. Mostly the abuser is a known person and even if it is not the parent, the child experiences a loss of trust of the parents and begins a search for a person who could be trusted. This leads to vulnerability to subsequent abuse and exploitation, allows for own children to be victimized by oneself or others, leads to

discomfort in intimate relationships, marital problems, aggressive behaviour and impairs ability to judge people which, in turn, leads to choosing wrong friends and disastrous marriages.

Child Sexual Abuse is a self-perpetuating phenomenon and cases suggest that adult males and females who have been victims of Child Sexual Abuse turn promiscuous and enter into unhealthy relationships. Females are more likely to choose husbands who abuse them and their children. As mothers they often show poor parenting skills, neglecting or abusing their own children.

There are several highly-rated international studies to prove some of these points.

R. Summit and J. Kryso in 1978, followed by J. Goodwin, T. McCarthy and P. Divasto in 1981, presented papers which showed that many mothers who sexually abused their own children had been victims themselves of Child Sexual Abuse.

L. Pincus and C. Dare in 1978, followed by L. P. Cammaert in 1988, had studies which showed mothers selecting emotionally inadequate partners if they had been sexually abused in childhood.

N. Groth, in 1982, stunned the international psychiatric community by pointing out that women who are sexually abused in childhood are open to selection by sex offenders who seek partners who are passive, emotionally vulnerable and dependant. These women put up no resistance at all as the male—intent on abuse of the children in his extended family—as easily distances his own child from the mother; his power over the woman allows him to operate as effectively even if she protests by using physical or emotional threats. Groth adds that the potential perpetrator does not, however, have to particularly sense out a woman who has been sexually abused in childhood. Since women in most societies all over the world are socialized to depend on others—mostly male—and to be obedient within the family, it is not very surprising to find many mothers of sexually abused children playing a passive role in the family. They are often dominated by their partner and see him as more capable, powerful and intellectually superior, more so if they have been victims themselves of Child Sexual Abuse.

M. Stern and L. Meyer have run a comprehensive survey for the National Centre on Child Abuse and Neglect in Washington, which points out that the non-availability of a sexually satisfying relationship with a consenting peer—meaning if a man does not get 'good sex' from his wife or girlfriend—is not a causal factor in Child Sexual Abuse. Most perpetrators try and sexually abuse children even while they are involved in adult relationships.

There are several studies which bring up the question of why mothers do not protect their children against Child Sexual Abuse in their own homes, even if they have not been sexually abused as children themselves. In the Indian context there is no such hard data available but, again, all the international observations reflected in the book fit the situation.

These factors, too, have been observed as being prevalent in the Indian situation. A mother who does not take immediate protective action for her child who is being sexually abused at home—by her husband, her father-in-law, her brother-in-law, her elder son, the male cousin—does not do so because she risks external judgements of her mothering, the inevitable breakdown of her family, the removal of herself or her child or her husband from the scene of the crime, retaliation by the accused and all the men and even the women around him, social stigma, continuous court appearances and loss of financial security.

All of the above coalesced in Ila Pandey of Karvi who is still on the run in and around Lucknow. Her daughters have been put in schools away from her so that her husband cannot get at them through her, their fees are being paid by an educational support group, Asha Trust, and other expenses are being met by the Lucknowies. Ila Pandey was often emotionally and physically beaten by her husband, she had breakdowns. This is now being sought to be proved as 'madness' in the courts by Jagdish Pandey and his brothers. Ila Pandey continues running, perhaps even she had not estimated how much she would have to when she confronted her husband with his relentless year-long sexual abuse of Gudiya, their daughter.

Ila Pandey is brave also because she has sought to overcome her own physical, financial and emotional inadequacies to protect her daughters from Child Sexual Abuse. Most mothers whose children are being sexually abused at home by their close male family members, specially fathers, simply look the other way. International researchers say that such women tend to be characterized as lacking in social skills and possessing a number of disturbed personality traits, even if they have not been sexually abused in their childhood.

Sahd in 1980, and Bennett also in 1980, found that such mothers had low self-esteem. Bennett added that these women had an 'intropunitive'—introspective—style of anger.

Herman and Hershelman, as also Harrier in a separate study, said in 1981 that such mothers experienced psychosis—they felt mentally unbalanced.

In the same year Frederichson added anxiety and suspicion to the list, and Herman and Hershelman followed up with alcohol abuse as one of the reasons why mothers did not stand up to the sexual abuse of their children in their homes. Goodwin, also in 1981, pointed to the mothers who had suicidal tendencies.

To be noted: the above are not the reasons why children are being sexually abused in their own homes; these are some of the reasons—and what has happened to Ila Pandey is the rest—why most mothers do not come to the immediate aid of their children. Applicable as much in India as anywhere else, especially in the light of Groth's theory that sexually abusive fathers choose partners whose resistance can be easily overcome. The disabilities noted by Sahd, Bennett, Herman, Hershelman, Harrier, Frederichson and Goodwin further significantly reduce the mother's ability to protect her children from Child Sexual Abuse.

And a mother who has been sexually abused herself in childhood turns into her own victim; the grown woman is the gaoler of the little girl, she paradoxically continues the role where the abuser left off. And so it gets handed down, generation to generation, feeling the impact of what just one man did—with perhaps just his finger—to one child a long time ago. That's how long term the effects of Child Sexual Abuse can be.

Traumatic sexualization (detailed on earlier pages in the list of long-term effects) is another outcome which can disturb not just the victim but an entire family for the rest of their lives. Psychiatrists dealing with adults who have been sexually abused in childhood—this is never revealed at the outset—are also contending with an array of sexual identity crises. A man cannot have sex with his wife any other way except lying on his side because that is how his driver did it to him; yet another responds sexually only to female on top; a third can 'take her only dog-like' because that was what the seniors brutally did to him in the toilets at his upmarket college in Delhi. Two college-going boys come into therapy for panic attacks at Dr Manoj Bhatawdekar's clinic in Mumbaii; they question their heterosexual orientation because they have been penetrated anally by both, the finger and the penis, by their uncles at home.

Supposing these teenagers had not found the courage to make it to a psychiatrist's clinic? Suppose they had done nothing at all except continue to suffer their anxiety attacks, marry, have sexual relations with their wives, then have anxiety attacks again, and begin to experiment with other men—or worse, with little boys—as a means of settling the question of their sexual identity? What would it have done to their wives, the rest of their families, the children whom they might procreate? This does happen, it happens a lot; a man's entire family in the future gets marked for abuse—sexual, physical, emotional, financial too—when he is sexually abused in his childhood.

Fortunately college boys as also young, working men—specially from middle and upper-class homes—are seeking professional help to understand their own sexual orientation, even if they have not been sexually abused in childhood, purely because they want the choice to be made by themselves and not social conditioning. If it turns out that they have strong same-sex orientation, they are happy to be gay. Unfortunately, not all these men are able to put off their families when it comes to 'settling down' and a hapless woman bears the brunt; but those homosexuals who are, indeed, able to hold their own are to be congratulated by Indian women. A man finding his own identity—even if through a sexual preference and not much else—means less trouble for women and their daughters.

Not a very nice thing to say, no? Because it is thinking of only women and girl-children; it is not inclusive of fathers and their sons, right?

Well, has there ever been a time when fathers, along with their wives, have not impressed upon their sons, almost conditioned them into thinking, that they—the male—possess that magnificent trump card: the power of choice? Mothers tell their daughters only this: the male will come and choose from a sea of simpering young girls like you; on a white charger he will come and whisk you off your feet, please perfect the art of simpering till he arrives.

The male and his magnificent trump card: that power of choice. So now, before he 'settles down', and even during and after, he also chooses little boys. But will this be enough proof for the parents of young males that they need to explain to their sons that they need to behave with other mothers' daughters, and other people's sons too? If those parents had done this before, maybe the statistics would not be as bad as they are today? And now that the world is turning on its head, or so it may seem to the parents of only sons, with older—and much elder—men actively seeking out little boys, what should the mothers and daughters feel?

But back to welcome signs, another one: men who have been sexually abused in childhood are also turning to psychiatrists. Dr Sujit Ghosh, whose clientele is predominantly from the middle and upper socio-economic section of Calcutta, is actively involved in the area of male sexual health as well. Therefore, men seeking help on issues related to sexual orientation and preferences are also being referred to him. Says he, 'Some heterosexual men who have come to me have revealed incidents of sexual abuse in their childhood. And some men with same sex preferences, who are not as yet comfortable with their sexual identities, at times do attribute it to their same-sex experiences in childhood.'

The psychiatrists from the University of Toronto and the Clarke Institute of Psychiatry, referred to in the earlier chapter, also say: 'Greater long-term harm is associated with abuse involving a father or stepfather and abuse involving penetration. Longer duration is associated with greater impact, and the use of force or threat is associated with greater harm.'

Savio would not even understand if all of this was very patiently explained to him; he is being exhorted to see a good psychiatrist but he will not do it. He was sexually abused by his stepfather for a long time; ironically, Savio's mother remarried as a very young widow so that her son would not feel his father's loss. When little Savio threatened to tell his grandfather, his stepfather held a knife to his penis, he smiled broadly as he said this, 'I will cut it off if you do'.

Savio is now a male model. He changes girlfriends often. He cannot get an erection to have sex with them without thinking of his stepfather buggering him. He beats up his girlfriend and then changes her for another because of this. He pumps iron, he exercises to the point where his body looks like steel. Often he and his close friend, a homosexual by choice, get together and hang out, sometimes Savio asks him to make love to him. At such times, when Savio is ejaculating he weeps-cries-shudders out just one word.

'Daddy!'

•   **s r i l a k s h m i**

Srilakshmi	Eleven years	·	Chennai

This is so very clear to me because it was my eleventh birthday. I wore a green and gold paavadai, the silk long skirt and blouse, lots of flowers in my hair, amma tried to put lipstick for me but I did not like it so I wiped it off. I danced around the house. In the night I was so tired that I curled up against my anna and went to sleep. I think he, my brother, was around seventeen at that time. I woke in the middle of the night because I felt his hand in between my legs.

'It's nice, isn't it?' He asked and yet told me, 'It feels good, doesn't it?'

I could not say no, I said yes. I began enjoying it too as I let my anna masturbate me, and I stroked him till he came. I was very happy but then he left for higher studies in America. Perhaps my mamas, my mother's two brothers, had discussed this with my anna, otherwise how would they know? Whenever I went to their house, my mamas would take turns to masturbate me, sometimes all of us did things with each other. But I did not mind their loving me together. Often I would be raw from so much rubbing because when I could not go to my mamas' house I would do it to myself.

I did not like it when old men tried to touch me. Once my appa's friend, a judge, came home to stay with us for a few days from Trivandrum. After dinner in the night, my amma sent me to his room with drinking water for the night and he said, 'Come here.' I went to him and he hugged and kissed me but I pushed him away when he put his tongue in my mouth.

They got me married in a big hurry when I was nineteen, my anna and my mamas were all there at my wedding, pretending as though nothing had ever happened. Perhaps they all knew that I had been caught in the act of masturbation with our car's driver and both of us were enjoying it so much. My husband is a straight in-out person, over in a minute, not interested in sex although I have tried quite hard to get him interested in these two years that we have been married. I feel unfulfilled and I masturbate but it is not enough any more.

•   **brother nature**

Dr Sujit Ghosh of Calcutta has dealt with a case which has registered deeply on his professional understanding of Child Sexual Abuse in the Indian context. It is, like Srilakshmi's, a case of incest.

Srilakshmi's is a case of multiple incest. Brother-sex: Then, maternal uncles' gang-sex. But polite society will describe what has been done to Srilakshmi as, simply, incest.

Incest. Such a sanitized word. Perhaps that is why they chose the word so that other than the victim everyone could relate to it sympathetically, in an oh-so civilized manner. Srilakshmi does not know the word incest, when she is asked to reply in one sentence what happened to her, she says, 'My anna and mamas played with me everywhere and put their fingers in me, I also played with them.' That is not incest, more so since the definition of incest does not even begin to understand what close male relatives can sexually do to little girls and boys.

Webster's, for instance, says incest is sexual intercourse

between closely-related persons; the crime of sexual intercourse, cohabitation, or marriage between persons within the degrees of consanguinity or affinity wherein marriage is legally forbidden.

Is any of what has been done to Srilakshmi visible in that definition?

Or what has happened to this girl which Dr Ghosh talks about?

'There is this upper-class family with an educated and professionally successful background. The family is nuclear, parents with an older son and two younger daughters. I was called in an emergency situation where the youngest girl had slashed her wrists and was admitted to a private hospital in Calcutta. She was discharged and sent home but within a week of being back at home, she attempted suicide once again.

'Nobody in her family could understand why she was doing this. Her final examinations were on then, she had to skip them. She was the quieter of the two sisters, more obedient, she kept to herself and tended to stay away from friends and parties; she was thought to be quite content otherwise. Her elder sister was quite boisterous, assertive, threw tantrums, had boyfriends and tended to get her way. The family thought that there was more likelihood of her doing something like this, if at all, in a fit of rage.

'Several intensive sessions revealed what was disturbing this young girl to the point of suicide. Her brother, the oldest of the siblings and close to twenty, was due home for vacation from college. The girl was dreading to share the room with him during his stay and had told her mother in as many words, but the mother had ignored her request. For a couple of years before the son left for college he had been sexually molesting his younger sister at night while pretending to be asleep. The girl was bearing it all, ashamed and ridden with guilt that she must be responsible for her brother doing something that is not good and sinful.

'This went on night after night and the girl would dread nightfall and having to go to bed. During the day it was a fine family, well known in Calcutta's social circles, the parents being successful professionals and financially very comfortable in life. When her mother was taken into confidence about what was bothering the young girl to the point of suicide, she went into denial. The mother's first reaction was how to protect her son from all this. She felt her son should not even get wind of what has happened leave alone be confronted on the matter. This led to the girl's mother shutting her off from professional help, the attempt to commit suicide was passed of as being related to examination stress.'

What becomes particularly damaging to an entire family in the Indian context is an elder brother sexually abusing his little sister. It is treated with the same mixture of horror and secrecy as the male breadwinner of a family being accused of sexually molesting a girl-child in the house. First, an immediate reaction follows from the fact that an allegation is being levelled at the son, a son, any son. Then, and almost simultaneously, starts the protection of the son of the house, the scion, the seed which will start the next generation of the family name. Then comes up the 'fact' that the girl has to get married and go away so why create confusion? Invariably in cases of a brother sexually abusing his sister, she is the younger of the two; so the facade of brother-as-protector cannot be shattered. This hypocrisy in Indian homes finds an echo in the cynical Hindi ditty sung at the time of tying rakhi, 'Din ko bhaiyya bhaiyya, raat ko saiyya saiyya.' ('During the day "brother-brother", during the nights "lover-lover".')

It need not even be added here that an elder brother sexually abusing his younger brother would probably not even be brought to light in the house.

Consider Pankaj's case. Pankaj's elder brother who is married, with children, is a well-known businessman in Ahmedabad.' Pankaj was four years old when he was moved in with his elder brother from his parents' bedroom. He shared this bedroom with his elder brother who often watched blue films featuring men and women, women and women, big men and little boys and girls. The brother masturbated while watching these movies, without exposing his organ to Pankaj. He never asked Pankaj to watch the movies, though Pankaj could clearly see the screen on the other side of his brother's bed. He did not even touch Pankaj.

Pankaj has grown up to have nightmares involving sexual acts with naked little children. He is married and cannot have sex with his wife without watching a pornographic movie. Pankaj's young and pretty wife is now also his brother's mistress.

'Brother Nature' is so serious an issue that it almost can't be found as a case history; that carefully does it get swept away under the family carpet; with that alacrity is the girl despatched to her 'own home' once she completes college; that younger brother, oh that was his initiation to life. There are also some powerful myths associated with the 'Brother Nature' phenomenon which are dealt with by counsellors Simon Hackett, Bobbie Print and Carol Dey who work with sexually abused young people in England.

These myths encompass views such as:

- sexual abuse rarely takes place between siblings due to the notion of the incest taboo

- sexual contact between siblings can be explained away as experimental
- sexual contact between siblings may be inappropriate, but is usually minor in nature
- young men who actively seek child-victims outside the home are more dangerous and have more problems than those who abuse siblings
- sexual abuse between siblings will go away if left alone, it should be dealt with by the family or can be managed by simply pointing out its inappropriateness
- sexual abuse between siblings is a symptom of an overly close sibling relationship
- sexual contact between siblings has an erotic content
- sexually inappropriate behaviour between siblings can happen, but is often a one-off, unplanned mistake, with no abusive intent

Generally speaking, older brothers who sexually abuse their little sisters tend to commit more acts of abuse over longer periods of time. There tends to be almost no direct disclosure in the home about this. If it comes out when the victim is still a little girl, the parents simply physically separate the two into separate sleeping enclosures for the night and treat the entire situation as either an effect of too much sex and violence on television (who shows brother-sex on television?) or go through a few pangs of guilt as a parenting default; the victim is forgotten. The older brother also tends to have other victims, inside the house if there are other younger sisters, or outside the house in the form of younger female relatives. His abuse quickly develops into hard-spectrum, that is finger or penile penetration; brothers are more likely to commit penile penetration than those who sexually abuse children outside the family. As mentioned earlier, invariably the brother tends to be the oldest of all the siblings as also 'trusted' by the parents, confirming the power dynamics of the abuse. David Finkelhor in his 1980 paper, 'Sex amongst siblings: a survey of prevalence, variety and effects,' says, 'The younger the victims of sibling sexual abuse, the more extreme the lasting effects.'

Srilakshmi is a terrifying example of this; the other girl, there is simply no way of knowing how she is coping on her own in a family comprising educated and cultured people. It cannot be nice for her, being that desperately alone in one's own home.

●_____ **prema**

Prema   Śeven years   **Bangalore**

Prema's mother died when she was three.

Prema's father remarried when she was four.

Prema had stepsiblings, a brother and sister, by the time she was six. Prema had no problems with her stepmother or vice versa, and even missed her when she went with her children to her village.

Prema is seven. Her stepmother has just left for the village with her children. Prema's father, an inspector of police, and Prema, are expected to join her for the summer holidays a few days later.

'Here,' says Prema's father, 'let me give you a bath today.'

Prema protests, no, no, she can bathe herself, she has been bathing herself all along, as also bathing her stepbrother and stepsister.

'I know, I know, but today I feel like giving you a bath. Cannot a father do this?'

Prema's father makes her undress, he spends a lot of time soaping her beginning-to-bud breast area. Prema is plump. He parts her legs and spends time soaping her behind, parting her constantly.

Prema's father bathes her every single day for those five days, sometimes thrice a day. He keeps her locked in the house as he goes out on work and returns to bathe her again. By the third time he has soaped his erect penis and inserted it into Prema's anus. By the sixth time he has vaginally penetrated her with it, bathing her again to wash off all the blood. Immediately after, he is sexually abusing her through every possible orifice, devouring her, muttering all the while, 'First you are mine, my oota, my food to eat, before any other man sinks his teeth into you.'

When it is the day to go to the village, Prema's inspector-father boards the bus alone to join his second wife and children. Prema has wrenched her hand away from his and run away from the bus station.

Prema is now a child-prostitute in Calcutta's Sonagaachi. She is not plump anymore, she has several sexual diseases including Aids. She says she never complained against her inspector-father at the police station because she knew they would suspend him and then what would her stepbrother, stepsister and stepmother eat?

• child prostitution

Should Prema be rescued from the brothel and if she refuses to go back home or if her family does not want her anymore, she will be put into a remand home. As will fourteen-year-old Seema who has been beaten and starved for three weeks in a Mumbaii brothel, she would not give in to the pressure. She was then put into a small room with a live cobra. She sat there, numb, staring at the cobra, for two days. She gave in. When, and if, she is found alive to be rescued, a remand home it will be.

Life in a remand home is no different. As Billa Number 61 discovered. A deaf-mute minor, she was found wandering around on Mumbaii's Churchgate railway station in a state of severe shock. She had been sexually abused several times during her journey from nobody-could-make-out-where to Mumbaii. She was sent to a remand home and given the identification tag of 61, no one thought of giving her some kind of human identity with even a temporary name.

Billa Number 61 was soon, and often, raped by the male cook of the remand home. He gave her fruits to eat in return which she accepted gratefully and happily, a small half-rotten apple today, a shrivelled chikoo the next.

Billa Number 61 felt hungry one afternoon, the food was never enough at the remand home, and she went to the kitchen for some fruit. She took off her salwar, hiked up her kameez and lay down with her legs spread wide on the cold, slimy kitchen floor. She waited, within a few minutes she would get something to eat.

When the cook was on top of Billa Number 61, two other girls came into the kitchen chattering and laughing among themselves. The cook got off, hiked up his trousers and offered them fruit. The girls ran out to call someone, anyone, in charge. When they returned with the warden, the cook was nowhere in sight. Billa Number 61 was sitting on the kitchen floor calmly eating a pulpy banana.

There was an uproar when this story got into the newspapers, committees were hastily appointed and several 'fact-finding' missions wound their way to this remand home, reports were written out, proclamations made, recommendations noted, several city non-government organizations working with and for children held meetings and were suitably outraged, the cook was sacked by the home and arrested by the police. Billa Number 61's case only recently came up for hearing; the cook, Shivaji Nanavare, was sentenced to ten years' imprisonment and fined Rs 23,000.

This incident happened in September 1997.

In February 2000, a nine-year-old mute inmate of the same remand home was raped on the same premises. This was discovered when she was admitted to the hospital with convulsions; she had been raped within nine days of being 'rescued' from the Dadar railway station and placed in that remand home. When she was admitted on February 25 to the hospital with convulsions, doctors also found other signs of sexual abuse apart from a deep bite mark on her face and abrasions on her body.

The newspapers reported on this crime; nothing much else happened bar a few murmurs of disapproval from the non-government organizations who raise money in the name of deprived children and ostensibly work towards their betterment.

But constable Patil read about it and quickly made his way to the remand home from his posting at the faraway Malvani police station. 'I needed to see if that other child was all right,' he says gruffly.

That other girl had been a resident of a small bungalow on the as-yet picturesque Marve beach. Her mother had died recently, her fifteen-year-old brother had turned alcoholic and was frequently thrown into the lock-up for drunken behaviour; this seven-year-old was just about learning to take care of herself, her home, her school, her studies and the domestic requirements of her brother and father when her forty-eight-year-old father decided to have some fun with her. She resisted, she fought back and tried to run away; he shaved off her hair and mauled her; she tried to run away nevertheless, he tied her to the bed post and raped her continuously for three days.

She finally managed to loosen her knots, untie herself and run away to the neighbour's bungalow, a not inconsiderable distance when you consider that beachside bungalows are suitably spaced away from each other and are surrounded by huge, rambling gardens. She reached the house of her seventy-five-year-old neighbour who could not believe what she was looking at. A naked child with red welts where her as-yet-to-form breasts should have been, a head criss-crossed with red shaving scars, her red eyes swollen with tears and that red reflected all over her body in the form of her vaginal blood which had not stopped dripping. The neighbour managed to get her across to Malvani police station; constable Patil and other police officials—who found themselves shaking with the rage of it—arrested her father Dilip alias Francis Fernandes on Christmas day. The little girl was sent off to the remand home. Her case made it to the papers too, prominently.

Did a single non-government organization claiming to be concerned about sexually abused children notice? Perhaps it was because of the holiday season, the turn of the century, the new millennium; merry Christmas and a happy new year little Miss Fernandes.

Some one did notice the story on the mute being raped in the same remand home as Billa Number 61; where is she now, Billa Number 61, who knows, does it matter anyway in such a tidal wave of evil? But some one cared enough to protect the nine-year-old mute from further evil. Majlis, a legal resource centre, filed a petition in the High Court pointing out that the girl, after being raped, was being sent back to the same remand home after her medical examination. Justices P.S. Patankar and R.J. Kochar directed the police to shift the little girl to Bal Asha Sadan, a home approached and requested to take the girl by Majlis. This was in March 2000. April 2000, within one month, there is a dramatically positive change in the girl. This mute child, 'rescued' from Dadar railway station in February, was put into the remand home where the entry medical report says 'hymen intact'. Within nine days she was bit, mauled, sexually probed, manhandled, assaulted and raped. She was then left to her own devices; except that towards the end of February she had convulsions and had to, perforce, be taken to hospital. When she was shifted to Bal Asha Sadan, she bit the other children there, she fought, she cowered under her bed when not having hysterics, she displayed sexualized behaviour, she wept, she would not allow herself to be touched, never mind undressed for a bath. April 2000. The child is a child again, she is mentally slow; but she is not mute, she never was. The power of true love in the form of real care.

Meanwhile: another non-government organization shelter run for destitute children, handsomely funded to save children from the streets. In the suburbs of Mumbaii, it is managed by a head who lives on the premises with his wife and children. He squeezes the breasts of a minor girl so hard that he leaves red marks. The girl, daughter of a prostitute, had been sent to this shelter on the premise that she would be safe from the kind of clients who frequented the area her mother worked in. This little girl's breasts were squeezed so hard that she was compelled to ask the shelter's assistant for medical aid.

What has happened to this little girl? The city's organizations who work with this attractively funded subject of Child Sexual Abuse—for seminars, more seminars, discussions with the same people or a round robin of different people, awareness campaigns among their colleague organizations—do not know. The girl has vanished. 'Well,' says the spokeswoman for one organization primly, 'we did call a press conference but the reporter who turned up could not get confirmation from the shelter's authorities. They denied it, you see.'

Oh yes, we see.

Why did they assume that journalists should be avenging angels on behalf of organizations who don't have all their facts in place? And why did they not group together and move the High Court on a Public Interest Litigation to have that shelter investigated by the police, the children within moved to another safe shelter, the child's sexual abuser arrested?

Another spokeswoman for another organization, but as viscerally committed to the cause, sniffs, 'Really! What do we know about law! We are just public-minded people working towards trying to save children from being exploited, how much can we do? Besides, that is not part of our charter, we cannot be using our funding for what we have not said. That would be misuse, you see.'

Oh yes, now we really and truly see.

As do the children on the streets who know these kind of stories well, as do child-prostitutes. When they run away from their homes because of the sexual abuse and are trapped by organized sexual-exploiters of children, they quickly pick up on the pitfalls of being 'rescued' by society, the very same society which brought them till here in the first place. They rapidly hone their survival skills within their new exploitative environment, the boys do it better than the girls.

Boys survive better. Is that why they are being preferred as child-prostitutes over girls for the tourist sex industry?

That boys are being preferred—in India and internationally—is now an accepted fact. The North American Man Boy Love Association (Nambla) has been formed with the express charter of facilitating sex with young boys: 'It should not be against the law for children and adults to express their love sexually. Children should be able to become sexual with an adult.' A thirty-page guide from men who like boys has sold out swiftly in America, 72,000 copies in thirteen months priced at five dollars each, titled *Where The Young Ones Are*. In India the guide is the middleman, the omniscient and omnipotent pimp. And now it is also the world wide web.

The report on The National Consultation on Child Prostitution organized in Delhi by the Ymca, Unicef and Ecpat states: 'There is growth of international networks of child sex abusers who are working together to share information on the safest places to visit in the world. There is also the development of a huge market for child pornography in the world of computers. India and other South Asian countries are slowly replacing South East Asia as the venue of choice for the tourist sex industry as there are fewer laws against child sexual abuse in these countries. Another reason is that European tourists believe that Aids among children in India is not as rampant. A large number of sex tourists are now seeking out India. The main destination in India for tourists seeking child prostitutes is Goa, with its combination of beaches and lax security at the airport for chartered flights. The recent trial in

Stockholm, Sweden, is one indication of how Goa is fast out-rivalling Bangkok as the new sex capital for paedophiles. When Lena Perned and her lover were put on trial along with eighteen others, she disclosed that they had chosen Goa because the Thai capital had become "too hot". Another popular destination appears to be Kovalam in Kerala. A German tourist was recently caught in the act but managed to bribe his way out.'

Remember 'Brother' and 'Father' Freddy Peat in Goa in April 1991 who also almost got away with sadistic sexual child abuse? He ran an 'orphanage' where the police found syringes, sedatives and aphrodisiacs along with pornographic photographs involving children. A young boy went home after visiting 'Father' Freddy and complained to his father of pain in his penis. The parent was shocked, so many young Goan boys from decent homes were going to see 'Brother' Freddy all the time! He lodged a complaint with the police. The mid-sixties Freddy Peat was arrested and 2,305 photographs seized, all of them featuring young Indian boys engaged in pornographic acts, some with older white women, most with elderly male foreigners. The police released Freddy Peat on bail within forty-five days on grounds of 'insufficient evidence'.

Child rights activist Sheela Barse intervened. She went immediately from Mumbaii to Goa in December 1991 and camped there. She sorted out those 2,305 pictures, all of them with little Indian boys save one with a little Indian girl. A girl-child, her mouth and eyes screaming in pain, being held firmly by two pairs of hands to be lowered, at the base of the picture, on a hugely stiff penis belonging to a third male. Sheela Barse's stomach never stopped churning. But she did sort out the photographs, she gathered evidence from the banks of foreign accounts, she spoke to landlords whose premises had been rented to shoot these pictures, she ran passport checks, she sent the drugs used on the children for analysis, she detailed the parcels which were mailed out from Goa's post offices. And she found the laws in the rusty Indian Penal Code under which the book could be thrown at Freddy Peat. She ensured the chargesheeting of Peat in August 1992 and his ultimate conviction in March 1996, when he was seventy-one years old. Sheela Barse can be credited with not only the first paedophilia conviction in Asia but also the highest sentence to be awarded in India in any case of sexual assault: twenty years.

Sheela Barse is still trying to secure those children justice. Peat was part of an international child-trafficking ring. A dozen foreigners have yet to be arrested and brought on trial to India. She says, 'I am in touch with Interpol headquarters at Lyon as also Interpols in some countries, I pass on information which they give me to the Indian authorities. I keep phoning the CBI in Delhi, I realize I don't need British Interpol to tell me that India is not serious about ending the problem. Thai police informs me that a paedophile is to pass through an airport and since India needs to arrest him on a specific case, I let the Indian authorities know. I give the flight details along with the date and time. I follow it up with phone calls. They say, "Oh, we missed him at the airport." I have been telling them since a while now that Himachal Pradesh, Thiruvananthapuram, Kovalam and Bangalore are being used much more these days by the tourism sex industry. I don't see anybody looking into the matter or even caring.'

No they have not cared, nobody from government has at any rate. Which is probably why it has happened again in Goa. Says Nishtha Desai, who is currently researching tourism-related paedophilia and is actively trying to change the situation in Goa by working with other non-government organizations, the police and local state government, 'A boy, around fourteen years old, was brought by a fifty-three-year-old German national from Mumbaii to Goa. They stayed in the same room in a Calangute hotel. The boy later testified before the police and a magistrate that the man attempted to have anal sex with him but was unable to completely penetrate because he began howling in pain. The man also had oral sex with him. Anal swabs taken from the boy and man revealed the presence of human spermatozoa. A taxi driver testified that he had driven the man and the boy to the hotel and the receptionist confirmed that they had shared the same room. The female assistant sessions judge found this German national guilty and gave him six years of rigorous imprisonment. The man went into appeal, and the male additional sessions judge ruled that it was not proved that the accused was indulging in unnatural offences against the child. The man left Goa and the country.'

Nishtha Desai's valid point is that paedophiles need fear no punishment from the Indian judicial system. 'In fact,' she says, 'a New Zealander has opted to be tried in India. Eoghan McBride, the sixty-year-old who was arrested in New Zealand in August 1999 because of an Interpol Red Corner Alert on charges of being associated with a child-sex ring in Goa, is alleged to be an associate of Freddy Peat. He said he wanted to be tried by Indian courts and was extradited by his own country, he was produced before the chief judicial magistrate at Margao on 29 November 1999. McBride has two New Zealand convictions. In 1991 he was sentenced to nine months periodic detention, two years supervision and psychiatric treatment after pleading guilty to six charges of indecently assaulting a six-year-old boy and an eleven-year-old boy. Both offences occurred when McBride was on parole from a two-year jail term for similar offences. At that time his lawyer acknowledged that McBride was a paedophile and said his client was prepared to authorise treatment that amounted to chemical castration.'

Neither McBride nor his lawyer needed to make good that promise since the Freddy Peats case hit international headlines in the same year, and McBride was named in it too.

'It is getting more and more difficult in Goa for its citizens,' points out Nishtha Desai. 'These foreigners stay long-term in and around the place and either bring children from Mumbaii or pick up kids from the beaches. They proposition the Goan school-going children or they simply take their pick from the children of the construction labourers from Karnataka. They also choose from the children of migrant vendors on the beaches or the young masseurs. They tend to come to Goa from England and Germany, avuncular-looking men distributing foreign chocolates.'

These men can fly straight into Goa on tourist-load charters; they can also go to Goa through Mumbaii, now an important hub for paedophiles. An entire South Mumbaii road—otherwise a commercial, movie theatre, residential strip—teems with young boys. Confirming this is Mansoor Qadri of Saathi which works with street youth. 'It begins from one end of the area which links to the upmarket and rich side of Mumbaii and at the other side is the Gaandu Gardens.' The garden is actually called something else, but in typically Mumbaii black humour has been rechristened the gaandu bageecha, gaandu means anal penetration.

Qadri also says he has heard of an all-boy brothel in the area too, which a lot of foreigners and 'office-going Indian men' visit but has yet to get confirmation. What he does confirm is what is being whispered: the elderly and heavy aunties who set out for drives during the early evenings from their plush areas on the other side of the strip, they swoop in during the city's rush-hour and quickly pick up one of the young lads holding a massage kit. The boys, like the rest on the strip, are between twelve and sixteen years of age, except that they stand specifically opposite one theatre, on the pavement next to a well-known clothing store. The aunties drop these masseurs back to the same spot soon enough so that they are well in time before their lords and masters get home.

Who cares, why should they care? There is money to be made all around, and so what if it is blood-money of the innocents? In Mumbaii, in the lanes around the Gateway of India, small hotels are run in a warren of rooms. Boys check in here by the hour, or stay the night with foreign male tourists who have checked in earlier. Well-dressed, young college boys also make money from the foreigners staying at the better hotels in the area. They are contacted by college pimps who do it to fund their drug habits.

Vikram does it because he is collecting money to settle abroad. 'It is easy money,' says this handsome fifteen-year-old who exercises and works out for an hour every day to maintain his well-toned body. 'I don't have to do anything except lie down and enjoy it while the foreigner fusses around over me. Then I have to just do it to him.'

Vikram's sister is also in the business, as a 'beer bar waitress' which can be read as a euphemism for a call girl. Her make-up and clothes make her look like a twenty-plus year old, she is all of sixteen. Their mother walked out on them when she caught their father red-handed in their bed, with a pretty boy from the neighbourhood. The brother-sister duo are 'a team' from the day their father raped him three years back. They protect each other by sleeping together in one room of their father's flat, in a high-rise at Mumbaii's upmarket Cuffe Parade. The sister does not like what she is doing in the beer bar, she prefers the foreign customers who would, in turn, prefer girls. She uses words like chocobar and cone ice-cream for oral sex and 'fuse uda dena' for very quick oral sex. She, likewise Vikram, refuse to believe that Aids can be contracted through oral sex. Both of them feel that if they share 'tenderness' in the nights, it is mutual and therefore all right compared with what their father did to Vikram. They make plans for when they will migrate. The 'Hansel and Gretel Syndrome' as some psychiatrists call this, after the children's folk tale about a devoted brother and sister.

Meanwhile, around the Chatrapati Shivaji Terminus, a boy-child sleeps alone. When he gets up in the morning and opens his fist, he will find money in it. This happens to him quite regularly, somebody putting money in his hand. He knows the other street-children who sleep near him do not get money in their hand because they sleep together, huddled, to protect themselves from strange men who come in the night. They come in big cars, smelling of nice scent, they press the money into his hand after they are done. The child thinks of the money, and the picture he will see with it in an air-conditioned theatre. He smiles in his sleep.

And in Bangalore, in the dead of night, an eight-year-old inert body is tossed out of a car onto a rubbish heap. In the morning they will find her, comment on the fact that she appears not to have been a street child. Perhaps, they will wonder aloud, she was kidnapped from another city? Or maybe she ran away? But why should she have done that, she looks like she came from a good home.

From a 'good' home. How will they tell? From the well-trimmed nails? From her clean ears? From her neatly cut hair?

How do you tell the class of a child from a tiny body pitted with cigarette burns?

Why, at all, do you need to tell the class of a child? It is a child.

A child. Someone's child. Our child.

Whom somebody has abused.

Somebody has used her like an ashtray and stubbed his cigarette all over her; somebody has then thrown her out of his car like garbage.

There she lies naked, her torn panties tightly clasped in her clenched fist.

notebook two

·

Click. Click, click.

She is under the bed, her grandmother is on it. She knows her grandmother's eyes are closed, that her mouth is moving silently as she prays. Rising around them in the room is a bluish grey swirl of incense, a whole big bunch of sickly-sweet smelling agarbattis lit and placed upright in a tightly-packed cup of uncooked rice. As her grandmother prays she rotates one hundred and one loosely-strung fat beads with her right hand. Her prayer beads, they click, click.

'Dadi, what are you praying for?'

Click, click, click, fast, furious, click.

'Dadi!'

'Hush, I am praying, can't you see?'

'I am under the bed dadi, how to see?'

An impatient rattle of the prayer beads, dadi is cross, 'Will you let me finish praying? Then I have to cook the evening's dinner and I have to clean the dishes and so much housework! Your mother will only come like a memsaab when I finish everything. Now let me pray, will you?'

'All the time you pray, why do you pray so much, God is not giving?'

'Hush, the mouth this child has.'

Her dadi is seated on the only bed they have, it would have been high and mighty if it was not so wobbly; a four-

poster bed which nevertheless lords over the ten feet by ten
feet square they live in, cook in, eat in, sleep in, bathe in.
For the toilet they go outside their room. They join the line
which wends its way through the corridor connecting ten
such rooms to each floor, four floors in all, a toilet at the
end of each. They are the smallest family in the entire
chawl, only seven to the room, and they are all poor in the
building. But they are about to become rich, her dadi just
says.

'I am praying hard so that we can leave this chawl
quickly and go to a nice place, into a big flat.'

'Big like a palace?'

Dadi laughs. 'That you can ask your husband to get for
you. We will have three rooms. One room for your
mummy, daddy, you and your brother, one room for your
dada and me, one room for your daddy's brothers.'

'I don't have a brother, how can he sleep in my room?'

'He will come. High time, anyway, your mother took
our family's name forward.'

'What, dadi?'

'Havey bey minute chup chaap bes, keep quiet for two
minutes and let me finish my prayers.'

'I will not go to the new house without my naram
takiya.' She says this clearly from under the bed, holding
her favourite pillow tight to her chin.

Defiantly: 'Won't go!'

'Don't be silly, you can't take that torn pillow with
you. Now let me finish praying or I will force you to go to
school the next time you pretend to have fever.'

She crawls tighter under the bed and burrows in the
folded bedding they stack there each morning after they all
get up. She puts her naram takiya on her lap, like a baby,
and pats it; soft and silky. Her mummy says her small
pillow is filled with goose feathers and covered with

English satin. Her mummy's mummy made it specially for her with her own hands; it smells like her fingers, lavender. She stays out of her dadi's way until her mummy comes home from school where she is a class teacher.

'She is under the bed,' her dadi sniffs. 'Six years old and completely uncontrollable, I do not know how you are bringing her up.'

'I will not go to the three rooms without my naram takiya,' she yells.

When they load the haathgaadi with their few belongings, they do not take the bed; they stack the two chairs upended and firmly truss them in place. She climbs on top of the chairs on the handcart and perches, her naram takiya hidden under her so that dadi does not see and demand that it be left behind. The haathgaadiwallahs pick up the hand cart's edges resting on the pavement, one man pushes, the other man pulls. The handcart rolls out of the area bearing her. She feels like a princess, she waves with her chubby fingers to the ghoshtwallah and the pavwallah and bald Dr Kamath who cured her of her double jaundice; and she waves at Derby Talkies where her mummy took her to see nice pictures. They are going to be very happy in the three rooms.

Click, click. Her dadi's prayer beads rotate, the half-burnt incense sticks form a quivering pile of ash.

'Dadi, what are you praying for today?'

'You are back from school? Go have your wash, I will make you tea. Eight years old and she does not know how to light the stove. When I was your age, I made my own tea and washed my own clothes.'

'All lies. God punishes liars.'

'What did you say?'

'I know your daddy was very rich and we were also

very rich when you got married to dada. Then people drank and drank and all the money went away.'

'And what else has your mother stuffed into your head?'

'I never said mummy said!'

'I know who is teaching you all this. But, yes, my father was very rich and my brothers are still very rich. We had big cars and so many servants. When I got married to your dada, they sent out invitations in ghoda gadis filled with dry fruit. My saris were all in Swiss lace and my petticoats of English satin.'

'Have you put a new cover on my naram takiya, dadi?'

'That pillow of yours, how much trouble it is giving me. Why you must insist on keeping it, I do not know.'

'Where is it?'

'I have given it to the mattress man to redo.'

'But he will steal all the goose feathers from it!'

'Then what can I do? To put a new cover I had to remove the satin of the old one, it was stained and smelling. And there was hardly anything left inside. I have asked the mattress man to mix it up with new stuffing and make you a new pillow.'

'But dadi, it will not feel the same!'

'Things do not, as you grow up. Now go and do your homework. I will finish praying and make you tea.'

'I don't want tea from you or anybody, I want my old naram takiya back, I want it back now.'

The lids fall over dadi's eyes, click, click, click.

Her two baby sisters and mummy are sleeping in their room. She quietly changes, drinks water from the earthen matka in the dark and cramped corridor which doubles as their kitchen and goes through it to the third room with her school bag. She sets everything on the low table and kneels against it on the floor. She pulls out her science and geography books.

Rotation. Revolution.

The room's door closes softly.

The earth rotates. It also revolves.

How can that be?

Something feels odd against her back; something goes up her dress and scoops itself into her cotton panties.

She is frightened, she makes to shout and a hand gently covers her mouth.

'Hush, it is only me.'

He has got off the bed, closed the door, knelt behind her, his one hand is over her mouth, his other is doing things she does not understand; and there is something hard, hard, sticking into her back.

'Hush, do not get frightened.'

She is bewildered. His tone and his hands do not match.

He is murmuring things as his hands seek to roam. There is something unfamiliar in his voice; not in the words but the pitch, pace and tone.

She wrenches herself free, yanks open the door, bangs it shut behind her, holds the door's handle tight, tight, tight, and squeezes her eyes tight; but the sadness crouching in the corners of the corridor creeps up on her and she lets go off his door's handle to run into their room.

In their room, she scrambles on to the bed and lies down next to her mummy and her sisters. Her heart is thudding, she feels like crying but everyone is sleeping in their room. She does not wake up mummy, mummy has not been smiling like she used to as a teacher, everyone has been shouting at her for not giving birth to boys.

When her mummy gets up, she asks her to get the books and school bag from that room.

How much is there to run in, run from? It is only three rooms and she feels like she is running, running. He waits for her to come from school, clad only in a towel so that he can expose himself better. The bathroom door's top glass-rectangle is shattered by her alcoholic uncle who threw his bottle through it. The other uncle now stares from it as she bathes, she cowers near the bucket.

He tries showing her pornographic pictures, big albums filled with huge coloured pictures of naked white women with their legs parted, holding up their breasts. In wedding-like albums. Why does no one else notice them? Why don't they know what is happening to her? Why cannot they see? Why do they leave her alone with him? How does he know when her mummy will not be at home? How does he know she will not tell her daddy? Where is everyone when he sets upon her?

Where is everyone?

Why is there so much silence in the three rooms when there is just him and her? Him making her stand in front of him, his fingers digging into her arm, hurting her, as he strokes himself, faster, faster, and then something white comes out?

Click. Click, click go her dadi's prayer beads in the other room. She is praying for her daughter who is married but unhappy elsewhere; she is praying for her husband, dada, who drinks; she is praying for her son who drinks and wreaks havoc; she is praying for her son who is schizophrenic and with his wife in another country; she is praying for her son who has only daughters to beget a son; she is praying for the son who is the apple of her eye.

She tells her dadi. She blurts it out because she cannot run, and hide, and duck, and dive, and scrape through, anymore.

Her dadi looks at her as if she cannot really see her. Her prayer beads rotate in her right hand, click, click, click.

She stands there, looking at the profusion of tiny white hair growing out of her dadi's chin in and around the big and black mole, trying hard not to listen when her dadi lapses into her mother tongue, 'Hoye, it happens, aam thaay, these things happen, kyarek ghar ma pan thay jaaye, some times it can happen in families, bhulee javanoo, forget it, tya nai jati, you stay away from him. And do not tell your mother, you will upset her. See how happy she looks now that she has gone to college to learn new things so that she can start teaching all over again? Remember how sick she used to be when she could not go out of the house? If you tell her anything she will stop going out of the house again and then she will not keep well again. That will be your fault.'

'I am going to tell my daddy.'

'Hush, you cannot do that. Your daddy works so hard, he slogs for all of us, do you want to upset him?'

'My daddy will stop him.'

'Then there will be a fight in the family and your daddy will have to leave the house and the shop. Who will feed your sisters then? It will be all your fault for not being sensible about it.'

The joys of a joint family.

She is running, she is running. From those hands which latch on to her buttocks like leeches as she silently struggles.

She is ten and she knows somewhat about these things. But she is still not prepared for the biggest, blackest pool of blood on the cracked, white tiles of the bathroom floor. The blood soaks her fingers like oil, she has begun menstruating.

Dadi sniffs, 'Too early, just ten and she has got her monthlies. Now we will have to get her married even sooner, or God knows what new ways she will find to embarrass the family.' Dadi begins tearing strips from an old, thick bed sheet, 'Here, you can use these.'

'I am not going to use that horrible material.'

'Achcha, you want silk I suppose, or should I get you velvet?'

'I want what they give ma in the hospital after the babies come.'

'That costs money, so much money every month.'

'Is it my fault that this has happened?'

'Nothing is a woman's fault. And everything is a woman's fault.' As she says this, Dadi's smile looks like it is in pain.

'Am not a woman! I am a girl.'

'Now you are a woman.'

Mummy explains to her how the babies will come out when she gets married. Husbands and wives make babies like this, mummy draws diagrams in curlicues and trellises, all mehndi-like patterns. She stares at them.

'What is a husband, ma?'

'A husband is the man whom you marry. Your daddy is my husband, I am his wife.'

'No ma, I am not asking this, I know this much. Who is a husband?'

'What do you mean, who is a husband?'

She feels confusion, she gropes for the words. 'Is my chacha my husband?'

'Silly girl, how can your daddy's brother be your husband? He is like your daddy, he is part of our family. Your husband will be a man from another family, he will not be as old as the men in your family.'

Suddenly she feels acutely sick, not just sick to her stomach but also in a deep, bone-and-muscle way.

And then her uterus begins mocking her. Every twenty-three days it twists and tortures, it makes sure that the pain tears right through her to remind her that she has to run.

Fast. Faster. Fastest. From those fingers with their nails cut in semi-moons, those fingers which flash out of nowhere, and shape themselves conically, to measure her growing breasts.

This is going to happen very often in her life, but she does not know it as yet. Whenever God decides to protect her, in exchange he takes away something that is special to her.

Her schizophrenic but brilliant uncle has to return from abroad, his distraught wife cannot cope with his condition alone any more. Her family comes down to the ground floor from the fifth floor where they live to talk to dadi and dada. Her father says, 'You did not tell us of his condition when you came with the proposal. True, we were impressed by his educational qualifications, his intelligence, his career prospects. But you should not have withheld such important information from us, how is a girl's father ever to know of a prospective groom's mental status if it is not immediately obvious?'

Someone loftily replies, 'It was not obvious because it was not so bad, in fact it was not bad at all. Perhaps you should ask your daughter what she has done to worsen his condition. Men improve after marriage, you know.'

The father looks hard at dadi and dada, 'I am not one of those men who will allow their child to suffer just so that the world does not get a chance to talk. My daughter is now like an unpaid nurse to your son, that is all her life has become. I am sending her an air ticket, she will divorce your son, that is that.'

All that loftiness rapidly hisses out of the room, like air from a balloon.

Quickly, in double time, a decision is taken. Bring him

back to India with his wife, they will stay in this house, they will both be safe here, dadi can help in keeping an eye on him so that the wife gets time to herself as well, her own family is just five floors above so won't that be nice? They can move into the third room, that is the best room with light, air and privacy; the occupants of the third room can move into the second room with its cracked bathroom panes and tiles, dadi and dada will continue to live in the hall-cum-bedroom. They will take care of each other, protect each other, obey each other, they will be one big happy family. In this house, safe haven; this lie.

For the son with his wife and three daughters rent a small place in an old building somewhere down the road. To get the money to pay up on the enormous advance rent and house deposit, sell the Poona house.

It is a tiny, tiny bungalow, almost like a doll's house in Poona, near the station, with a guava tree in the hanky-sized front garden. She loves it, all the holidays spent there are bliss. And now she must not even feel a wrench as it gets taken away from her so that she can go into another home where she will be safe. Away from this house, safe haven; this lie.

When they load the three haathgaadis with the family's belongings, she swings up her youngest sister and sticks her on to a stool strapped onto one of them. She makes the haathgaadiwallah rock the handcart. Her sister squeals with delight, she feels her spirits lift. They will be happy, just their very own family in their very own house down the road.

This is her hall. This is her kitchen. Her bathroom, her toilet, both separate. This is her mummy and daddy's room. And this is the room where her sisters and she will sleep.

'No,' says ma, 'you have to sleep in the hall.'

'Why can't I sleep with my sisters?'

Her mummy tells her.

No, she says, no. No, no, no.

'What is wrong with you?'

Please ma, no.

'Look, we are a joint family, are we not? We have to share each others joys and sorrows, don't we?'

Her mummy sounds so tired, she looks so weak.

She does not know what to do, she does not know what to say; she does not know what to do with the panic bubbling deep within her stomach.

Her mummy says, 'He is your chacha after all, your father's brother, not some stranger, what possible problem can you have when he is one of us?'

Us: that impossible word sliding sharp, deep, like a razor into her.

She blurts, 'Ma, no. He will hurt the girls.'

'Hurt? Have you gone crazy? What rubbish are you talking?'

She bursts into tears, she can taste the bitterness on her own lips, she can feel her body trying to escape from its dirty skin.

Ma's gaze: angry, incredulous.

Her mummy sits down heavily on an as-yet-unpacked suitcase. She is white as a sheet.

'All right,' she finally says. 'This will take time, a little time. You know how everything is. Meanwhile, remember what I have told you about how babies are made.'

He has not done anything like that, ma, not even close. Not let him.

Her mother looks relieved, she gets up from the suitcase and goes into her room.

She goes into the bedroom which was supposed to be

her safe haven, she sits there, on the edge of the bed, but does not cry anymore.

Her entire system is registering an invisible assault: she sits there and realizes that it is she who, in bringing up the problem, has turned into the problem itself.

Her mother says one of her daughters is not well, she needs to sleep with all the girls, they all sleep in the hall; he sleeps in the bedroom. Her father says nothing.

She does not talk to him, it is as if he does not exist for her as she buries herself in her school and its homework and her books, happy novels filled with sunshine and fun families, Enid Blytons and Nancy Drews and Billy Bunters and Williams where uncles are not like this, where fathers are fearless. She becomes a member of libraries where books can await her, reliably patient and tolerant of her capacity to devour them. She reads, she soaks in books, she reads in bed, in the toilet, in the bus to school and back, she reads in good light and bad light, she reads like it is her lifeline, which it is. She gets the thickest spectacles, a very high number.

She does not go anywhere near him while he stands in front of the mirror in his towel to shave and then go in for his bath in the mornings; she keeps away from him, right at the very end of the room while they all have dinner together. She cannot eat banana anymore, and Bombay duck, its white wetness makes her feel ill. But she eats everything else, more than she should and can, specially sweets and chocolates which find hidden places in her to nestle and deposit. Slowly, methodically, miserably, she eats.

Now she is very fat and with the thickest spectacles.

'Who will marry her?' wonders dadi aloud.

Mummy speaks to daddy, mummy speaks to dadi. The

alcoholic uncle is sent to live with them instead.

Mummy picks up plates of food as he flings them drunkenly around. Together, mother and her eldest daughter wash the lemon yellow walls with soap and water where the khichdi mixed with dahi has splattered and oozed down.

Mummy opens the door late every night when he bangs, and abuses, and leans on the bell. She cannot bear to clean up his vomit, the smell makes her vomit too, ma cleans it all up.

Mummy gets pregnant, it should be a boy this time they all tell her. Mummy stands in the sun, downstairs, because in the house the uncle is in an alcoholic stupor and partially undressed. It is only noon and she has come home from school because her uterus is mocking her. Ma tells her that this has been happening often. She stands downstairs on the road, in the blazing sun, numb, while heavy lorries laden with steel girders and double-decker buses crammed with people rumble past her. She phones her daddy from the grocery shop downstairs, they do not have a phone upstairs as yet, and she phones him at his neighbouring shop because he does not have a phone in his own. Her daddy is out on money collection because he needs it to feed such a big joint family. What kind of message can you leave in someone else's shop, in what kind of words which would convey your agony, your urgency, your utter helplessness?

Her mummy gives birth to a dead son.

I am sorry ma, so very sorry that you lost your son because of me.

Something has gone wrong with her. She does not recognize herself any more. Or is this the girl she is actually supposed to be? 'Bad blood,' as dadi has sniffed. 'Bad blood, it cannot be from my own family's side, of this I am sure.'

She cannot stop eating, she has become so fat that her thighs rub, and burn, against each other. She talks loudly, she screams, she swears, she is disrespectful, she is not interested in her studies when earlier she was among the highest scorers, she has just slapped a girl in school and threatened to break a bottle over the head of a teacher.

They pack her off to a boarding school, an expensive place in Mussoorie, where girls from grand families have been sent to polish up themselves. She becomes moody. 'Uncommunicative,' says the principal to mummy and daddy in a letter. She collects money quietly, she sells her gold ring and earrings at a jeweller's on the Mall, and she runs away from the boarding. By a bus, then a train, then a plane from Delhi, everyone stares at this fat girl with thick spectacles in a smart blue blazer travelling without any luggage. She comes back home.

It is afternoon when she arrives, the door is locked. The neighbour tells her that her mummy is in hospital, she is having another baby.

Her newest sister is brought home and when mummy feels strong enough, she takes her to a child counsellor. After days and days and days of making her answer stupid questions and giving her childish games to play, the counsellor asks her, 'So you will feel better if your daddy tells that man that what he did to you was wrong?'

That is all it will take?

She nods.

The child counsellor tells mummy something and then mummy tells daddy. Nothing happens.

Why do they give her so much power one minute, and then persecute her the next?

Now she knows—fully and well—that it is only she who has to protect herself.

And now the school wants her to leave, she has already been given three white cards as warnings, followed by the serious three pink cards which means the school means business when it comes to recalcitrant children. Three white cards plus three pink cards means you have to leave, she is fourteen years old.

'But where can I send her?' asks ma in despair of the principal Sister Esperanca. 'She is almost at the end of her schooling.'

Sister Esperanca, her face kind and concerned under her nun's cowl, takes her hand and asks, 'What would you like to do?'

'Why should you care? You have been signing all those white cards and pink cards, haven't you? So why should you care what happens to me now onwards?'

'Shameless girl!'

Sister Esperanca gestures for ma to stay silent. 'It is important in life to take the consequences of your actions. As your principal my job was to keep warning you as long as I could, without other students taking advantage of the school's kindness. You refused to listen, you acted according to what you thought was right. But it was not, we kept trying to tell you that. Now you must face the results; as you sow, so shall you reap. Now I will ask you again, what do you want to do with your life?'

'I want to work. I have to take care of myself. I do not want to study, it is a waste of time, I want to start working and earning money and collecting it to look after my sisters and to buy my own flat.'

Sister Esperanca smiles tenderly, 'So many words from one so young.' She addresses ma, 'You should be proud to have such a strong daughter.'

Ma says, 'I am . . .'

She is?

'. . . but she has to finish her studies first. She can do what she wants after that, I will support her once she is professionally qualified.'

Sister Esperanca nods, 'Yes, that is correct. Girls must be professionally qualified today to look after their own futures. My child, would you like to finish your schooling in Poona?'

Oh yes, please, since it is Poona.

'We have a fine convent there, with a small boarding school where you will be happy. It is the ideal environment for you, I can speak to the principal there.'

Ma cuts in, 'Yes, yes, that is a very good idea. I have a relative there, I can request her to be the local guardian.'

Sister Esperanca smiles again and pats her hand, 'I will not ask you to be a good girl, I know you are not a bad girl. But I will ask you to be less angry, will you control your temper in Poona, my child?'

'I will try. But then they should not purposely make me angry.'

'My child, the world is filled with people who want to do only this, purposely make other people angry. We must not rise to their bait. Still, you have said you will try. You promise to try?'

'I promise.'

Everyone is happy, specially she.

So that's all it took, would have taken.

'But ma, I love him. I want to marry him, he wants to marry me.' 'You are too young to get married.'

'Ma, I am nineteen years old, not all that young. Besides, what objection can you possibly have? It was you

112

who appointed her as my local guardian there, he is your own relative's son. You know how much she has stood up for me in school?'

'Yes I know, she told me on the phone that you were caught reading love comics in the moral science class and she told the nuns, "Well, good morals are about pure and undiluted love, so why should anyone object to such reading material?" Very nice, but I wonder if she would have been so accommodating if it was her own daughter.' Ma sets her mouth primly as she says this.

'C'mon ma, don't get all hoity-toity, you know we both like her, she is a strong woman. And he has been good to me throughout college, you let me go to college in Poona because you felt theirs was one home I could safely go to. Besides, it's not like I am marrying a cousin or uncle or something; she is, after all, your distant relative. They are rich, they live in a fancy bungalow in Poona. What more can a mother ever want for her daughter?'

'I do not know what other mothers want for their daughters and I do not care. What I do know is you have fared well in school and college, are you going to just waste all these good percentages?'

'You mean to say there are only dumb housewives? That only the ones who graduate badly get married? All the ones who fare well go off for higher studies?'

'I do not want you to go for higher studies just for the sake of an additional degree. You need to be professionally qualified, just being a stupid graduate is not enough any more.'

'So what happens if I am not professionally qualified?'

'Don't you remember what was decided in front of Sister Esperanca?'

'How does it matter since I do not need to work? He is rich, very rich, you know that.'

'You might need to work in the future.'

'Yeah, like you, in fits and starts.'

Ma flushes, she says, 'How do you know you are not making a mistake?'

'Like you did?'

Ma bites her lip, she says, 'So based on what you see as my mistake, you think you are not making one?'

'Well, at least he is not a weak man, attached to his mother's apron strings. He will stand up for me and my children when we need it.'

Ma laughs, 'Now I am convinced you want to marry him for all the wrong reasons.'

'If you are such a bloody expert, how come you screwed up your own life?'

'Let us see, perhaps I won't be alive, but let us see how differently you do things when you have children and yet want to take even a single decision for your own life.'

'Yeah, right, now dump your stupidity and your husband's weakness on us. And try and live your life through mine; whatever you bloody missed, do it by trying to control mine.'

Ma's upper lip curls, her nostrils flare, this means she is seriously angry. 'Okay,' she says abruptly, 'promise time.'

'No promises. I am getting married, look at this big diamond ring he has given me. It's a rock.'

'Good, maybe soon enough he will give you more than a rock, he will give you a full quarry to wear on your fingers since that is all you seem to be interested in.'

'Well, what else is there to life for a girl, for God's sake! Grow up, marry, have babies, look after them the best you can, give and attend good parties, grow old as gracefully as possible and play cards at some posh and pricey club in the sunset years of your life.'

'You forgot to say look good and stay slim.'

'Don't rub it in, ma. I know I am very fat, okay? Besides, he is huge himself and if neither of us mind, why should you have a problem with it?'

'I don't have what you call a problem. Marry him, play cards at the club. Do it, do it all. But first get professionally qualified, work for one or two years after that. Stay engaged to him till then, spend weekends with him. I will not object and I am sure neither will his mother. Marry after you are twenty-one, I will say nothing, promise.'

'You promise?'

'I promise. You promise?'

'I want time to think.'

'All right, tell me tomorrow.'

'Tomorrow? Mummy don't be absurd, how can I take such a big decision without consulting him?'

'Him? Listen to this girl, she is already talking about a "him". Call the fellow by his name, the man is to be your husband, talk about this man like he is God and he will start pretending to be one.'

'You should know, right?'

'Go away, go to bed, tell me tomorrow.'

'Oh, all right, I promise.'

Mother, daughter; daughter, mother: interchangeable most times. Between these two women can spring a strong affinity and an equally strong tension. The bond, a result of a recognition that neither women can express. The tension, an outcome of what one woman must always suspect, for the other to deny; because they are supposed to not be friends.

These have been clear, dry and cool nights. Starry and sharp. The air spiked with a special silence. She has slept like a baby through each, no nightmares, no dreams, not

115

one; waking only to walk to her hotel's window to see if the night is still there; wishing star intact.

She smiles, it will end soon, she must spoil it herself to end it, she must destroy it before it can get snatched away from her; she must only be a tentatively accepted visitor in her own fantasy.

She smiles. He gives her a sidelong glance and looks back to the road, he changes gears to negotiate a turn at Jubilee Hills and observes, 'You have been smiling throughout our drive.'

'Yes,' she says simply.

'What were you thinking of?'

My naram takiya, she wants to say, its cool comfort and yet its sensuous satin against my cheek; like your cognac eyes on my face.

A baby with you, she wants to tell him.

It's her fantasy, say whatever she wants.

'I am waiting,' he says softly over the purr of his car's powerful engine.

'You are a wonderful man.'

He laughs, easily, naturally, in bass, 'Why this compliment?'

'My blood sings under my skin when I am with you. You know this. Yet you have done nothing to take advantage of the situation. And I know your blood hums for me.'

He says something in Telugu, his timbre like liquid gold.

'I did not understand that.'

'Bombay woman, what do I make of you?'

'Is that what you said in Telugu?'

'No.'

He moves his hand from the gear stick to her knee.

'Put your hand on mine,' he says. She does. 'Now take

it away.' She does.

He moves his hand back to the stick shift, he says, 'What did you feel?'

'Skin. And bones.'

'You could not have felt my bones, they melt when you are near me. I adore you.'

Something pricks her eyelids; quickly, quickly, spoil this. 'Adore? That's a really old-fashioned word.'

He looks at her, sidelong, those cognac eyes caressing her face, 'You are very different, Bombay woman; stay this way, so strong.'

The last thing she says to him, she knows she will never see him ever again, 'You will always be very special to me; remember that, always.'

What she does not say is what she has known from the first day of their intensely brief friendship: something is finally setting itself right.

What can you explain when you do not want to understand it yourself, she thinks as she clicks the seat belt in place. The aircraft is ready to fly her away from Hyderabad, she leans back in her seat and closes her eyes. Waiting for take-off.

This has been happening from the time she was nineteen, every time she has sat in a plane. Or walked on a road. She is in her early thirties now, she has travelled the world and the seven seas. She waits as the plane taxies on the runway.

She waits for the aircraft's sophisticated engine to pick up speed, and sound; deeper, deeper the sound, deeper, until at the very centre the sound of its silence. Even as she has walked on the pavements of cities all over the world, she has known this sound of silence: she has looked up at the sky and there it has been, a plane flying in the limbo of deepest silence.

Not like the comfortable silence she had been shaken

from by her guardian's son when she was studying for the last year of her college in Poona.

'Hey, get up, you are fast asleep over your books.'

'Oh God, what time is it?'

'Almost three o' clock. You want a drink?'

'A drink? You must be crazy, I have a paper to give tomorrow morning, I mean this morning, in a few hours.'

'Oh come on, have a small one with me; I will drop you at your examination centre tomorrow morning.'

'Thank you kind sir, but that your mother's driver does anyway.'

'One, just one small one.'

'Where did you celebrate your birthday?'

'A party with my friends at a farmhouse, we had a few drinks. Come on, have a nightcap with me.'

'Seems to me you have had more than a few. And don't open that bottle here, your mother may well walk in and yell at us both.'

'She is asleep in the main house, we could see her coming from this east wing if she does, come on have a drink!'

'No. Get lost, will you? I need to complete revising this last chapter.'

'Okay, give me a kiss and I will get loshsth.'

'You are so drunk you are sloshing your words. Go away.'

'One khish.'

'Oh go to bed, please, you have no idea what you are saying.'

'Bed, with you.'

'What?! Fuck off you fat pig. Drunk, fat pig!'

Her uterus mocks her. Why did you get in his way? Why did you not run?

Why did you not run, run, run, you knew by then how

to run, didn't you?

Why did you let yourself get overpowered? Not a scream, not one shout for help?

Why were you a mute spectator to your own devastation?

If you do not shout, you have no business to feel violated.

You should just clamp on your lip hard to taste blood, to not feel the pain.

Intensely tearing pain, searing your insides.

A few minutes before she can get into the car to be dropped to the examination hall, he pulls her from the main house to the east wing.

'Look,' he says, pointing. On and around the divan, with the table lamps on either side of it still switched on, scattered books and sheets, rolled away pencils and ball points and fountain pens, a bottle of royal blue ink after emptying itself on the divan.

'Look,' he says, pointing to the royal blue stain.

'Look,' he says laughing, pointing to that ink stain.

'You were a virgin all right! But you didn't bleed red, you bled royal blue. I got myself a royal virgin, with blue. blood!'

And he laughs, and he laughs, he slaps his thigh in merriment.

She tries to find another sound to shut out his laughter. Above the house, her head, a plane flies, its drone deepening. Until there is an epicenter of silence in her ears.

The plane has taken off from Hyderabad airport, it semi-circles over the city, dipping a wing gracefully, giving her a view of the city she has come to care for. Somewhere down there, he is leading his own life, without knowing how much he has done for hers.

The sound of the engine, from inside its sleekly gleaming

metal body, is steady; restful pulsing under steel skin; no dark, angry, punishing silence.

Ma was right; if she had not got herself professionally qualified, started working and known another life with its different identities, she would have wound up marrying that fat pig for all the wrong reasons.

Today is her fortieth birthday. She is with her friends in Khandala, celebrating what is supposed to be the beginning of a momentous period in a woman's life. Right now she is at the nearby Lonavla market, inhaling the heady scent of chocolate and walnut fudge at Coopers as the next fresh batch is packed into boxes for the hordes of tourists thronging the tiny store. She looks around the marketplace and sees her abuser.

It's not like that she has not been seeing him on and off when she goes to their shop, it's not like she has not been speaking with him when she phones the shop for her father and he picks up the receiver. Is that mockery creasing his voice?

Once she had even tried to confront him on the phone. 'You don't know what you have done?' she stammered.

'I do,' he had replied, with cold, calm and complete contempt. 'I have looked after all of you, so many of you. I have worked in this shop to pay your mother's hospital bills. I have tolerated a lot of nonsense from all of you. Go to hell, take your father with you.' He had put down the phone. He did not bang down the phone, he put it down gently.

Today is her fortieth birthday. They hardly ever went for holidays as a family after ma died, every hill-station felt empty without her. This time they—her father and her sisters—planned to visit Khandala and Lonavla together, they used her birthday as a happy excuse.

Her father opted out at the last minute saying there was no one at the shop.

She made three points to her father. This was being planned since a while so he could have given others at the shop prior notice. It did not matter if there was no one there since he was not officially the partner anymore. He did not need to work so hard since all his daughters were now earning.

Her father mumbled something in response.

A sunny morning in Lonavla. The smell of fresh chocolate fudge. Her. Her abuser. Her father who has, as always, chosen to support her abuser over her.

Just a few more footprints on a heart, no big deal.

That evening they celebrate her birthday, she and her friends. She looks deep into her glass of brandy as the night falls over Lonavla and Khandala.

A clear, dry and cool night. Starry and sharp. The air spiked with a special silence. Carrying with it a memory, cognac eyes. Stay strong, Bombay woman.

She cuts the cord. She imagines her veins opening up and blood pouring out.

She opens her veins in her imagination and lets her blood flow freely.

As she dies, the child grows colder.

Soon she will be a mature adult; not a silly child who keeps feeling orphaned.

3 June 1999. She opens her eyes at the hospital and focuses on her angel of mercy who has performed her hysterectomy. Now her uterus can no longer mock her.

She looks at her husband; her eyes, they sting and shine. Now she is free to love him, live in him unreservedly.

Ma would have been dotty about him. Would ma have let her go through with this? She would have promptly come into the picture, always sticking her Parsi nose straight into my business.

Ma died three days before her twenty-eighth birthday.

Ma tried to wait for things to get better, in many ways they did after daddy got a shock about losing his son. It went straight home to him, that he had his own family, his wife and daughters who could not be continuously persecuted by his own weaknesses which included his brothers and mother.

They even got a new television in the house and fresh paint on the walls in all the rooms; she had chosen light lavender for the one she shared with her three younger sisters.

But a heart can mend only so many times as it breaks. Ma's heart had ultimately imploded when she was forty-nine.

After ma's death, several practicalities of life start flinging themselves at her with a vengeance. Ma you sent me off to work and never taught me how to cook, nor the bloody difference in the dals. This is yellow dal, this is small yellow dal, and what do I call this pink one, okay, baby dal.

The rest she dealt with mechanically, her mind on the most important things that needed to be done. She had to protect her sisters. She had to protect her father from himself. She looked up legal books, she studied the personal laws binding women in all religions, she looked at the rent laws since the flat was in the holy joint family name, she spoke to experts about partnership laws since her father was a partner in the shop.

This was not about rights—there is far too much inequality for anything to be really right—it was only about fairness.

Her sisters saw this as unnecessary aggression, disrespect

to their father, an attempt to 'take our mother's place'. She protested, there were fights, often they were resentful.

She knew she was being over-protective about her sisters. Better that, than none.

Her sisters are grown-up women now, working, owning their own apartments; when everyone gets together, they try hard not to miss that feeling of another time. The evening paper would slide from under the door, ma would receive her millionth phone call of the day from daddy and then make tea, steam the patrel; the girls would troop in from school, their uniforms happily dirty, their plaits askew, their ribbons undone. Suddenly there would be a five o' clock feeling in the house, food would leave a special taste of happiness on the tongue which had nothing to do with eating.

In those moments there was something close to perfection.

If only they could have all gone on like that.

If they could have held their lives at that level.

If ifs and ands.

●   **mothers & men**

Brave, brave child.

All of twenty-one, her hands playing tourniquet with her test papers. She gets the best grades in her third year of arts, she goes to the classiest college, she reads the best books; they teach her about human psychology and sociology, why men are contemptuously tolerant of women; the finest in feminist literature which has helped her figure out why her father did what he did to her. This, she has understood with finality.

'It started when I was six. I have an elder brother, and two younger ones who are twins. He wanted to control us, as completely as he controlled our mother. He would call out to her, she would go to him, into their bedroom and close the door on us; always we would be on this side, and they on that side of the closed door. Outside the door mother was like a shadow, his shadow in his house. I spent more time with my brothers and their friends, I was a tomboy. My father resented the fact that I was not submissive, he wanted to break me. Later he started the same thing on one of the twins; he picked on the one like me, also rebellious and outspoken.

'I told my elder brother a long time back, he did nothing, he let me down. He is twenty-four years old now; our father used to beat him, it stopped only when my elder brother started going to work. My father used to do things with the maid, it was so open, but my mother did nothing. I told my mother about what my father did to me when I was sixteen, I thought she knew all along, I always thought she knew and would do something, anything, to stop it; mother cried when I told her, she was uncontrollable when the twin told her it had been done to him too. She took action then, she filed for divorce and for the house in the name of her children.

'My father is now fifty-three, he is not as professionally active as he used to be, he was an important person in the travel industry, he still has a travel agency which does well. I was in awe of my father, sometimes I was frightened of my father although he was very playful and rarely ever drank alcohol. It took me all my strength to confront him when I grew up; I confronted my father, he said, "I was playing with you, Jennifer. I thought you enjoyed it." He told the twin, "I was soothing you. Remember how you got convulsions?" I left my father's house after that, I lived with an aunt, then mother called me back. I returned because I wanted my father to understand that I would no longer be giving in to his patriarchy and power games.'

Honor thy father and mother, every Sunday morning Mass Jennifer hears this in church. It is an important thing to believe in as the sun shines on a week-weary world renewing its faith in itself on its day of rest. Honor thy father and mother at all cost, to not do so is to admit that parents are both sly and sorrowful, parents are abusive; they have betrayed their child. Jennifer does not need a sermon on Judas the great betrayer in church anymore, she has working knowledge of what is betrayal. There is no defence mechanism called denial here, there is no denial at all to protect Jennifer from anything so painful. Those who do not have a wall of denial around them appear fearless. The harder for this kind of wall to come down; walls of denial can come down with a crash, a wall of fearlessness is so achingly vulnerable, lower it please only brick by painful brick.

Her dark eyes, repudiating everyone and everything; those cheeks red as she triumphantly stands her ground, uncomforted; that head held high with its angrily, closely cropped hair: is that a child still visible in that woebegone face?

'I must tell you at the outset, I am a lesbian.'

Yes.

'You are not surprised to hear it?'

Who can honestly say that there is any real advantage in being loved by a man?

'I realized this when I was nineteen years old, since then I am part of a gay group. We are not the most functional group but we are all right, we manage.'

Good, it is in everyone's interests to be up and about, there is nothing to be gained by settling into a miasma of primitive feelings. Perhaps she will eventually set up her own house with a girl as wonderful as her.

'Oh no, I cannot live with the idea of just one partner, I need to have a variety of women.'

Yes.

'You are not shocked to hear it?'

Sad is the word, overwhelming sadness as one observes a perpetuating pattern—promiscuity can be one of the by-products of hard-spectrum sexual abuse at the hands of a father. But this must play itself out for Jennifer to truly know.

Time must do that; it will, spitefully, just when Jennifer has settled into a comfortably familiar pattern of surviving with some degree of relief.

Till then Jennifer must purposefully tread a path, so purposeful must be Jennifer's tread that no one must realize that the journey has been far more taxing than anyone can ever guess.

No one must see that side that can suddenly move them to tears; twenty-one-year-old Jennifer being tossed between vulnerability and tough-minded disdain.

Beside the extinguished childhood of her daughter, the mother's future appears radiant.

She has just come in from the office, her career has never been better, her personal life is also on the up after a long time, the worst is behind her, it can only get better, just that one rough bump left.

'The children are really helping me, they have moved me out of the bedroom from behind that closed door, I sleep with them now. They tell me, "Don't worry mummy, maybe you will find another man who will be good to you." I loved him, you know, I really loved him; ours was a love marriage and I so wanted a happy house and small family. We were a big family and well-off financially, but not such a happy one. We were six sisters, I was the youngest and also the quietest, I never remember speaking much except to my mother; my mother was frightened of my father, she was submissive because he was so dominating. But she was a great source of comfort to me when I would go to her with the problems with my husband, "Bear it, Genevieve," she would say, "bear it, since there is no other way".

'I bore it, I kept a good house, I went to work and did well in my career. He resented it, he even got me pregnant with the twins because of it, I did not want more children after my first two but he forced it upon me. I continued to work after the twins and even did better.'

She sounds genuinely surprised that she could have been so focussed about her work.

A pause, then she continues, 'He would display his resentment in other odd ways; when my grandmother died, he did not let me go for her funeral. I remember, he was in one of his moods and he flew into a rage so I spoke to my mother on the phone and decided against going. When my mother died, he said, 'She is gone and she has taken my peace of mind with her.'

Why did she do nothing at all about the husband and the maid?

Her voice, mild as milk. 'I did not know.'

Really?

Her voice modulates without transition into the tearful. 'The maid came to work in our house when she was around nineteen, she was there till she was twenty-five years old, he gave her clothes and good food, she got pregnant, he threw her out of the house. The maid's mother told me all this when she came to ask me for money for the maid's abortion. I asked him afterwards why he did all that, he said, "Well you were at work, were you not? And the maid kept threatening to leave, somebody needed to be there to look after the kids and their needs." '

Why did she do nothing at all about her husband and her daughter?

'I did not know.'

Truthfully?

'Really.'

It is okay to tell the truth now, nothing can be taken away from Genevieve if she tells the truth. There will be no harm to anybody, there will be good. Eventually.

How final is finality; Genevieve perceives this for the first time in her life because no one has asked her this before, it is her call, she answers it, as if an adult has asked a child a question, she replies, 'I wanted all of us to be a happy family. I thought so, on some days I felt that he was not doing good things. But what could I do to stop him, he was so big and strong and he was always overpowering me.'

Exactly what she did when she was told that her son,

too, was being sexually abused by her husband—file for divorce, file for the house and custody of all the children. Apart from filing a police complaint which she has yet to do vis-à-vis the criminal aspect of Child Sexual Abuse.

'I did try once, to talk to him, I wanted to stop him. He threatened me with my life, he said he would kill me or one of the children. I spoke to his family, after all what are families for?'

What, indeed.

'As a child I was always taught that families are for support. Aren't they?'

Families are also about offering endless possibilities for pain.

'My husband's brothers ignored what I had to say, to this day they are supportive of him. One of my husband's sisters said he had done it to her too, she had to take psychiatric help after her marriage, she is lucky, her husband is a very understanding man. She had told her brothers soon after he had done it to her as a child for the first time, no one had paid attention to her.'

Did she speak to her own family, her sisters?

'No.' Her voice falters. 'All of them are not happily married, most of them have too many problems of their own, with their own husbands. I am not really close to them for that reason, when my mother was there it was different, she held us all together in a family bind.'

Her good mother, she the bad mother; Genevieve closes her eyes and moving her head slightly, tries to push the thought away, it won't go.

A wave of grief soaks her so thoroughly that she begins crying, softly, the tears chasing each other down her fair cheeks. She weeps, she talks, she weeps; a mother saying she is sorry, but promising she did not set out to be a bad mother; a child remembering her own mother; an adult remembering a childhood and yet an adult who has preferred to forget how her childhood worked, how it is supposed to work but refuses to for unhappy children. She talks, she weeps, her eyeliner streaking lightly over the discreetly coloured face, her lipstick blotching against her lace-edged handkerchief as she presses it against her mouth and tries hard, so very hard to keep those memories away.

She fights every morning to keep those memories away, when she looks in the mirror, lipstick ready in hand, that last final touch before leaving for work. Her drawn countenance, its expression wary, as if any minute her face behind its mask might disintegrate: every morning, such a bad moment to be pushed away.

And now, finally, someone is asking, a person who is willing to listen, someone she can tell who will not invalidate her; how final is finality?

A low-slung bungalow with running wooden verandahs surrounded by a huge garden filled with lush green trees and shadows; on the back verandah a chair, Burma teak and Rangoon rattan, a cane lounger to sprawl in during the afternoon's somnolence, a male cousin around twenty-two, she may be eight or nine. When she is thirteen, the cousin is suddenly stopped from coming home to meet any of the sisters. All that time: she on his lap, his finger from his lap gently guiding itself through her panties as he read her stories from her favourite storybooks.

Another low-slung bungalow, another huge garden around it filled with the glistening shadows of the night and a great silence which emanates on such nights; inside the house she furnishes her own silences, transfixed on a cane easychair in her bedroom, the door closed, on the other side, another closed door. On the other side of that door, the momentary gleam of an eyeball from the motionless figure on one of the four beds, three of them tense in their impersonation of sleep, on the bed tucked away in a corner small but womanly breasts cringing under a crumpled t-shirt as her knees are wide open, prised to open wide as any grave, playtime for a father.

She cannot get off her chair, she twists all her rings on her pink-tipped manicured fingers, she moans, 'Do something, oh please do something.'

Do what?

She is fiddling with her fingers, appearing to knot them with each other, then to unknot them as they knot themselves again. A low moan, 'Stop it, please, I beg of you, make it stop.'

Genevieve, it has stopped, it is okay, you are safe now; breathe gently, Genevieve.

She asks, 'Can I undo that?'

No.

She asks again, a child, 'Can you make it go away please?'

She can do that herself.

Eagerly, that child again, 'I can make it go away?'

Yes, but not in the way she thinks. There is no law in this world which can protect adults from their childhood abusers; it is a crime for which there is no punishment.

There is no triumph in anyone's voice as this is being said.

Her eyes, an adult's now, cloud over. Her voice is as soft as sand running through an hourglass.

'Shit,' she says.

Delicately, elegantly, with gravel now in the sand, 'Shit.'

It must not be like this, to know and try so hard not to hurt.

It should not be like this, to know and hurt so hard.

It should not be like this, to not know, then to know and yet hurt, hurt, hurt.

This is not how stories should end: that special taste, that smooth sensation of the purest truth spreading on the tongue; quickly rushing from behind to smother this sweetness, acridity.

Bitter, bitter chocolate.

notebook three

·

Tanuja   Nine years   Varanasi

My friend and I went to the temple but she refused to come
inside when the priests called us. She said the panditji was
not a nice man and she was scared. Scaredy-cat. I went
inside to take the laddoo prasad the priests were offering
us. One of them filled my hands with the prasad and lifted
my frock. He pulled down my chaddi and started pressing
me. The other pandit said, 'Sambhaalo, pakdey jaaongey.'
That's when I realized the pandit was doing a wrong thing
and started crying. But when I reached home I stopped
crying because I did not want mumma to know that I had
disobeyed her by going to the temple alone.

After that when mumma took me to the temple with
her, that priest looked at me and smiled, and he told
mumma I was a 'goon-waali bachi' and ran his hand over
my face. Mumma was happy he called me a virtuous child
and said, 'Panditji ko pranaam karo.' I did not and she hit
me on my head. That other pandit started laughing. I
began crying very badly. I would not stop crying and
mumma started shaking me at home very hard to tell her
what it was, so I told her. She said, 'Chup kar!' But I told
my dudda when they were planning to have a pooja in my
house and call that pandit who laughed at me.

My dudda and his friends went to the temple and beat
up the two priests like anything. I was very happy. My

dudda said he wanted to go to the police station and send the priests to jail so that they never laughed at little girls again. But my mumma said, 'Then nobody will marry your daughter.' Still my dudda is the best dudda in the world.

● what the law ignores

If Tanuja's father had taken the matter to the police station, the pandit would have been locked up for a maximum of two years, or fined, or both. Tanuja's case, whenever it came up in court, would classify as Assault or Criminal Force to Woman with Intent to Outrage her Modesty. Section 354 of the Indian Penal Code.

According to advocate Flavia Agnes of Mumbaii the legal sections invoked in cases of Child Sexual Abuse can be:

- 293. Sale, hire, distribution or circulation of obscene objects or literature to children. Punishment: jail up to three years or fine up to Rs 2,000 or both.
- 294. Obscene acts or utterances in public places. Up to three months in prison with a fine.
- 302. Murder. Punishment: death or imprisonment for life.
- 323. Causing hurt. Up to one year's imprisonment.
- 324. Voluntarily causing hurt by dangerous weapons or means. The latter would be any substance which is dangerous to the human body to inhale, swallow or receive into the blood by any means. Imprisonment for up to three years, or fine, or both.
- 325. Causing grevious hurt. Up to seven years.
- 326. Causing grievous hurt by dangerous weapons. Up to imprisonment for life.

- 342. Wrongful confinement. Whoever wrongfully restrains any person in such a manner as to prevent that person from proceeding beyond certain circumscribing limits is said to have wrongfully confined a person. Imprisonment up to one year, fine up to one thousand rupees, or both.
- 343. Wrongful confinement for three or more days. Up to two years in prison.
- 344. Wrongful confinement for ten or more days. Up to three years in prison.
- 354. Assault or use of criminal force with an intent to outrage modesty. Alternatively referred to as Molestation when the archaic language of the phrase— Outraging of Modesty —outrages the user. Up to two years.
- 363. Kidnapping. Jail up to seven years.
- 366. Abduction. Procuring of a minor girl. Generally used on pimps. Jail up to ten years.
- 375, 376. Rape. Penile penetration in a vagina is the only kind which constitutes rape legally. Digital, oral or object penetration are not considered. Punishment: from seven years onwards. This can be lessened too. A court has reduced the jail term of a rapist from seven years to six months when he agreed to pay compensation of four lakh rupees after negotiations with her father who used her 'future subsistence' as reasons for entering into the dialogue. The court agreed, 'The compensation is necessary for a woman who will never get married in future.' Additionally, Hindi movies are not the only place where the woman is married off to her rapist and he, consequently, allowed to go scot-free.
- 377. Unnatural offences. Generally considered in cases of sodomy. Up to five years.
- 417. Cheating. Up to one year in jail.

- 452. House trespass after preparation for hurt, assault or wrongful restraint. Up to seven years.
- 458. House trespass or house breaking by night after preparations for causing hurt. Up to fourteen years.
- 503, 506. Criminal intimidation. Threatening with injury to a human body, reputation or property. Up to two years or fine or both. If threat be to cause grevious hurt or death or destruction of property by fire, the imprisonment can go up to seven years.
- 509. Indecent behaviour. Violating modesty with word or gesture. This would include exposing penis or other sexual parts of a body, applicable for the grandfather at home or the 'flasher' standing outside a school waiting for children to pass to expose himself. Up to one year in jail.
- 511. Attempt to rape. Half the punishment awarded for rape.

Please look very carefully at 375, 376.

This law needs urgent changing in connection with Child Sexual Abuse.

What is it when a tongue or a bottle or finger or candle or carrot or banana is inserted into a child's vagina or anus?

What can it possibly be if a penis is inserted into a child's mouth?

Rape.

The rape of the child's body, the rape of the child's innocence, the rape of its very childhood.

Look at this even as a simple situation. A slap is an offence. A slap with a stick in the same hand is a greater offence. That is, use of body part plus object is a greater offence. Then why is a rape with an object not a greater offence than a rape with a penis?

Enormous complications come into play in India when the truth needs to be told as it is. For some reason—perhaps our innate duality or other-worldliness, these being polite words for hypocrisy—anything that leads to the truth and nothing but the truth in our country is perceived as a threat by a very large section of people.

But it does need to be said: unless a child is ruthlessly raped, society—parents included—prefers not to see what the men do as sexual; society also prefers not to see it as an assault. It is both, sexual and an assault. Rape, as the law sees it now, is the putting of a penis in a girl child's vagina. Is this not an aggravated sexual assault? And the putting of anything else in any orifice of a child's body, is that not an equally aggravated sexual assault? Men do not set out to just rape our children thereby being covered in our country's legal context; they set out—purposefully—to sexually assault our children. Let us get this straight: our children are being sexually assaulted also by men whom we know. And there needs to be a law which says precisely this.

Therefore, the words 'sexual assault' need to be used in place of rape in 375, 376. This will be applicable to women, men and boy-children too. If the law changes the word 'rape' for 'sexual assault', all kinds of penetration including digital and oral can be included. Widening the scope of 375, 376 and making it gender neutral would also help all those little boys being sexually assaulted by men in their own homes and on the streets, and would assist the little boys being sodomized by paedophiles in Goa, Mumbaii and elsewhere in the country.

And this too needs to be done. Just as the law makes a distinction among rape, gang rape and custodial rape (whether a woman's rape takes place in a police station or hospital), it needs to differentiate between Child Sexual

Abuse by a parent and its extended family, and comparative strangers. Child Sexual Abuse by parents and close relatives is a far more serious offence because of the kind and depth of emotional scarring it causes to the psyche of the victim. The differentiating clause already exists in 376, all that needs to be added for the child is that father, grandfather, brother, maternal and paternal uncle or any other person in a position of trust of the child is to be seen as a greater sexual assaulter.

Punishments should be from ten years to life imprisonment.

Once 375, 376 are made all-inclusive, watertight and gender-free, it eliminates the need for 377, which can be scrapped. Little boys being sexually abused by adult males, be they heterosexual, homosexual or bisexual, can be assisted under the redone 375, 376.

Now please look at 354, Outraging Modesty. Why is it called this, because it is non-penetrative and therefore cannot be harmful to a child? If a girl's breasts have been fondled, would that be merely the outraging of her modesty? If a boy's testicles are being fondled by an elderly uncle, would that be merely an outraging of this boy's modesty, or would they say a boy cannot have 'modesty' since only girls have it? If a grandfather asks his granddaughter's visiting friend to touch his penis with her hand, what would that be?

This law needs to be correctly addressed so that it is correctly applied in police stations and courts. Call it 'unlawful sexual contact'. And give it a minimum of three years as punishment.

These two laws need restructuring, and this is long overdue. It will happen, it must. The Government of India must give its citizens-in-the-making a legal future; the victimized child must have a voice. For this, Parliament must restructure the laws.

And when this happens, children in this country will be better protected legally. One child must go through hell for other Indian children to benefit; a little child did. Her sexual abuse by her father went on for even longer because daddy would take her to a hotel and do it, daddy would also invite his male and female friends to watch. One day she went with her sisters, her mummy and her mummy's sister for a little picnic in one of Delhi's parks, and as she sat there on the green grass surrounded by her toys and her potato chips and soft drinks and cake, feeling comforted by the healing rays of a gentle sun, she found herself telling her mummy about the picnics that daddy took her for with his friends.

When her case reached the courts, they could not understand how to categorize it. Daddy had invited his friends but they did not do anything to her though they did things among themselves while watching blue films on the hotel's video. Daddy himself had not put his penis into her but he had put in quite a lot else. What was this in black and white categories? It did not come under legal rape, that was for sure. The law, clearly, had not caught up with the atrocities being perpetrated on the children it was supposed to protect; a legal review was urgently required. Sakshi, the organization working with children and women victims of sexual violence, pointed this out and followed through with recommendations. It is now a case almost forgotten; but that family has yet to recover. Daddy tries to control his other daughters emotionally from the distance he is at, they wind up quarrelling among themselves at home. Tragically, ironically, cruelly, he had earlier even encouraged his other daughters to fight with the one he had abused, by making the ones whom he spared feel 'un-special'. His wife who has weathered enough, including her own parents telling her to drop the case against her husband, is back at work; but every now and then she does hear a remark flung in her direction. Earlier, she used to find hand-scrawled notes left on her desk: 'Kya, he stuck it into your daughter instead of you?' 'Humey bhi kuch khidmad ka mauka do.' ('Give us a chance too.')

And the girl herself, how is she? She has short-term effects, she is displaying some of the beginnings of long-term effects of Child Sexual Abuse but she is recovering; how much she will recover will only be revealed as she grows. Think about this little girl being taken to court, down those dark yet clattering corridors, her face being covered by her counsellor Hemlata's dupatta because she has to be carried past her daddy's angrily hissing relatives cursing her under their breath. Think about this innocent heart being battered by a battery of her daddy's lawyers in court. Think about her when the laws change, and when they do, please send up a thank-you prayer for her. She will be the reason why your child will be legally secure vis-á-vis Child Sexual Abuse.

And she will be the reason why all the other existing laws which can be applied to Child Sexual Abuse will be taken far more seriously in the future.

Asha Bajpai who researches and teaches law in Mumbaii points out that, broadly speaking, laws to deal with Child Sexual Abuse can be sourced from the following:

- The Constitution of India
- The Indian Penal Code (as spelt out above by Flavia Agnes)
- The Immoral Traffic Prevention Act
- The Juvenile Justice Act
- The Indian Post Office Act (child rights activist Sheela Barse used a part of this Act as well to nail Freddy Peats since his pornographic material was being sent,

and accessed, through the country's regular mail system)
- Foreign Contribution Regulation Act (also used by Sheela Barse in context of the flow of monies by Freddy Peats to manage his paedophilic, pornographic business)
- International Conventions

'International conventions could also be considered by practising lawyers,' suggests Asha Bajpai, 'as there is a very clear Supreme Court of India ruling which says they can be invoked provided they do not violate any citizen's fundamental rights as guaranteed by the country's constitution.'

Several women must suffer, they must emotionally and physically bleed before their sisterhood can somewhat benefit. This appears to be what has happened in the case of the international conventions ruling. Remember Bhanwari Devi? In Rajasthan? She was a 'saathin', a grass-roots social worker; she protested against child marriages in her area, rampant as they are in Rajasthan. She was rewarded with a gang rape and the court refused to believe that she had been gang raped, proclaiming that 'high-caste men' are not likely to 'touch-low caste women'.

From Bhanwari Devi's gang rape came this realization: that this paid social worker had been subjected to the most hard spectrum of sexual harassment for doing her job, and while she did it. Before, she had been continually sexually harassed verbally while on her job, she had often complained, no one had paid attention. It is now called the Vishakha case and has sparked off a debate at the court, followed by intense discussion on an international convention which India has also signed—the United Nations Convention on the Elimination of Discrimination Against Women, or Cedaw—and many years have passed with more cases and more discussion in courts and among women's rights groups and it has slowly but steadily built up opinion. These efforts are now understood as laws against sexual harassment at work; remember this, every working woman—and her husband and children—in every part of India where, and how, it all started, send up that small prayer of thanks for all these women—beginning with Bhanwari Devi. A miraculous mixture of silk and steel, they have suffered to provide us with legal weapons which make it possible for our women to stay sexually safe at work.

International commitments which can be invoked to deal with Child Sexual Abuse cases, commitments to which India is signatory, include:

- United Nations convention on the rights of the child
- United Nations convention against all forms of discrimination of women
- Universal declaration of human rights
- International covenant on economic, social and cultural rights
- International covenant on civil and political rights
- Optional protocol on civil and political rights
- Convention against torture and other cruel, inhuman or degrading treatment or punishment
- Slavery convention
- Abolition of forced labour convention
- Convention for the suppression of traffic in persons and of the exploitation of the prostitution of others
- Convention on the political rights of women
- Convention on the abolition of slavery, the slave trade and institutions and practices similar to slavery

There is just one proviso to any of these conventions being invoked, the judges should also be aware of them. Sakshi conducted an extensive Gender and Judges survey in 1996 in which they monitored reactions of judges from various courts. While the study covered a relatively small number of judges, a total of 109, they were selected from a wide cross-section, and consequently reflected the views of judges from regional and judicially distinct backgrounds as well. This report has since been dubbed The Purple Report for the colour of its spiral-bound cover.

A small sample of the contents of Sakshi's Purple Report:

- 74 per cent of the 109 judges surveyed said preservation of a family should be a primary concern for women even if there is violence in the marriage
- 49 per cent felt that a husband who slaps his wife on one occasion in the course of their marriage does not constitute cruelty
- 48 per cent said there are certain occasions when it is justifiable for a husband to slap his wife
- 55 per cent felt that the moral character of a woman is relevant in sexual abuse cases
- 68 per cent felt that 'provocative' clothes are an invitation to sexual assault
- 9 per cent said that when a woman says 'no' to sexual intercourse, she often mean 'yes'
- 34 per cent felt that dowry still has 'inherent cultural value'
- 11 per cent maintained that daughters should not inherit property on an equal basis with sons
- 22 per cent categorically disagreed that there is a concept called 'gender bias'
- 50 per cent felt child sexual abuse is not common; the judges said this 'uncommon offence existed only amongst uneducated, depressed and over-sexed people

or people with a prostrate gland problem', they also felt such abuses were most commonly carried out by servants and least commonly within the family

Not surprisingly, 78 per cent of these judges had never heard of the Convention on the Elimination of Discrimination Against Women. Cedaw, which is its acronym, is the first international attempt in law to define women's human rights in terms of women's reality. This convention was ratified by the Government of India in August 1993. The debate and discussions around this convention in women's groups have since been given space in the media; these judges were surveyed in 1996, after an entire three years of information dissemination and time to keep abreast of progress in their respective fields.

If some judges would much rather be ignorant of the Convention on the Elimination of Discrimination Against Women, they are not likely to have heard of any of the other conventions either. In which case they would be loathe to allow any point on it, no matter how valid it may be to a case in court of Child Sexual Abuse.

Lawyers, too, can be equally ignorant of truly fine rulings by learned judges in connection with cases of Child Sexual Abuse.

There is, for instance, a ruling which very clearly opines that if a child maintains it has been sexually abused, corroboration to this effect need not be sourced, the case can proceed beyond looking for technicalities. This is the case of 1983, Bharwada Bhogibhai Hirjibhai versus the state of Gujarat. He had sexually abused his little daughter's child-friend who had come to their home to play.

The judge's opinion:

'In the Indian setting refusal to act on the testimony of a victim of sexual assault in the absence of corroboration is adding insult to injury. Why should the evidence of the girl or the woman who complains of rape or sexual molestation be viewed with the aid of spectacles fitted with lenses tinged with doubt, disbelief or suspicion? To do so is to justify the charge of male chauvinism in a male dominated society. On principle, the evidence of a victim of sexual assault stands on par with the evidence of an injured witness.'

And there is this absolute path-breaker by the Supreme Court which ruled in March 2000, that non-injury to the rape victim does not signify her, or his, consent. That is, the absence of injuries on the body of a rape victim is not necessarily an evidence of consent or even of the falsity of the allegation. The Supreme Court set aside a Rajasthan High Court judgement acquitting a rape accused on the ground that the absence of injuries on the victim was a material fact not excluding the possibility of her having been a consenting adult. Said Justices R.C. Lahoti and S. N. Variava, 'The High Court has committed a clean error of law. Courts have to display a greater sense of responsibility and be more sensitive while dealing with charges of sexual assault on women.'

The case was about a man who had raped a fifteen-year-old girl. The Sessions Court heard the testimony of this girl and her father, and corroborated it with the medical evidence. The accused went in appeal to the Rajasthan High Court which reversed the Session Court's sentence of seven years' rigorous imprisonment and a fine of Rs 2,000. The Rajasthan High Court said that the lodging of the first information report was delayed and the person to whom the girl narrated her story was not examined by the prosecution. The girl's father approached the Supreme Court for justice; it was granted.

Justices Variava and Lahoti observed, 'An unmerited

acquittal encourages wolves in the society being on prowl for easy prey, more so when the victims of crime are helpless females. It is the spurt in the number of unmerited acquittals recorded by criminal courts which gives rise to the demand for death sentences to rapists.' The judges added, 'If the prosecution has succeeded in making out a convincing case for recording a finding as to the accused being guilty, the court should not lean in favour of the acquittal by giving weight to irrelevant or insignificant circumstances.' The judges said the delay in registering the first information report had been satisfactorily explained and 'mere delay is no ground by itself for throwing the entire prosecution case overboard'. Justices Variava and Lahoti also pointed out that it would have been preferable if the woman before whom the child narrated her story could be examined but no dent was caused in the prosecution's case by her non-examination.

There is also this judgement by Justice S. Radhakrishnan of the Bombay High Court on 14 August 1998.

This case highlights that old adage: 'Don't just get angry, get legally even'. The lawyer advised the client to deal with the case as a civil one; all Child Sexual Abuse cases are criminal cases but it was too late to put the daughter through a conclusive medical test. The lawyer felt that the situation was still an important one as a civil case, for this would once and for all sort out many of the matters connected with the problem.

The case has Afra Fernandes as petitioner with Flavia Agnes as her advocate, versus Anthony Fernandes as respondent who did not attend court, nor did he have anyone to represent him though he was served with adequate notices.

The court heard Afra's account of how Anthony would get drunk and beat her up, how he began walking around the house naked and with a knife, how he had been sexually abusing one among their five children. The young daughter took the witness-stand and spoke of her sexual abuse by her father. Afra also produced the receipts of the various complaints she had registered at the local police station against her husband of his various acts of cruelty. She also showed a bill and receipt issued by their building's housing society in both their names, the husband and the wife, proving that the flat stood in the name of both, petitioner and respondent.

Justice Radhakrishnan observed: 'All this evidence has not been controverted and challenged, and the respondent has not appeared and cross-examined. Under these circumstances this evidence will have to be accepted, as uncontroverted.' Justice Radhakrishnan then granted Afra Fernandes judicial separation under Section 22 of the Indian Divorce Act; he gave her custody of all her minor children; he restrained Anthony Fernandes from selling or creating a third party to the rights of their flat; and this is the most important—Justice Radhakrishnan restrained Anthony Fernandes himself, as also 'his agents, servants and relatives', from entering 'the said matrimonial home'.

In other words, now if Anthony Fernandes enters the home he owns jointly with his wife, he can be kicked out of his own house and thrown immediately into prison.

This is how it should be, because to allow Anthony Fernandes to enter would be—to use legal parlance but unfortunately a line not used often enough in the courts—'against the best interests of the child'.

Advocate Flavia Agnes would agree that this was, in some ways, a 'dream case': a very obvious situation created by Anthony Fernandes, his absence in the court leading to this ex parte decision, and a very learned and committed judge in Justice Radhakrishnan. So many factors do not always come together in the court, most times matters go against the best interests of the child. No one has understood this more than Flavia Agnes as she stood on the Bombay High Court premises with tears streaming down her face.

It can take a lot to make Flavia Agnes cry, she is not the pushover she used to be when she was married and being beaten to pulp by her husband. She took it until she was in her late-thirties, and then she decided to become a lawyer. She left her children at her husband's home, a very tough decision but one that had to be executed since she was leaving penniless to live in a slum, educate herself, start afresh but with every intention of reaching out to her children as soon as she could. She threw away her husband's surname, she rejected the idea of using her father's surname, she simply took a second name which would stay with her unalterably. Her fortieth birthday was very special—her first year as a qualified lawyer. Today advocate Flavia Agnes is fifty-one, a grandmother of children settled all over the world; right now she is standing and crying in the hustle and bustle of the Bombay High Court.

A civil case was listed as coming up only much later in the day; perhaps it would be well past lunch before it did. Advocate Agnes accordingly went to deal with the divorce aspect of the same case in the court at the suburb of Bandra during the morning. But by the time she could reach the High Court in the city centre for the afternoon session, there had been a board collapse; the term used when cases listed on the board are dealt with dizzyingly quickly though not necessarily for the obvious reason. Advocate Agnes' case had come up and gone in the morning. It was that of the daughter of the mother seeking a divorce. Advocate Agnes' contention was that the child not be forced to spend time with her grandfather because he had sexually abused her; it would go against the best interests of the child. The court would not believe that the grandfather could do such a thing and the grandfather's battery of lawyers were working overtime to secure weekend visitation rights of the girl to her grandfather's house.

Mulls Flavia Agnes, 'When the case has several connected aspects to it like this one, I am not sure whether the answer lies directly in taking the child's sexual abuser to the criminal court. But then again, the onus of proving that the child has been sexually molested by a person from her own house in practise falls on the child in a civil or criminal court. Sometimes I wonder about whether it is even worth dragging mothers and their children through such cumbersome and lengthy court procedures. But then if you don't believe in the courts, what do women and children have for themselves? Then: only might is right. Neither women nor children have that male physical might, so they must look to the courts for the rule of law.'

The rule of law goes completely against the best interests of the child in the time taken by the judicial system. Of what use are the best laws in the land if they cannot be applied with alacrity? For instance, the average time taken for a case of rape to find its way from the lower courts to the Supreme Court can be between ten and fifteen years. Correlate this with the forty-eight cases of Child Sexual Abuse reported between 1992 and 1994 in the newspapers. The children averaged between eight and ten years of age, incidentally, the youngest of these children was six months old. By the time the cases come up for their initial hearing, bar the six-month-old child, the rest would most probably no longer be minors.

Like this girl, living with her elder brother in his marital home at Kalyan in Maharashtra. She was continuously molested by him during the nights, she fought back. He raped her at knife point. A few nights later, when he attempted to rape her again, she screamed. He threw her out of the house. That was in 1985, her case came up for hearing on 14 February 2000. She stood up in court after fifteen years and said, 'I have not given any statement to the police, the contents of the first information report are not true.'

In 1986, a complaint was filed in Mumbaii that fifteen-year-old Bhuvaneshwari had been raped by her stepfather when her mother had gone to Nagercoil in Tamil Nadu to visit her married, elder daughter. The case came up in court in March 2000, the rape victim is now twenty-nine years old, married and with two children of her own; she reverses her statement in court.

Even if there is no reversal of statement, the child is not adult as yet, the mother of the child pursues the case because justice must be done and truth must prevail, her doggedness can meet with emotional death. In a Child Sexual Abuse case in May 1996, a judge of the apex court declared that mothers who allege such crimes against the father of a child are 'mentally sick' and are 'unnecessarily spoiling the child's future prospects for marriage and a happy life'. In another case, a sessions court judge dismisses the allegation as one of a 'promiscuous imagination'.

The worst case to date has been that of Mehra versus Mehra, the judgement of which was delivered on 31 July 1996. Nowhere in the judgement is the mother's point of view mentioned, thus if a student of law has to read it as a case study, or a lawyer has to look it up in the way it is listed in the legal books which discuss cases and their outcomes, this case would appear quite contrary to what it actually was.

This is what actually happened. The woman from Delhi, living with her husband Mehra and their child in America, discovers that her husband is sexually abusing her daughter. She approaches the police there who medically examine her child and confirm the abuse. She confronts her husband, he does not stop sexually abusing their child. An overwrought woman gathers her daughter's things, she runs away from America on a flight to Delhi and the safety of her own family.

This is how it is seen through the judgement, as quoted in Sakshi's Purple Report. 'The tone of the judgement is determined by its opening observations on Child Sexual Abuse: "Some eerie accusations have been made by a wife against her husband." From the outset the perspective of the court is that "incestuous sexual abuse" by a father is "incredulous". Such disbelief ultimately governs the court's unquestioning acceptance of one version (the father's) and unequivocal dismissal of another (the mother's). The mother is described as a "vengeful" woman merely because she spoke of her marriage as "extremely painful and unhappy". The assumption being, women in unhappy marriages have no recourse but to falsely accuse fathers of sexually abusing their own children. The worst outrage is the father's allegation that the mother herself molested the child to implicate him. That allegation was used to counter the finding of an Indian paediatrician that "on examination of the genitals of the child . . . a wide vaginal opening—wider than would be expected of her age group" was present. Surprisingly, the court chose to ignore the paediatrician's finding as well as a first police report filed when the family was in America which stated that the complaint of Child Sexual Abuse was "founded". Instead the court accepted the father's oral—repeat, oral—submission that an American doctor said the child had not suffered such abuse. No document was ever filed to support this submission.'

Naina Kapur, the director of Sakshi, remembers this case well. 'The mother was being accused of sexually abusing her child, she was utterly distraught even otherwise; there is this odd acceptance of the idea that a woman at such a time must present a composed and balanced picture.'

The woman got her divorce and custody of her daughter, they now live in Delhi. The father went back a free man to the United States, perhaps to even remarry, have more children and carry on with his life as before.

Look at the laws again. Think about the around one hundred documented cases in this book itself. Even if all the laws are rewritten to be truly sensitive to children who are victims of Child Sexual Abuse, can a child ever get justice?

No. A court of law can only give a judgement, never real justice to a child who has been sexually abused.

And yet judgements must remain as the final yardstick. Because justice, if it cannot be truly done, should at least be seen to be done.

Like in the case of a doctor who forced oral sex with several little girls of his neighbourhood. One eight-year-old refused to suck his penis, he undressed her, placed his penis just inside her vagina and sucked her lips until he ejaculated. The lower court refused to consider the complaint as rape, said 'no normal man would have been able to restrain himself from full penetration', and dismissed the case as 'concocted'.

The case went on for several years at a high court. Here too the accused was acquitted on the grounds that 'the absence of ruptures negates a case of rape', and that the accused had only outraged the modesty of the girl. The court further defended the accused saying, 'Now that the doctor had got married and was not indulging in nefarious activities . . . no useful purpose will be served by sending him to jail.'

The case reached the Supreme Court eleven years later,

the girl was now nineteen, and the doctor was finally given seven years in prison.

There are several judgements which destroy the very notion of justice when it comes to girl-children and sexual abuse, far too many to be narrated here which refer to virginity as being a girl's only virtue and marriage being her only goal. All judges are clearly not sensitized to gender issues.

To address this, post their Purple Report, Sakshi also conducted a gender equality and sensitization programme with a small group of judges. Well into the workshop when all the judges were relaxed, they were asked to think about their first sexual experience which was the most pleasurable to them. After a while they were invited to speak about that experience. There was immediate reaction.

'How can you ask us to speak about something so personal in public?'

Sakshi then made just one point.

If the judges could not speak of something which had given them so much pleasure, how did they expect a little girl to speak—loudly, clearly, without confusion—in court of her sexual abuse that has caused her so much hurt?

This must remain among life's greatest ironies. One of the judges who did brilliantly during the workshop and appeared to be the most sensitized, subsequently dealt with a Child Sexual Abuse case. He refused to believe that a grandfather could do anything at all to harm his little granddaughter.

• secondary victimization

Now let's go back to Tanuja and the pandit. Tanuja's father lodges the complaint with the police, and the inspector on duty wonders aloud, as a chief justice once did, 'what modesty such a small child could possibly have that it can be outraged'. The policeman advises Tanuja's father to not lodge a case as there would be a lot of 'bey-izzatti'.

'The policeman simply will not be interested in the case because our law is still based on physical evidence,' points out lawyer Meghna Abraham, an Oxford fellow on children's law. 'The Indian police, anyway, is not trained to understand anything other than law and order. To get parents to approach and then deal with the police, the state is going to need to set up a very special kind of police force for children, like the Child Protection Units abroad where the policewomen do not even wear uniforms.'

And special children's courts where all, and only, offences against children by adults can be speedily tried. This is not to be confused with juvenile justice courts; these would be children's courts where all crimes—including sexual—committed by adults upon children would be speedily tried. British courts, for instance, have a very clear rule that crimes against children must come up for their hearing within three weeks, after which the defendant has a maximum of ninety days to plead his case. The courts are also very child-friendly. A few American states have also begun to amend the legal codes to meet the special needs of child witnesses. For instance, some judges no longer wear the formal robes or even sit on an elevated platform; everyone sits around a table at eye-level with the child. More family members are being allowed into the courtroom to be with the child, care is being taken to see that the child does not see the offender before the hearing. Washington state has courtrooms where children sit on the floor with toys, the judge sits with them; the room is equipped with a one-way mirror and the defendant can see the child but not the other way around while the judge takes the child's testimony. In Israel, children do not even appear in court if they are part of incest cases. A counsellor is assigned by the police department to get the child's statement and that counsellor then testifies on behalf of the child in court.

What is working very well in England as also America—even though it is not yet admissible evidence in court in the latter—is video taping. Video taping is so very simple, quickly done in a simple room with simple questions to the child; no suggestive questions need be asked like, 'Did the man show you his penis?', open-ended questions which authoritatively yet affectionately guide the child into truthful answers are all that is required. In England, this video is played in court and everyone watches it while the child is not present. If the defence lawyer wants to cross-examine the child, he does so in a special room which is linked with closed circuit television to the courtroom.

There are countless advantages to video taping the child's testimony, including the one where even if the defendant changes his lawyer, the new lawyer would still have to watch the video tape before subjecting the child to a fresh cross-examination even if the case goes into appeal in the higher courts. Admittedly, though, fresh cross-examinations can pose problems of their own because children can, and do, construct the same thing in different ways if there is a gap in time. There is, however, one distinct, though addressable, disadvantage to video taping a child's testimony. A child is being asked to speak in front of a camera about something horrible which has happened to its private parts; would even an adult be able to handle a similar situation without feeling a mixture of inhibiting emotions? But the child's parents and counsellor can reassure the child, and can help it through its uncertainties and fears by preparing the child for the video tapings. And better a child face a non-judgemental camera than a roomful of strange, hostile adults.

If children's courts—as distinct from how it is now, a child-victim's case being lumped along with lakhs of adult cases, in serpentine queue—are not set up, Tanuja's case will take its toll on the child. It will also take its own time to come up for the pandit to be convicted, the hearings will drag on.

'Jhootee!' shouts the pandit's lawyer as Tanuja forgets and says he touched her there with his left hand. 'You are lying, last week you said it was his right hand!'

Tanuja goes into distress, all around her are male officials even though it is an in-camera hearing to which she has a right. In-camera for a child is still too many people whom she does not know in a room which is smaller than the court room but as strange: a judge, some policemen, court officials, the pandit's lawyer. And the pandit, glaring at her from across the room. Tanuja tries to block out the abuse to cope with it. She is asked, repeatedly, to say what happened. Indian laws do not allow for a child's evidence to be audio or video recorded once and for all and presented in court. Indian laws do not take into consideration that getting children to repeat the story can not only further traumatize the child but also affect clarity and the truth—the child's truth, the real truth—can get lost in the process.

'Secondary victimization is the key reason why we do not actively encourage parents from reporting the matter to the police,' says Javita Narang of Ifsha in Delhi which counsels Child Sexual Abuse cases in both, children and adults. 'We work so hard with re-building the child's confidence through counselling and one trip to the court destroys it all. Fresh dates are constantly set and there are so many instances of children growing up into adults before the judgement is actually delivered.'

The secondary victimization of a child can be far

worse, if not as bad as, the actual sexual abuse itself. It is something being actively considered in western courts dealing with Child Sexual Abuse cases. Counsellors working in these courts have xeroxed a poem by a twelve-year-old girl child and put it up on their noticeboards.

I asked you for help, and you told me you would
If I told you the things he did to me.
You asked me to trust you, and you made me
Repeat them to fourteen different strangers
I asked you for help and you gave me
A doctor with cold hands
Who spread my legs and stared at me
Just like my father.
I asked you for protection
And you gave me a social worker.
Do you know what it is like
To have more social workers than friends?
I asked you for help
And you forced my mother to choose between us.
She chose him, of course.
She was scared, she had a lot to lose.
I had a lot to lose too.
The difference is, you never told me how much.
I asked you to put an end to the abuse
You put an end to my whole family.
You took away my nights of hell
And gave me days of hell instead.
You have changed my private nightmare
Into a very public one.

• prevention than cure

Very clearly, prevention is better than cure when it comes to Child Sexual Abuse. It has to be a matter about prevention rather than punishment.

And this prevention lies in the hands of each and every parent, the father and the mother.

How can you protect your child?

- remember this at all times: Child Sexual Abuse is a crime situation where the fact is known only to the abuser and the abused, where the abuser enjoys advantages of age, relation and social prestige, where the offender is a mature person and the victim is a child

- teach your child to speak up and ask an adult several questions if it is not comfortable with what is being done to, or around, it; questions like 'what are you doing?', 'why are you doing it?', 'should I tell my daddy?' can have their desired effect

- please explain all this to your child in a one-to-one tone with the usage of simple language and in a manner which does not make the child feel like it is mentally deficient to understand such things; do not explain all this to your child in 'totlaa', or what you think is child language; you would be embarrassed at the number of children who find adults speaking to them in 'aley ley ley, mela laja' language as exceedingly stupid

- establish a comfortable and free atmosphere at home so that it encourages your child to disclose anything he, or she, may have felt as a violation, especially if it has been felt within the family: remember, your child's silence is what the abuser has been trading on

- find the language to explain Child Sexual Abuse to your child, use simple terms specially for genitalia like breast, anus, vagina, penis, bum; please do not continue using the words you taught your child while potty training it like 'chi chi' and 'ka ka' for vagina and penis and anus; it is also very wrong on the part of a parent to be teaching a growing boy words like 'little brother', 'bell', 'chilli', 'parrot' et al for penis, it may sound cute to some parents but is enormously misleading for the child's understanding of its own body
- teach the child the difference between a 'good touch' and a 'bad touch'; this is crucial
- let the child know that it is not the child's fault if someone does a 'bad touch'; and that you are there for the child if it wants to come and tell you if it feels frightened or confused about the 'bad touch'
- help the child understand its right over its own body, specially the right to say 'no'
- do not force your children to hug and kiss others, this sets a critical pattern for abuse later
- intervene on your child's behalf when he, or she, cannot say 'no'
- know where your child is at all times, be familiar with your child's friends and daily activities
- train your child to check with you each time it has to go out of the house and to inform you where it is going, with whom and for how long
- let the children in your building understand that they must use the 'buddy system' while playing downstairs, each one keeps an eye on the other
- believe what your child tells you, be alert to small changes in behaviour
- observe the adult who is paying an unusual amount of attention to your child

- also observe your child if it is being suddenly over-affectionate to an adult, check to see if gifts and chocolates are being given without your consent
- ask the child not to go near strangers or be friendly to them if they offer gifts or chocolates
- repeat this bitter chocolate message firmly; children do not always obey their parents and it is important they understand this
- give your child emergency telephone numbers where he, she, can call if they sense danger
- ensure that your child's school runs non-graded and no-test sex education courses which include Child Sexual Abuse information for junior classes; senior classes would be given additional information on Aids and nurturing respectful relationships between genders
- ensure that your child's school and college appoint professionally qualified child counsellors who are trained to handle cases of Child Sexual Abuse as well; do not expect teachers to do this job for you for two reasons: if you as a parent do not want to address such issues, why should a teacher want to do it; also: teachers cannot always be expected to go beyond their brief specially when they are working in overflowing class rooms run in factory-like schools and colleges

Sex education in schools in India still tends to be a taboo topic with a set of parents. In fact, it is this set that stops several schools all over the country from imparting sex education to their students, the principals of such schools complain of the educated middle and upper-class parents of their pupils who would much rather not have sex education in schools for fear that their children will turn 'naughty'. The children themselves, though, want sex education. Or as they tend to call it: Sex Ed.

In a March 2000 poll survey conducted by Mumbaii's Bhavans College through a cross-section of students, teachers and parents from the city's schools on compulsory Sex Ed in schools, 62.23 per cent of the students voted for it. Possibly fearing that they would have to give a test or examination on Sex Ed as an additional subject, 29.13 per cent of the students feel it should be optional. More than the students are the teachers, 71 per cent of the teaching community feel Sex Ed must be made compulsory in Mumbaii's schools. An important statistic this: teachers continue to feel that they have a responsibility to fulfill, besides their duty, that of the psychological health of the children they teach; possibly this happens because teachers are by now used to parents expecting miracles in schools while facilitating very few themselves and at home. 'What,' parents are known to protest, 'are the teachers doing?' Well, what the parents are doing is evident in the next set of statistics; 66.52 per cent of the parents say Sex Ed in schools is a good idea. Why? Because they find they cannot discuss the subject at home with their children. Why? Because their own parents could not discuss it with them. Why cannot they learn from the mistakes and omissions of their own parents and start afresh with their children? No reply to that. Well? Replies the father of a twelve-year-old son who agrees with the parents in the survey, 'Okay, admitted that we are like our parents, but that does not mean our children have to be like their parents. Therefore, it is better they get their information from their schools on sex and the risks associated with it. These are the days of Aids, our children must understand.'

A small percentage of the parents, of course, continue to oppose Sex Ed in schools, at home or, indeed, anywhere else; the reason they give in the survey, 'Against our Indian culture'. Centuries of tradition and glorious heritage winning over Child Sexual Abuse and Aids information here.

Parents like these tend not to live in real time, and there are such 'culturally sensitive' parents everywhere in India. When workshop organizers conduct Child Sexual Abuse sensitization programmes in schools, parents are invariably wary but the children almost always respond with alacrity. Like when Jabala of Calcutta ran a similar programme in city schools, several children disclosed their sexual abuse and requested the workers of Jabala to speak with their parents about it; they also asked for one-to-one counselling so that they could absorb what had happened to them.

Dr Nandita de Souza of Sangath, which works with children and their families in Goa, says, 'I cannot overstate the importance of sex education in homes and schools. I always stress that if parents want to keep their children sexually safe then they must educate them, either themselves or through the school; parents have begun understanding this now. It is also vital that sex education in schools addresses the issue of Child Sexual Abuse beginning with the younger children.' Sangath has conducted three workshops for the parents, staff of an orphanage and teachers, 'We focussed on the development of a child's sexuality, which behaviours are normal and what could be a cause for concern. We also teach parents how to talk to their kids about sexual abuse. The most important task for parents is to create an atmosphere of trust and openness at home which would encourage children to ask questions and share information about whatever concerns they may have.'

To correctly understand the signs of Child Sexual Abuse in a child it is primarily important to know the stages of sexual development in a child so that the parent can be in a position to assist the child more efficiently. Just as children learn that various body parts have diverse functions and produce different sensations, they become aware of the feelings that arise from the manipulation of their genitals. Anything that is pleasurable is likely to be repeated. This is normal self-exploration as children learn more about their own bodies. Child psychologists say that children develop their own sexuality in distinctly different ways—a little girl may like the idea of constantly sliding down banisters or swooping into the sky on a swing; a little boy may feel turned on during his first motor-cycle ride or even when watching fire engines. Almost all children by the age of five are playing games of 'house house' or 'doctor doctor'.

A stray thought. The child is playing 'house house' with other children, any one of them could have been sexually abused by their father or close male relative in their own house; what kind of twist can this game take even as the children play it?

Another thought. The number of 'doctor sets' available in toy shops are testimony to the number of parents who want their children to become doctors when they grow up, no matter if the child displays piffling aptitude for the field of medical healing. The child has yet to grow up, parents have already started collecting money for the huge donations they will readily pay so that their child can become a doctor. They proceed to the toy shop and promptly pick up a 'doctor set' to present to their child as a play apparatus. The child is at the sexually explorative age, it has been sexually abused by the family doctor, it has some plastic instruments in its hand which its parents insist are part of its 'doctor doctor' game. Playing 'doctor doctor' can turn serious; and what about child and adolescent patients when this child grows as an adult, practising doctor?

A child's sexual exploration of itself as a human being can include trying to stick fingers or small objects into several openings of its body like the nose, ears, belly button or genitals. By the age of seven children want to know where they came from and play games which would include 'you show me yours and I'll show you mine'. By twelve the boys are into ejaculation contests between themselves and girls use their own body language. In other words, both sexes may begin to experiment with sexual behaviours and may be interested or disinterested, alternatively, in the process.

What would be abnormal for children of any age is to be obsessively preoccupied with their own bodies or that of others. Or if their behaviour turns coercive towards others or injurious to themselves. This is what parents should understand, to be able to differentiate their child's normally developing sexuality from the possible presence of Child Sexual Abuse.

Sensitizing parents, along with the teachers, to a child's sexuality can have a greater impact. Sangath's awareness programmes have increased referrals of Child Sexual Abuse from Goa's schools. Among the cases which have been referred there were those of three girls below fifteen years of age who presented with persistent urinary tract infection, headaches and 'daytime bed-wetting'. Enquiries revealed that all three had been sexually abused: by a male at home, by an older male mate in the school and by a bus conductor.

Sex education in schools, followed by an intensive course in the first year of college, is imperative in today's times. Indian children are also sexually maturing much faster than they ever did. With specific reference to Child Sexual Abuse, the unfortunate flip side to this is that any of these victimized children may mistake the sexual abuse for love and care-getting at an even earlier age. All relationships, subsequently, could be lust first, love later, if at all.

Ergo, what is needed—at priority level—is Sex Ed in both schools and colleges. For the beginners at junior school, very basic Sex Ed which would comprise information on 'good touch, bad touch' and other aspects of Child Sexual Abuse. At the senior school level, Sex Ed not about birds and bees but about Aids and the body's orifices, the penis and the vagina and the babies which can come out as a consequence. At first year college level, Sex Ed about meaningful sexual behaviour where love must come first, so that respect and trust can be what cements a meaningful relationship and not lust.

Oh yes, the parents might agree, jolly good idea, let them—the teachers—get on with it. What are those teachers doing?

It is not enough that Sex Ed be taught in schools; parents—through their Parent Teacher Associations in schools—need to keep an eye on what exactly is being taught in the name of Sex Ed.

A middle-age Mumbaii mother, accidentally pregnant, miscarried the foetus. Her school-going son looked accusingly at her to say, 'You did an abortion, you are horrible!' The boy was being taught in his school, as part of his Sex Ed classes, that abortion was evil.

Teachers and school principals need to monitor the details too. In an all-boy senior school in Chennai, at a Sex Ed workshop presented by a non-government organization there were references to 'experiments' being 'alright', because 'this is the only way to find out once and for all what your sexual preference is'. The teacher, also a parent in the same school and sitting behind as an observer, stepped in and pertinently pointed out that this would create social and gender anarchy as it was encouraging the boys to be both immoral and bisexual.

At a Mumbaii college the Sex Ed questions were equally loaded in favour of sexual experimentation. The college principal disallowed the two-day workshop from going ahead, dryly noting that there was more to Sex Ed than the act of sex itself. He added that he did not want his students to be identifying themselves as practitioners of safe sexual acts but as people who cared about their partners and as professionals in comprehensive fields which would help them get ahead with their future.

In other words: a life which goes much beyond ejaculation and orgasm. The kind of Sex Ed for kids which would help them understand that sex is not about penetration or not, good sex or bad sex, or less or more; but loving and cherishing, holding and hugging, warmth and real friendship. Do even the parents know and understand this?

Dr Shekhar Seshadri of Nimhans is also working in the direction of young adults, specifically young males in colleges, understanding that there is more to being a man than penetrative sex and sexual violence. He has been closely involved with the conceptualization and story board of the four nation masculinity film project, supported by Unicef and Save the Children. This masculinity project has short films by documentary film-makers Rahul Roy of India, Farjad Nabi and Mazhar Zaidi of Pakistan, Tsering Rhitar and Kesang Tseten of Nepal and Manzare Hassin of Bangladesh. The films address the different issues which frustrate and frighten young men in these countries; the films do not directly address Child Sexual Abuse but anything that can help the sexually uncertain male deal with his confusion and contradictions can go a long way towards protecting a child from sexual abuse.

Dr Seshadri is similarly working towards true masculinity awareness workshops in colleges, as also corporations, around the country. Says he, 'There has to be an alternative model to masculinity. We cannot have parents telling little boys, "Why are you crying like a girl?" We should not allow teachers to separate boys and girls on the playground, this is really a tragedy because the boys grow up losing out on the friendship of so many women. It needs to be said out very loud that sex is not about making love and making love is not about penetration, ejaculation and orgasm. It needs to be understood quickly that genital sex cannot be connoted as mainstream sexuality and that virtue cannot reside only in a woman's vagina, it can well be in a male body. Virtue, after all, is an internal state, virginity is a choice and the vagina is an anatomical structure. There are two messages which need to be changed. That maleness is not a natural endowment, rather a precarious state which you must achieve at all cost. That the penis has a mind of its own and once aroused it has to do its own thing.'

Any message that can underscore the point that males need to stop fucking little girls and boys, along with their childhood, is welcome.

• dealing with disclosure

Child Sexual Abuse is no longer about only that most unequal of power and gender structures—a big man and a little girl. It is also about a big man and a little man. And then several years later—the little man as a big man and another little man; the victim as perpetrator, and thus perpetuator; male handing it down to male.

In short, Child Sexual Abuse is not solely a 'woman's

problem'. Women are expected to protect their children, and children are generally taught by their mothers to protect themselves from men. But what about the men themselves? Specially the men who are not, and will never be, perpetrators—and then the perpetuators—of Child Sexual Abuse? There has never been a greater urgency than now for these men to start playing their role in not allowing Child Sexual Abuse by those men, men they would much rather dismiss as perverts.

If these men do not act, they will be responsible for the birth of more broken boys in the future.

Parents, therefore, have jointly to watch out. Even then disclosure can be both, chilling and heart-breaking.

A three-year-old comes up to her mother who is dressing up to go out for dinner that evening with her husband and says, 'Mommy, show me your titties.'

'What?'

'Show me your titties, mommy.'

'Chee-chee, who taught you such dirty things?'

'S'not dirty, dadaji says it.'

'Dadaji says it? To whom?'

'To me.'

'And then what do you do?'

The little girl quickly pulls up her T-shirt with both her hands and dances around her mother's bedroom. 'My titties, my titties, my titties, yea, yea, yea!'

The mother calls her five-year-old son. 'Does dadaji tell your sister to do this?'

'Yes mommy.'

'What else does he do?'

'He does funny things to her panties, then he washes her panties.'

'Does he do anything to you?'

'No mommy.'

'Are you sure?'

The daughter chips in, for her it's a game, 'He's lying mommy, he's lying. Dadaji tells him to show him his popat (parrot), then he holds it.'

This is a tableaux which recently unfolded for a young mother, like a thunderbolt from the blue right into her happily married life. Especially grim was the magnitude of the abuse, that it had gone on for so long and neither she nor her husband had an inkling of what was being done to their children by their grandfather.

Every international study being examined, every child psychiatrist spoken to, is of the firm opinion that prevention is better than cure. But having positive goals is not enough for a parent; intervention and then the effectiveness of this intervention is equally critical.

G. Caplan's conceptual model of prevention in mental health, which he presented in 1964 as 'Principles of Preventive Psychiatry', has been widely employed the world over in relation with Child Sexual Abuse:

- primary prevention: preventing the child's sexual abuse by eliminating its causes; by developing positive competence in the children (as described in the earlier chapter 'Prevention than Cure'); by increasing awareness among parents, teachers and other caretakers of the child that child abusers are to be found at all levels and classes of society and in all ages; by recognizing that little boys are as much at risk as girls; by establishing a more conspicuous social vigilance about Child Sexual Abuse so that potential abusers might be deterred; by insisting on establishment by the state of an effective and immediate penal policy which removes from circulation child sexual abusers because they represent a disproportionate and long-term risk to the child population

- secondary prevention: by identifying abuse sufficiently early for effective intervention to put a stop to it; by creating an atmosphere in schools and families through formal and informal means which would make children feel able to report abuse; by providing them with a vocabulary for at least the parts of their own body so that they disclose what they are experiencing; by removing the offender from the child's home; by understanding, with a very clear recognition, that children rarely lie about sexual abuse
- tertiary prevention: by developing treatment programmes so as to reduce the possibility of future psychological impairment which would include communicating with the child that the blame and responsibility are not theirs even if they 'co-operated' or 'consented'; that is, to minimize the consequences of the abuse without minimizing the abuse itself through formal interviewing and 'treatment' which is maintained at a minimally intrusive level by people who provide a sympathetic and undramatic yet supportive response to the disclosure: this would include the police, the courts and mental health professionals

Parents play the most important role in primary prevention and then in secondary prevention. Studies show that if the sexual abuse of a child is nipped in the bud, it inflicts the least damage on that child. But parents, for all practical purposes, cannot always be with their child. Therefore, it becomes all that more important for them to be closely involved with as many aspects of both primary and secondary prevention. The starting point is, as always, the home. Parents need to be friends with their children, use the open house concept for their own children, and an open mind concept too. So that the children can talk. And disclose.

What should you do to ensure that your child would, indeed, want to talk to you about its sexual abuse? What should a parent or guardian be doing to facilitate any kind of disclosure by a child? Here are some strategies to deal with disclosure; much of this has been advised as approaches for counsellors in the Child Protection Units run by the British police so that they can encourage the child's disclosure of its sexual abuse. Absolutely no reason why they would not work as well with parents who can make for the best counsellors for their children.

- first the environment: make yourself available
- give your child the confidence to approach you
- consider the atmosphere of the place where you and the child are going to deal with its disclosure; is the height of the chair you will sit on too high, are you going to sit behind your writing table, etc; do the talking at the child's physical level
- then the attitude: let your child know it is doing the right thing in telling you
- listen actively and avoid thinking about your next question before you have 'heard' and 'understood' what your child is saying
- accept your child's information as the truth
- avoid showing your revulsion or displeasure
- do not promise confidentiality when you know you are going to speak to your husband or wife about it later; if the child is insistent on 'promise promise', simply smile and take the conversation forward
- support your child by helping it realize that it is not to blame; explain that it happens to other children too
- then your own interaction: do not promise what cannot be delivered by you
- avoid leading questions while the child is disclosing,

e.g. 'did your uncle touch you like that?'

- use the child's words to confirm that you have understood certain things, 'so you are telling me you are frightened of him, isn't it?'
- do not make judgemental statements like 'why did you not tell me before this?' or 'you should have screamed for help' or 'he should not have done that to you'
- and now you need to take action as the child's trusted parent; keep a detailed record after the initial, and following, disclosure like date, time, place, non-verbal behaviour, exact language used by the child; you might need this in the future
- decide how serious it is in an exhaustive conversation with your husband or wife and what steps you both will take, without your child's knowledge, to correct the situation
- also decide if your child needs to see a counsellor and choose the right one yourself instead of taking your child through a hit-and-miss approach; you need to be limiting the number of people the child has to talk to so that re-victimization is avoided
- inform the child of the steps you have taken which directly concern its disclosure
- keep up the level of continuing support and contact without appearing over-protective
- and this is where you truly score as a parent over any counsellor no matter how qualified; your warm conversations, your cheerful smiles and some happy hugs to the child can go the longest way

A word here about the counsellor, be it a psychiatrist or any other kind of mental health professional. This bears repetition: please do not entrust your child's emotional future to someone who has not trained in post-Child

Sexual Abuse mental health. There are no college or university-level courses in the country specifically on this subject, an addition would greatly assist future mental health workers. Those who work now with children who have been sexually abused in India are self-taught, through books on the subject from abroad as also from workshops to share their experiences, training under child psychiatrists working with children who have been abused and applying this on-the-job experience on the other abused children whom they counsel.

As a parent what you would definitely want to do when looking for a child psychiatrist or counsellor is first check whether the professional has comfortably handled a number of Child Sexual Abuse cases. The second, and this is equally important, whether the doctor is too busy; you cannot allow a situation where the doctor lines up his child-patients, makes them wait for long in a queue and then talks to your child for a few distracted minutes. The third, and perhaps this should have been the first point: whether the doctor avoids prescribing medicines as the first, or even the second, resort, and if he does, is he able to effectively explain his reasons to you.

The other points you need to observe as a parent taking a child for counselling: the professional should take seriously and respect the information communicated by you about your child; the professional ought to be flexible about enlisting you or your spouse, or both, as part of the treatment team, as observers and reporters on the response to the treatment; should you suggest a change in treatment, the counsellor should not react by feeling threatened with your views, in fact the mental health professional should encourage a dialogue so that you, yourself, feel less overwhelmed by the entire procedure of what is happening to your child and you.

There are some child psychiatrists and counsellors who encourage parent participation in the counselling; please do not assume that the mother of the child is the only choice at that time. Fathers have been known to shepherd the situation with more joviality and alacrity, thus helping the child swiftly.

What do you do if your child has been abused?

- do not panic or over-react to the information disclosed by the child
- do not criticize or blame the child, it would be unfair to say, 'I told you not to do that!'
- do not say or do anything which will make the child feel guilty about the abuse
- support your child's decision to speak out
- be sympathetic and supportive, this will help your child make additional disclosures and discuss his, her, feelings
- suppressed anger is the single greatest cause for distorted emotions after sexual abuse; do not hasten to get rid of any feeling of anger, it is a natural reaction to abuse; encourage the child to ventilate those feelings and help him, her, to channelise it in a positive manner
- do not minimize the magnitude of what has been done to your child
- a feeling of isolation is common after Child Sexual Abuse; encourage your child to participate as always in his, her, favourite games and activities
- do not make any false promises to your child
- consult a doctor to check for physical injuries if you think it necessary; do not take too long to get to the doctor, a child's body heals quickly; get a written report from the doctor
- if the doctor's report states physical injuries and you want to lodge a complaint at the police station, discuss

it with your spouse thoroughly, and then explain it as simply as possible to the child

- as parents it may be complicated socially and emotionally to take a stand against the abuser, particularly if he is a family member; but it is still important for the parents to do it so as to reinforce the child's understanding of wrong and right
- do not think that understanding the abuser will in any way help your child, it might just work to the contrary; you have to remain child focussed
- do not link apology with forgiveness; if the abuser says he is willing to apologize to the child, do not insist that the child forgive him
- stand by your child; do not re-victimize your child by getting into arguments with your family member who has sexually abused the child in front of it; families fall apart when such cases are disclosed, relationships between several families collapse as well, e.g. a father and his sister fall out when it is discovered that her husband has been sexually abusing the father's child; do not be bitter about your family falling apart in front of the child as this will make the child feel responsible and guilty for the situation
- never imply that the child should forgive-and-forget the abuser in order to heal
- do not bring religion or religious figures into the picture; religion does not solve problems, if correctly absorbed, it can only help make human beings strong to solve their own problems; when adults are not mature enough to understand this, how can children?
- consider the need for counselling or a professionally-qualified child psychologist; remember to consult your child on the gender of the doctor, an abused male-child might not necessarily have a problem with talking to a male doctor

- if you decide to speak with the police, the child need not come to the police station with you to report the crime

If your child has been raped, as a parent or guardian you have the right to make the following demands:

- Demand that the police visit the scene of the crime.
- Demand that the rapist be arrested.
- Demand that he be medically examined.
- Demand that you be allowed a legal representative for your child.
- Demand your child's right to have an in-camera trial; that is, a special room and not in an open courtroom.
- Demand that there be a screen or curtain in between the child and the perpetrator so that the child is not frightened by his staring eyes or presence; give your child its favourite toy or little blanket to hold and feel comforted with during questioning.

Those were your rights as a parent; these are your responsibilities so that your child's case is strengthened and you effectively assist the police in discharging its duties:

- This is the most difficult one: please stay calm when you get to the police station.
- When you report the crime at the police station, remember this is only the first step.
- The police will note down what you have to say as the first information report (FIR).
- They will then investigate.
- This investigation will include the panchnama; the medical examination of the accused and your child; a chemical examination for substance, blood, semen, etc; a statement by the witnesses which must not be signed by them but you need to make sure that they come to

court when called to verify their statements; an identification parade.

- They will file the charge-sheet.
- After this, the police will arrest the accused.
- Please remember: the first information report must very clearly state the date and time of incident, the specific place of incident, the description of the offence, the name of the accused, the names of the eye-witnesses if any, and the name of the complainant.
- Remember that the description of the offence you put on the first information report is what your child will have to remember till whenever the case comes up in court for hearing; therefore keep it as uncluttered as possible.
- You must take a copy of this first information report from the police with their stamp on it, and the report's number from them.

All Child Sexual Abuse cases are criminal cases, therefore, they would be seen as crimes against the state, and it would be a state lawyer who would defend your child. That lawyer is called a public prosecutor; your own lawyer can only assist the public prosecutor's thought processes outside the court, your own lawyer cannot represent your child in the criminal court. However, the accused can get his own lawyer. Should you be filing for any related civil matter, your own lawyer can represent you in the civil courts.

At the end of this book is a Helpline, a guide if intervention is required for both children and adult survivors of Child Sexual Abuse. The doctors and counsellors mentioned are experienced professionals in the handling of Child Sexual Abuse cases from upper and middle-class homes, they have been found to be most capable. If you

live in a town or city not listed in the Helpline, please help
the upper and middle-class children in your area by
identifying at least one counsellor who could be briefly but
suitably trained by any of the organizations mentioned in
the listing as specializing in counselling. The presence of
that one trained counsellor in your city can go a long way
in establishing better future citizenry. Another good idea
would be to speak to your child's school or college principal
and Parent Teacher Association to invite one of the
organizations listed, that is closest to your city, for separate
student and adult awareness workshops; the police
commissioner of your city and his wife can also be invited
to attend as parents-cum-special guests should he then
want to think of a similar awareness programme for the
police-parents in his force.

There is no twenty-four hour crisis intervention listing
simply because there is none anywhere in India which can
effectively assist you in dealing with Child Sexual Abuse if
it happens outside office hours; given its nature, this
happens too. Even during working hours there are less
than a handful of non-government organizations which are
completely experienced in assisting you organize your child's
case with the police, apart from the medical and legal
aspects of it.

•   **child protection units**

The answer, however, does not necessarily lie in summarily
increasing the number of non-government organizations;
there are already far too many of them in India which do
not always walk their talk. Specially in the area of children
where they tend to vanish when it comes to timely
intervention and action for the suffering child. What use

child-centred non-government organizations stuffed with paid staff and high-flying heads which appear to continue on the strength of their positive goals rather than on a systematic evaluation of their effectiveness? To whom, then, the greater good?

Also, not the answer is a 'strategic alliance' with the police; the very phrase conveys a cover-up of the actual issue, that the interests of a young citizen of India are not the concern of its police. There are, anyway, enough horror stories of how this 'strategic alliance' does nothing at all to help the child in distress. One example: a child cell set up in collaboration with a police station in a metropolitan city in India pleased that police commissioner because it did something for his caring image; it added importance to the non-government organization because the newspapers gave it publicity and this, in turn, got it more publicity as champions of the cause of the sexually abused child. What did it mean for this child who was forced into oral intercourse by her neighbour? Another neighbour saw this neighbour leaving while adjusting his fly, the little girl's grandmother found her inside the flat gagging on the semen, the little girl's family approached the police station and the policeman on duty, since he had been told that such child cases must be referred to the child cell, phoned the social workers concerned who took the usual amount of time in getting there, not intentionally long but long enough considering the travel time it takes in a large city. Meanwhile, the utterly distraught child and her parents waited. The ladies arrived and assisted in the filing of the first information report, a case was registered of molestation or outraging of modesty, and that was pretty much that. The ladies took their leave, the family was left to fend with its own feelings and return home to a situation where other neighbours, including the perpetrator's family, had begun passing angry and loud comments about them going to the police for 'such a matter'.

The social workers did not enter into discussion with the police or the family on what laws could be possibly applied quite simply because they were clueless on the laws of the land. It did not occur to any among them that they could approach any lawyer in the city who would have been happy to explain the relevant laws, and its pitfalls, to them. Oral sex with a child could have well been classified beyond 'outraging of modesty' which would get the accused a maximum of two years. It could have been classified as 377, an unnatural offence, 452 which is house trespass since he did it to the girl in her own flat and which would have got him up to seven years, or 511 which is attempt to rape.

The social workers of the cell followed on 'our case of that poor little girl' every now and then by keeping track of what was happening in the court on it. Tch, they went in unison, tch, tch, these laws are such a mess; they said this when the case finally came up and the judge let off the accused for lack of proof.

No, such a 'strategic alliance' between social workers and the police is certainly not needed.

Nor should it be that social workers think they should be the ones to decide whether a sexual abuser goes to jail or not. Because this is how the bleeding hearts brigade can actually wind up confounding the issue. A girl is sexually abused by her father in Mumbaii, she is molested. The mother is not at home, the neighbours hear the girl crying out and intervene; they rescue the girl, they beat up the father, he runs away, he returns after a few days. The social workers go into a huddle—should the father be handed over to the police or not? No, they decide, the father need not be arrested, they offer several reasons why.

First, the girl has been molested, not raped; punishment for this crime, if proved, is meagre at best. Secondly, the man is a first-time offender, and therefore quite likely to get a suspended sentence. Thirdly, the man is the only breadwinner, he is the father of six children, if his wife permits a case to be registered against him, the possibility of him abandoning his family, running away again, and perhaps even abusing another child is very high. Finally, the girl would have to live within a society who in all probability could blame her for what had happened.

And thus these social workers play both God and police, they decide that the man need not go to jail. Says one of those social workers, 'We took this decision in the interests of that child.'

Congratulations.

What about the fact that the father can do it to the child again? And to the children of the neighbourhood? Or perhaps the children in some other neighbourhood? 'This does not mean that the man is allowed to continue molesting unchecked. The social workers would have to pay daily home visits. Two or three of his girls would be placed in boarding schools. The mother would have to be helped to get contraception since the chances of the man agreeing to use it would be slim to non-existent. Even the neighbours would be enlisted to keep a watch on the man and his movements, be it within the family or out.'

Wonderful, even if typically woolly-headed optimism.

Word gets around in that neighbourhood. Two months later, three boys in the vicinity, ages fifteen to seventeen, rape an under-ten years old girl.

Why did this happen? Is there any connection between the two cases? Cause and effect? What message went out in the neighbourhood—and specially to the neighbourhood youth and children—when one man molested his daughter and several people got together to keep him out of jail?

Larissa Pitter, a social worker who monitors Child Sexual Abuse cases in Mumbaii, then presents the other point of view, the practical one, 'Suppose those social workers had decided to go with the case and have the man arrested, who would stay with such a case for the five years or more it takes for it to come up in court? And which non-government organization would guarantee counselling for that child for all those years it needs to be taken to court?'

Deepika D'Souza, director of the India Centre for Human Rights and Law, thoughtfully makes what is the most crucial point of all: 'In all this, that little living, breathing and frightened child gets completely lost.'

On no account must that child get lost.

Under no circumstances must that child's right be submerged.

To ensure this a penal policy needs to be established that removes from circulation child sexual abusers because they represent a long-term risk to the child population in India. This, in turn, would also deter potential abusers. It is widely recognized that compulsory child abuse reporting laws in both the United States of America and the United Kingdom have led to professional alertness and intervention, and this has led to even greater public awareness. Most states in Australia and Malaysia are required to report known and suspected cases to the local child protective services agency. In the Netherlands, Belgium and Luxembourg there is a 'confidential doctor' within the health care system who receives notification of all forms of maltreatment. All of this has meant that treatments to children once being hidden or considered acceptable in homes have become unacceptable and the more severe forms of maltreatment are thrown into sharper relief.

The laws need to be amended, so that every limb of the legal system and every court in the country acknowledges Child Sexual Abuse. But after the laws are amended, far more needs to be looked into; or else the amended laws can turn into toothless tigers.

India's police needs to professionally open its umbrella to be truly child-inclusive, child-assist and child-friendly. 'Sympathetic police support must be ensured,' points out Dr Kiran Bedi who has set up a foundation to guide the children of prisoners through their formative years; information on Child Sexual Abuse is regularly imparted to these children.

Child Protection Units (CPU) must be set up in each city of the country; centrally monitored and updated by a senior police officer like perhaps Dr Bedi herself. (No, in this book it is not she who has thought of the idea of CPUs for India nor does she know of her name being suggested as a CPU Chief.) The Child Protection Units would handle all cases against children by adults, be they sexual, physical or emotional. Such Child Protection Units don't need too much of an investment: one brightly-painted room, one working telephone and smartly turned-out police officers who are conversant with English, Hindi and their state's language. Not just-hired constables who have enlisted in the police because they cannot get a job elsewhere, not women constables simply because they are women; but police officers who at least look like they can win the war against all forms of child abuse, including sexual and physical. It is of the essence that these police officers be educated beyond the standard tenth level; not just literate but educated because they are going to be dialoguing with children and their parents from all classes, not simply those from the slums.

These police officers would run the Child Protection

Unit round the clock and would be sensitized to Child Sexual Abuse as also a child's physical and emotional abuse, as separate and combined issues since a child's sexual abuse also has its echoes in physical and emotional abuse. The sensitization programmes can be done by the organizations working in the legal, police, medical and counselling areas of Child Sexual Abuse. Such sensitization programmes can also include the medical examiners and that very important, but largely forgotten figure, the public prosecutor. One sensitization session would definitely include the difference between abuse of a child by a stranger and its family member; the latter coming with a different set of dynamics and requiring more skills in case investigation.

Each city's Child Protection Unit would have a bank of child counsellors attached to it, drawn from the organizations working with Child Sexual Abuse in the city. Counsellors must necessarily come with a working knowledge of Child Sexual Abuse trauma; children who are brought with physical wounds—and not necessarily a torn vagina or anus—may have been sexually abused with a finger or intense fondling. They are not likely to reveal this outright. But a trained counsellor can coax out disclosure with even a doll or puppet-play situated in a non-threatening room. She can comfort the child and bring out the puppets to tell open-ended stories. The child will finish the story by talking about its sexual abuse, almost always in the third person.

The only disadvantage of this would be the hurry associated with the disclosure. Mumbaii child counsellor Veena Fernandes recalls the time a 'did he, did he not sexually abuse his granddaughter' opinion was required within a fortnight. 'I made good progress and I did not push the child, allowing her to find her own ways of trusting me,' she says. 'But there was this deadline so during the third session I pushed a little, and it all came undone when the child simply withdrew. I had to start all over again.' The child did disclose, that dadaji had given her a Barbie doll and chocolates, that he took her for bath and touched her here and told her to touch him there. Veena Fernandes ascertained where 'there' was with the help of an anatomically-correct doll and wrote out her report. She also went to court to speak with the judge who refused to believe her, the judge would not even make eye contact with her; maybe he would have—the eye contact followed by the belief—if she had come from 'within', from a Child Protection Unit, for example, as the child's case manager.

These case managers, as the counsellors can be designated, in a Child Protection Unit can get called in on a rotational basis as soon as a child abuse is reported, be it sexual, physical or emotional. The same case manager would 'stay' with the case till its closure all the way, till the court declares its judgement, and this would also help the child have on-line counselling and comfort during its visits to the courtroom for cross-examination. At the CPU, the child's case manager would get the child to disclose, and would help the police officer in the video taping of a child's testimony. The video taping section would be like that of the counselling section, chosen from the city and attached to the Child Protection Unit on a freelance basis and paid accordingly; thus cutting out the need to specially hire and train and then maintain sections by the police force itself.

The video tape prepared by the Child Protection Unit would be final. The defence lawyer must see it and then he can cross-question the child only once, irrespective of whether the child has been sexually or physically abused, strictly in an in-camera hearing with a protective partition or curtain placed between the child and the accused. This protective screen is being allowed after being used in a Child Sexual Abuse case in Delhi; no reason why it cannot be used in physical and emotional abuse cases either.

All of this needs to be done. Step by step. Together. Do it simultaneously. Do it separately. Just do it.

And then while all of this is done and working reasonably well, all that would be left to set in place is special children's courts, Child Protection Court (CPC), just one in each city. A Child Protection Court which would be for the children only, dealing with crimes against children by adults. Just an ante-room perhaps in an existing court, brightly-painted with a smiling judge whose attitude is child-friendly and who appears easily accessible. Who disposes of cases quickly, in a maximum of ninety days. Who dispenses justice for a wronged child.

A Child Protection Court is as important as a Child Protection Unit. Or else everything else done for an abused child turns into a graveyard of good intentions.

●   **dimple**

Dimple   **Five years**   **Delhi**

My five-year-old daughter Dimple came to me a few days back and said the neighbour's man-servant was 'trying to do kissy' with her and she did not like the taste of bidis he smoked, so I must tell him to stop. The child was so assertive, and yet so innocent. Dimple watches a lot of television and perhaps this is where she has learnt to articulate so clearly, though the kids in our building are equally confident creatures. I told my husband about the neighbour's servant and he dealt with the matter by telling the neighbour to sack the servant.

The neighbour turned around and said, 'You can either go to the police or deal with the servant yourself, don't make this our problem. Behetar yahi hoga key aap apni beti ko sambhaal le.'

My husband came back and told me the same thing, 'We better keep an eye on our daughter.' And that was that.

Dimple is much too young for me to try and explain things to her. But somewhere, I think, she has already understood that she needs to have a hands-off relationship with men. When she grows up a little, I shall explain to her all that I can about sex and sexuality and body parts. Women should know about their sexuality and how to assert it, I understand this now after reading so many books on the subject. That is why I have no problem at all if my daughter decides to have protected sex before she gets married. I don't do this myself but I have so many women friends who sleep with younger boys if their husbands don't know how to bring them to orgasm. Sometimes they do it just for the variety. That's fine with me, women have a right to their sexuality. I have two unmarried female friends who have decided to be mistresses of married men. If the wives of the married men don't have the guts to do anything about it, why should my friends deny themselves the love and the security? After all, they are given money too, to run their homes and look good even though they are working women.

If, God forbid, Dimple is sexually molested again despite my best precautions, I shall tell her that I understand, it has happened to me too, and I shall comfort her. My mum never comforted me because I never told her. Once I did try, though, to tell her that one of her card-playing friends in our house was trying to do something to me with all my clothes on and his too, and she said, 'You want to cut off our nose in our society with such loose talk?' And she slapped me. Dad would be too busy with his parties or his office to care. I grew up with everything, a fancy house, cars, good clothes and food, fancy friends and games, everything including a retinue of servants who would sexually abuse me.

When I got pregnant, mum and dad got a shock. They had me aborted and got me a 'governess'. It was quite funny, I was in college by then and I had a 'governess'. My first, and only, lesbian encounter was with her and both of us enjoyed each other's bodies thoroughly until we were caught one night by my father and he threw her out. We should have been careful, we were making love in the bathtub. In college I smoked, drank, rebelled, had affairs with the most unlikely men, got pregnant again, aborted, went on the pill, and fell in love with the man who much later became my husband. He was going around with my friend in college and since he did not believe in contraception—he never has, he thinks women should take care of such things since it is their problem—he got her pregnant. I helped her through her abortions with him and that is how we got close. He understood me and cared for me the way I was, and I was comfortable with him because I did not feel dirty about my past when I was with him. I too aborted before he decided to marry me. It has been a comfortable marriage.

Yes, it was a slightly difficult time for me when I told him about my sexual abuse as a child in a drunken night we spent together on our third anniversary. He reacted and had a string of affairs, but I did not mind after the initial depression. Because he continued to look after me and give me lots of money and have sex with me. Every now and then he has affairs even today, I know this, but it's okay because he comes back to me every night and that's what matters, that he continues to care for me.

And he protects me from my parents—he is so courteous with them!—as he does from our son who is older than Dimple and growing up to be a difficult person. Our son fails every now and then in school, he gets into fights, he is so rude to me but since he is respectful to his father I feel it is best that they handle it among themselves. My husband respects me even more for this decision. He says Dimple is my problem since our son is his. That is okay with me, I am not the sort of woman who will run away from her responsibilities. In fact, in between, when I was working I realized that it was disturbing my family life, specially my husband who needs to see me at home when he walks in at six every evening from office before leaving for the club from which he returns in time for dinner. So I left my job, although it was well paying with very little to do. And my husband would keep calling me at the office almost every hour, asking me what I was doing. The telephone operator and my office colleagues were very envious, they said, 'We envy you, your husband really loves you.' I told them I was the happiest woman in the world. They said I should be, I have a husband, a daughter and a son. I always say I would have preferred two daughters. Daughters you can protect, sons what can you tell?

I shall ensure that Dimple too grows up to be as happy as I am. That's my promise to myself.

●   **dimple's brother**

Is there an untold story in the preceding chapter?

There are two of them.

Dimple's mother is so completely in victim mode that

she has absolutely no intention of not deriving her power from this role.

She has been in scattered forms of therapy since many years, she enjoys this thoroughly—the undivided attention that the women counsellors give her. She has taught herself to use the right phrases from the books she reads on feminism and sexuality and she uses this jargon judiciously, appropriately. She plays psychological hide-and-seek with counsellors when they begin cracking through her veneer and point out that she is exactly like her parents and husband, never there for their children. Dimple's mother leaves home by noon almost every day to play cards, discuss books and films with friends at assorted coffee shops, watch movies, do 'social work' and attend work-sessions on 'finding one's self'. Sometimes she does not come back in the night, having spent it at the homes of her various 'emancipated' women friends where they discuss ways and means of writing the ultimate book on women's liberation. She keeps in touch with her children about their studies and the servants about the dinner menu on her cell phone.

Dimple's mother delicately, and graciously, changes counsellors when their sessions reach the point where a mirror is held up to her. It is high time, the mirror tells her, that she realized she is leading a pathetic life and worked, instead, on improving the future instead of worsening it for herself and her children. Dimple's mother asks with intentionally subdued passion, 'But what about me, the child in me who feels her parents have let her down?' Then she changes counsellors to move on to the next one where she elegantly lights her cigarettes, flicks her untied hair in an exhausted manner and proceeds to plumb for new depths of deprivation as she goes through her routine of appearing to emotionally bleed herself for what she sees as her audience. She sighs, she shudders, she gasps.

And she refuses to admit that she was simply not there—in affection, emotion and strength—when she walked in on her son being sexually molested by their cook.

She sent her son to bed, sacked the cook when she could get another a few days later, and told her husband nothing. She told him about Dimple because her survival instincts about her own marriage galvanized her to do so.

Dimple's brother hesitantly, one weekend when Dimple's mother had gone to find herself in an out-of-town workshop, spoke to his father. He cried, his little body convulsing with his sobs, as he pressed his fists into his eyes so that he could prevent his tears from pouring out of them. His father gripped his shoulders—father and son, one Sunday morning as the sun lit up their tastefully-appointed living room on Prithviraj Road—and said, 'In the future, you tell me. Together we will bash up the bastard who dares to touch you again.'

Dimple's brother is one among twenty-five per cent of boy-children under sixteen being sexually abused in India at any given point of time. He is fortunate to the degree that his mother's complete self-absorption compelled him to speak to his father who was supportive, even if fleetingly. What the father is really saying to his unhappy son is this, 'Well, we will wait till someone does it to you again and after he does, tell me and then together we will do something about it.' What he should be saying is this, 'I am sorry I was not there for you when that happened, be assured I am there for you hereafter if you need my help in anything. Now, there are some things which you and I need to talk about, like growing up and what good touch and bad touch is all about and what that word sex really means. How about you and I sitting down this Sunday to talk about it?'

If Dimple's father had to say the latter, and then follow

through with the Sunday talk, the difference it would have made to Dimple's brother would have been phenomenal.

As it would to this eight-year-old boy playing near a Durga Puja pandal in Calcutta. A masked man whisks him away into a car, drives to a nearby secluded spot and sodomizes the boy. The boys fights, struggles, he tears the mask off, it is his grandfather's closest friend. He staggers home and tells his parents what they insist is a lie. A masked man? The boy lapses into silence. A few weeks later he develops a speech defect.

Most sexually abused boys do not get the immediate intervention and assistance they deserve. This is sad because it is that much easier for a boy-child to get help since the family's 'izzat' does not depend on his 'purity', unlike the way Indian society judges a female. Tragically, though, a boy-child has his own social constraints set firmly into place by his male peers: to sound as though one is complaining about any aspect of sex—instead of simply pretending to enjoy it all—is to be a 'sissy' or 'chhukka'. Thus, most boys do not prefer to see it as Child Sexual Abuse.

Assume for a minute—after setting the sexual ethics of it firmly aside—that this is perfectly all right, young men being initiated into sex by a randy aunt or female cousin or even a male uncle or physical instructor at school. If they do not see it as any kind of abuse and therefore do not suffer side-effects, then where is the problem?

There isn't a problem, and there is absolutely no reason why one should be constructed in the guise of Child Sexual Abuse. This is equally applicable to women survivors of Child Sexual Abuse who feel close to nothing—except a very healthy rage which they ventilate and are happier for it. Sections of surveys also indicate a fortunate percentage of women and men who are no worse after their sexual experiences as children with their cousins, assorted aunts and uncles, other known persons and strangers.

The problem comes with the assumption that an equal, or more, number of children will experience no short or long-term effects of their sexual abuse in the future since the country is far more liberal sexually than it ever was.

This assumption would be incorrect—and grossly unfair to children—for the same 'liberal' reasons. With urban Indian children getting sexualized almost as soon as they enter their teens today, they are more aware than adults of the rights of the space surrounding their bodies. They are exposed to far more on television, through magazines and the internet, through the print media, than ever before. Homosexuals and lesbians are cogently presenting their case and talking about what they see as valid reasons for choosing these alternative sexual lifestyles. Condoms are freely available. Sex is not the four-letter word it used to be, it has turned into another misplaced and much misunderstood three-letter word spelt as f-u-n. All of this is sharpening teen instincts about the ethics of modern sexual behaviour. The information explosion on Aids is assisting greatly in this direction.

And all of this is reflecting in a greater awareness on fondling and how much with which boyfriend or girlfriend, 'okay sex' how often. Modern sexual ethics, in short.

What was okay until recently for one section might not be so-okay shortly for a lot more.

This is already being reflected in the attitudes of children. In Dr Shekhar Seshadri's survey of young boys 15 per cent report Child Sexual Abuse; the boys also report their experiences with older males as both unwanted and unpleasant.

Older males themselves are beginning to disclose their sexual abuse as children. 'A much larger number of men than one would expect,' points out Chennai's Dr Vijay Nagaswami. An individual and marital psychotherapist, Dr Nagaswami is counselling an overwhelming number of males from upper and middle-class homes who have suffered sexual abuse as children in one form or another. He adds, 'A few come directly with their disclosure though this is rarely the presenting symptom. My experience in dealing with adolescents and adults who come in with other problems is that some or all of this can be traced back to their having been sexually abused in childhood. A large amount of this Child Sexual Abuse has happened at the hands of family, relatives, persons trusted by the child like servants and family retainers. And it has happened at the child's home.'

Home, where the maximum harm is. Where a few children—mostly boys—are now trying to fight back.

A thirteen-year-old Pune boy has reported to his parents that a female cousin has been seducing him since quite some time with gifts and games. The reason for the disclosure? The little boy said he did not want to get Aids.

An eleven-year-old Bangalore boy being sexually abused by his neighbour since the last several years, walks up to his home and punches him straight in the stomach with a warning that he should never, ever, be touched again.

Children of commercial sex workers are also attempting defence, albeit with tragic twists. Perveen is the fifteen-year-old daughter of a Bhopal prostitute. She was a group dancer for public functions and had to deal with several attempts of sexual abuse. Her mother stopped her dancing and set her up as a house-maid where she is being regularly sexually abused by her employer, his wife ignores Perveen when she tries to talk about what the man-of-the-house is doing to her. Perveen has now decided to go back to dancing, even if it incurs her mother's wrath. 'If I have to face such things in both places, I might as well do what I enjoy, my dancing,' she says.

And this, too, can happen.

A twelve-year-old Chennai boy is initiated into sexual activity by a twenty-one-year old married woman, his neighbour. Their affair lasts for two years, even through the first few months of her pregnancy. The woman has no idea whose child it is, the boy-child's or her husband's, but there is no assumption other than the obvious in their neighbourhood. The woman gives birth to a girl and does not resume the affair. The boy tries, she puts him off, first citing her post-pregnancy status and then her daughter as reasons.

The boy is now sixteen, the little girl two.

The boy rapes the little girl in revenge.

• exit cycle

The eight-year-old boy from Calcutta who develops a speech defect is also likely to display several other signs of short-term and, then, long-term effects of Child Sexual Abuse; as he grows, he is also likely to stay trapped in the survivor's cycle (see chapter 'The aftermath').

Dimple's mother, reprehensible though she may sound, is also in the survivor's cycle; and here she is likely to stay. She derives what she sees as her power from playing the victim's role while perpetuating emotional abuse in her family. A small thought here: why does Dimple's mother sound so reprehensible? Because she is a woman, a mother? Take away the theatrics of Dimple's mother—don't the fathers of other children behave similarly and with far less reason?

The truth is that Dimple's mother needs real help, not

medicine, just a good psychiatrist; make that a very good psychiatrist because Dimple's mother happens to be an intelligent woman, not blazingly intelligent but above average enough for her mind to need another which can match hers. The truth is also this: Dimple's mother will shun all help from those who truly care for her; all that friends can do is draw her attention to the problem and then not feel depressed when she intellectualizes the entire situation for them or simply cuts them off.

Mumbaii psychotherapist Dr Rani Raote, who also counsels adults who have been sexually abused in childhood, says, 'This does happen; women who have survived in dysfunctional relationships tend to react negatively when they enter a functional one. They may even try and spoil it for themselves with some kind of psychobabble. Such cases can take an even longer time to heal, because you can only heal if you really want to heal.'

Wanting to heal would mean getting out of the survivor's cycle, that coldly comforting space. Where one's skills have been honed and sharpened to do precisely that: survive. And to get till here has been such a long, painful journey. Now, just when there is this odd sort of comfort, to leave it?

To exit; into the future?

No.

Too difficult.

Very frightening.

International therapists working with Child Sexual Abuse adult patients have realized that an adult identifying herself, or himself, as a survivor over any length of time can be as damaging. The child victim becomes a survivor through the process of developing defensive strategies which endeavour to protect her, or his, inner core. These defence mechanisms include repression, denial, detachment and dissociation; such defence mechanisms often result in the adult survivor not having access to memories of her, or his, sexual abuse. However, in adult life these once adaptive defences start creating problems of their own. Like nightmares, intrusive recollections of the event acting as if or feeling that the event is recurring, alternating with memory lapses, anxiety problems with relationships because of the earlier detachment, to name just a few.

Which is why specialists working on the subject of Child Sexual Abuse now strongly feel that an adult victim of Child Sexual Abuse should 'grow up' while healing. There should be renewal, and then the person should move on. To be identified as a complete person rather than as just a survivor or a victim of Child Sexual Abuse.

Here, from *Recollecting Our Lives*, Dr Shekhar Seshadri presents the exit cycle, or how to reclaim the self.

It is four steps to self-acceptance, an absolute resolution of all the consequences that stemmed from that sexual abuse in childhood. Adults reading this, who have been sexually abused in childhood, may feel free to start work on any of the four steps first, just please remember to work on all four aspects.

- Empowerment.

The sexual abuse was not my fault. I can shed the guilt and shame; they are his, not mine. I did the best I could as a child living under those conditions. I am remarkable for having endured that abuse and its consequences.

- Survival skills.

I can be myself to myself and others. These survival skills have helped me to survive. Now I can choose which ones to keep or change and which to put aside.

- Clarity.

I was sexually abused. I can separate out who I am

from what I have thought and felt about myself because of being abused. I have personal rights. I have the right to set and enforce boundaries and limits. I trust my perceptions. I am much more than a sexual abuse survivor.

- Self-awareness.

I value and use my thoughts and feelings. I can make mistakes; everyone does. I can learn new things and be flexible. I appreciate myself.

And from these four of the exit cycle which reclaims the self, comes:

- Self-acceptance.

I know myself. I like who I am. I respect myself for having gone through the abuse(s) of my childhood. I am strong and able to learn and change when I want or need to. I deserve to be loved and respected by others.

Exit.

Exeunt. To quietly exult.

Dr Rani Raote sums it up with, 'The honest attempt should be to work towards self-worth, and this is applicable for everyone, irrespective of whether they have been traumatized or not. In the final analysis self-worth is what a person should possess; and self-worth is that which takes the longest to achieve. Women who have been sexually abused in childhood have a lot of trouble with self-worth. Until there is an active working towards self-worth, adults— and those who have been sexually abused in childhood are no exception—will try and lock themselves into labels; they will give themselves labels which, though unflattering, will sound familiar to them. They will feel familiar with these spaces, and this familiarity will make them feel that they are comfortable.'

This can have alarming consequences. Like the mother

who, while sorting out the laundry to put into the washing machine, saw blood on her son's underwear. She did nothing, said nothing, she was paralyzed in a familiar space, she was in complete denial. Her children grew, her teenaged son one day had a roaring fight with his father, his younger sister overheard. And discovered that their father had been sexually abusing both of them. To his son the father would say, 'You want to make me do it to her instead?' To his daughter the father would say, 'Let me do it to you otherwise I will do it to your brother.' The sister went in for therapy as an adult, she benefited from it; the brother went in for therapy, he abandoned it thereafter.

There is absolutely no age for beginning to heal; Dr Rani Raote has a woman who came in to heal at fifty-seven years of age. She came with depression, a sense of futility and alienation, a relationship problem with her dysfunctional husband. Sessions revealed that she had been sexually abused by their family's trusted male servant when she was seven years old, he kept abusing her till he left, when she was twelve years of age. Her most vivid memory of this, an apparently unconnected one. Eyes. She recalled the driver's eyes, as she was being driven to school by him: sitting in the backseat, she would find his eyes on him, he would be adjusting the rear-view mirror so that he could see her, look at her, mock-undress her with his eyes.

Those eyes; their violation.

This fifty-seven-year-old lady is better now, and better equipped to manage her dysfunctional husband without being sucked into it.

'Blockers' is what this lady is called by the psychiatrists and therapists—shrinks as these specialists are also affectionately nicknamed since they are supposed to scale down the magnitude of the problem.

Blockers are those trapped in their survival cycles but

having completely blocked out the reason why. They come in for help later in their lives, in the late-thirties, mid-forties, fifties and sixties; they come because they do not like themselves the way they are, they cannot understand why they are like that but sub-consciously they know something is not right; in fact, it is terribly wrong. Typically speaking, blockers go with the following symptoms to see their shrinks. These have been identified in three sub-groups by Helen Sheldon in 1988 for the *British Journal of Psychiatry* as:

- depression, anxiety, sleeping difficulties, eating disorders, self-harm, alcohol and drug dependency
- a feeling of isolation, alienation, distrust, fear of men, repeated victimization in adult relationships and difficulties in relationships with their own children
- avoiding sex, or on the other hand, promiscuity, prostitution.

What would you do if such a blocker was your friend and she, or he, had the kind of 'flashback' which the lady had about the driver's eyes in front of you?

This may sound incredible but the blocker has come to you and spoken because she is ready to heal. Flashbacks are a very important part of healing.

What will you do?

You will really have to see if this blocker needs professional counselling. She, or he, may not. But if she, or he, does, you would be a friend if you found her a counsellor and then went along with her. Adult survivors of contact or hard-spectrum Child Sexual Abuse need specialized handling because it is, at once, about the adult and the child in that adult. Please do not try any pop psychology, and please do not take her to any support group of which you may be a part. There is a very real danger of her becoming dependant on the support group and seeing it as an end unto itself instead of one of the means to an end. Besides, no matter how enabling your support group is to you, it is not the exit route for a victim of Child Sexual Abuse even if the head of the support group has been sexually abused herself, or himself, in childhood. Adult victims of Child Sexual Abuse need one-to-one counselling and they need it by people who have been trained to handle the subject.

Meanwhile, listen to this friend, just listen to her without judging her. A thought is going to filter through your mind if she tells you the building's lift man sexually abused her—yeah right, so what was she doing when the lift man was lifting her uniform? She was in terror, that was what was happening, this child in a lift whose door glides shut and the lift starts going down into this dark chute of a tall building and she is trapped in a small metal cage with a man who senses that she can be comfortably victimized, or re-victimized since that happens to a lot of children. He can smell her fear, no one can hear her silent scream.

So don't judge, just listen. This may be the very first time she is disclosing her secret even if she does it almost dispassionately. There are so many very silent victims of Child Sexual Abuse in India today who need someone to hold their hand and point out that it is now safe, that what happened was in the past. That it was not their fault. Repeat it to them: it was not your fault. If you think you can assist them, until you can get them to a good counsellor, please stretch your imagination. You may find it very difficult to believe some of the things which will be said.

And prepare yourself to witness great pain; once the floodgates have opened and the victim begins talking, you will be submerged under overpowering pain.

•   ## to the victim

Are you being flooded with memories right now yourself? Are you an adult victim of Child Sexual Abuse who has never spoken to anyone before this? You are not alone, this book proves it to you. And you understand now that it was not your fault, don't you; it was not your fault at all.

Perhaps you have come till this page with enormous anger, that this has happened to you possibly because your abuser might have been abused himself or herself. Perhaps you are disturbed that this is an attempt to show up your perpetrator in a 'humane' light.

It is not.

Be rest assured that your perpetrator, even if he or she has been sexually abused as a child, is still slime; he is absolutely despicable. What the perpetrator does, no matter what the cause, is not right; nothing justifies Child Sexual Abuse, nothing exonerates a child's abuser.

What you could do, instead, is please think of those truly special men and women who have been sexually abused in childhood, who are not sexually abusing children in turn. They may be reading this book alongside you. As would those people who fortunately for them have never been scalded by Child Sexual Abuse nor would they ever even think of sexually abusing children. These are all good people; please remember—even as you hurt as much as you do—that our country is still a safe place for children because of such good people.

Do you have anyone whom you can turn to right now—a good friend of either sex perhaps whom you would like to talk to before you decide whether you want to see a counsellor? If you have no one at all, for the moment try deep breathing. Very deep breathing, like in yoga, will help; pranayama, this breathing is called, is a life force. Books and cassettes are available on the subject; for this moment you can simply breathe out with a hiss from your nostrils while keeping your mouth closed; then breathe in with another audible sound. When you breathe out, your tummy should go inside, when you breathe in, your tummy should come out as your lungs fill with oxygen. Please do this very slowly, you might feel dizzy otherwise.

If you are alone, it is perfectly all right, nothing can harm you. If you have people around you, that is all right too. But if you have suddenly come in as a blocker, please create an additional small space in your home for yourself. Just a special chair in a special place, a colourful cushion which you like, anything; this is your safety space which you must use as the memories start. At this point, you must start watching your intake of cigarettes and alcohol. Feel equally free to start dropping what is not essential in your life, this includes unsupportive people who have always vexed your spirit. Pray, not too hard, just simple mental chats with God; and soon enough this too will pass because your most frightening thoughts of today will by tomorrow be those of yesterday. And tomorrow will not be the same as it is right now.

Child psychologists suggest the write-it-down or draw-it-out technique. There is much healing power in the written word, several children as also adults are known to disclose their sexual abuse by writing it down. Write about that experience as it happened; you smelt cigarette on his breath, write about it; you heard the television in the next room, write that too; put down every sensory detail you can remember. Write as much as you want, write as little as you want. Write it from the middle, from the end, from the beginning. If you don't remember completely what happened, write what you do remember. You will come to parts that are too difficult or too painful, try and write them down. If it is still too difficult, write that you cannot write it. If you write for too long and start to ramble, bring yourself back gently. Write for as long as you want, take as many breaks as you want. Take as long as you want.

Now go away from what you have written.

Come back later, some other day, some other time.

Add to it if you want, do not cut out anything you have already written.

Do you think you have got it all down? No? Take some more time, complete it.

Then burn it. Burn all of it, a nice little bonfire of that which bothered you so much.

If you have decided to speak to a friend about it, that's fine; you suffered alone as a child, you do not have to do it again. But please remember that you need to speak to someone who will listen to you, as in really listen. So when you are considering whether to speak or not, or whom to speak to, ask yourself the following questions:

- does this person care for and respect me?
- does this person have my well-being in mind?
- is this someone I have been able to discuss feelings with before?
- do I trust this person?
- do I feel safe with this person?

Once you have chosen, tell this friend that there is something personal and vulnerable that you want to share. Ask when is a good time to talk, point out that you need a little time, not a mere five minutes between appointments. When you do talk, feel free to tell your friend whether you want to be asked questions, whether you want advice or not, whether you just want to talk, talk, talk for now. And tell your friend this is in confidence; if you decide that other people should know, you will choose the time and person.

Talk. Talk to your friend. Liberate yourself from an environment which encourages silence—specially from women and children—as culturally correct.

Talk and you will find that such telling can be transformative, even for the non-blockers. Ellen Bass and Laura Davis in their book *The Courage to Heal* point out why:

- you move through the shame and secrecy that keeps you isolated
- you move through denial and acknowledge the truth of your abuse
- you make it possible to get understanding and help
- you get more in touch with your feelings
- you get a chance to see your experience, and yourself, through the compassionate eyes of a supporter
- you make space in relationships for the kind of intimacy that comes from honesty
- you establish yourself as a person in the present who is dealing with the abuse in her, or his, past
- you join a courageous community of women, and men, who are no longer willing to suffer in silence
- you help end Child Sexual Abuse by breaking the silence in which it thrives
- you, eventually, feel proud and strong

While you talk, get angry. That's another culturally incorrect construct in our country: women must not get angry. Anger is the backbone of healing, go ahead and get angry. But please differentiate between physical anger, verbal anger, abusive anger and the one you really want—healing anger. Direct your anger accurately and appropriately at the person who violated you. Often anger gets directed at parents, specially mothers, because they are seen as the greatest of betrayers; you feel that your sexual abuse happened because they were collusive, contributing, weak, passive, withholding or inattentive. Maybe they were, and you need to work that out within you too; it is not only your right that you express and validate those feelings but it is also an essential part of your healing. However, unless your parents were your actual abusers, please do not direct all of your anger towards them. Remember, the abuser holds—always, always holds—the ultimate responsibility for your sexual abuse when you were a child. Thus it is he, or she, who deserves your legitimate anger.

When you think about your abuser and allow yourself to get angry, you will be filled with seething anger; if you observe yourself carefully, you might also find it to be destructive anger. You do not need destructive anger; you have been through enough destruction. Deal constructively with your anger by doing any, or all, of the following to heal:

- talk, talk, speak, talk, speak to a good friend
- try the writing technique described above
- then create an anger ritual with what you wrote, burn it; or tear it into tiny, then tinier bits
- go for a long, brisk walk
- join exercise classes, and visualize yourself punching and kicking the abuser while you do these exercises
- dance, at home, in the disco, at parties; dance an anger dance like a Shiva taandav

Feel free to create your own outlets for your anger; some have even broken old dishes and felt better. Just remember at all times that your expressions of anger need to be positive ones.

If you decide that you must eventually see a professionally-trained counsellor, please choose one who has worked with Child Sexual Abuse cases. Please do not place your trust in those who have not worked with adult or child victims of Child Sexual Abuse. Even if they have been sexually abused in their childhood themselves. And please do not feel the need to talk about it in front of groups, you are not a member of the Alcoholics Anonymous which encourages men to stand up and admit they have been wrong. That technique works very well for alcoholics because they have, indeed, been wrong. You are not. 'Non-specialized counselling can do a lot more damage,' points out Anita Ratnam who works with college students all over the country on different aspects of Child Sexual Abuse.

If the abuser is still around, healing is not about settling scores with him or her. Healing is for one's self. However, there is a very recent case where confronting the abuser has been followed through with family support and it has made all the difference to the victim. Kalindi Muzumdar who has been working with Child Sexual Abuse cases since a while handled this case where there was a 'confrontation' between a twenty-five-year-old victim and her seventy-year-old perpetrator.

The victim and her friends, three of them, would go to the fourth friend's house as children at Mumbaii's Marine Drive. This was when they were all around ten years old. The grandfather of the house sexually abused every one of them, except his own granddaughter. This happened regularly. It took fifteen years for one of the victims to disclose this to an adult although all the victims spoke of it, in hushed tones, among themselves as little girls.

After a lot of preparatory work with Kalindi Muzumdar, the twenty-five-year-old told her parents about her Child Sexual Abuse. Her parents were supportive.

'What can we do now to help you? We very much

want to help you,' they said.

The girl spoke to her friend whose grandfather had abused her. Her friend chose not to believe her.

'Ask our other friends whether he did it to them or not,' said the girl to her friend.

Slowly, the friend did. The other girls said yes, it is true, but we don't want to have anything to do with it now that we are older and leading our own lives.

The friend spoke to her family, they would not believe her. But she stood convinced.

A family meeting was called and the girl was invited, her family was prepared to go with her but she preferred to do it alone. She walked into the home where she had been sexually abused as a child and stood in front of the grandfather as he sat there, surrounded by his family.

'I am sorry,' he said. 'I am deeply sorry for what I did to all of you little girls.'

The girl is healed today. As is the woman who went and spat on her father's grave because he had sexually abused her when she was young. Both these women bear scars, of course, but a scar is the best indication that a wound is no longer open and bleeding, it has closed because of the healing.

Such confrontations with perpetrators don't always go off so well, in fact they do not go well at all. The abuser has done what he wanted to, a long time ago; he is not likely to confirm it should you confront him now. Certainly you can—specially if you feel other children can get hurt by him—tell your family and his. This would be disclosure. Do not confuse disclosure with confrontation; you might even find that disclosure is more than enough.

Making a disclosure in the family, if a family member has sexually abused you as a child, is very tough. Please make the decision to disclose to an entire family, or one member of it, only after you are very sure that you are strong enough to do so. Remember to expect nothing from it, the family might well go on treating your abuser like before. You will need to feel very stable, very centred, very cool and collected when you are doing this disclosing because you might not be believed. Or there might be no reaction at all, it might be as if you said nothing at all of any consequence. On the other hand, there might be a situation where several parts of the family may simply stop talking to you, they might start excluding you from family gatherings. Are you strong enough; are you working on making yourself strong enough that what you disclose is by far the most important thing than any negative reaction?

If your abuser is not a family member, the disclosure within your family and his will be much easier. As will the confrontation, but you really need not bother with it. What will you get at the maximum from a confrontation? What can he do to set right what he has already so badly wronged? You will not be able to send him to jail; it is too late for that. You will get an acknowledgement of responsibility; you already know your abuser to be him. You will get an admission that what you say is true; you already know it to be true. You will get a change in the relationship; you have already instituted that change with your disclosure to yourself and the families. What you might get, which you have not got till now, is an apology; can you be certain that the man is apologizing from his heart, that he really feels sorry for what he did and that he understands what he did to be wrong?

There are not all that many international studies done on perpetrators; the few existing ones find themselves as up against a stone wall when it comes to the crunch: getting the man to feel sorry. Getting them to say sorry is no problem, it is a social demand for that moment and the abuser simply goes with the flow to get out of the sticky situation he finds himself in. Getting the abuser to really feel sorry—so that they do not do it again—does not quite work that way.

It does not even work when they come out of good therapy. There is a teacher, declared cured by one of the best psychiatrists in the city, who simply went back to buggering little boys in suburban Mumbaii schools; the man had also sworn on his religious beliefs as also his child's head that he would never, ever, do it again. And there is this father, who sexually abused his daughter, who told counsellor Kalindi Muzumdar, 'I did it because it was all right to do it, and it is all right to do it because Brahma did it. Brahma also fell in love with his daughter, he created Lakshmi and kept turning to look at her which is why he has three heads.' It made no difference to the abuser that what he was citing was not history but mythology. 'It is about the gods,' he insisted. He was equally indifferent that he was looking at it incorrectly, he did not care that there is nothing in mythology to support his distorted view. Sounds familiar, doesn't it, even from adult situations?

What, in the final analysis, is a person who perpetrates Child Sexual Abuse?

He is a bastard.

What worth can a bastard's apology have?

So why would you yearn for an apology from a bastard?

Instead, concentrate your energies on that person who is special and worth your attention: yourself; and your own healing.

•   healing by yourself

Perhaps you are one of those healing on your own, with no disclosure, no assistance, nothing at all and the minimum of fuss.

You are brave. You are strong. And you are, quietly, a role model for many.

Like Meera, who is also healing on her own. Meera has taken a conscious decision towards natural healing; each time she looks within, she mends.

Meera laughs when this slight adaptation of an African lullaby is read out to her on the phone:

> Hush, little baby; don't say a word,
> Mumma's going to buy you a mockingbird.
> And if that mockingbird don't sing,
> Dadda's going to find you a wedding ring.
> And if that golden ring turns to brass,
> Baby can get herself a looking glass.

'How slight is this adaptation?' she asks.

Very slight, baby and daddy are interchangeable for mummy; the irony laced with bitterness would remain intact.

Meera is healing in her own way, through a very quiet if scarring process. And now she is trying to make very sure that her daughter does not need to scar. Meera is an Ahmedabad housewife and recently had to bring up the topic of Child Sexual Abuse with her politician-husband. Her husband was insistent that she let their seven-year-old daughter go for a weekend to their friend's house in another city.

'But we don't know what other kind of people will be there,' said Meera softly.

'What do you mean?' growled the husband.

'Please humour me,' she replied, 'please sit down and listen to what I am saying.'

The husband sat down, lit his cigarette, closed his eyes to humour her.

'Imagine your little girl watching her favourite cartoon programme on television. A hand gently pats her little thigh. The hand travels, still very gently, to the upper part of her body to check on her development. The hand comes back to her thigh and fingers slowly crawl into her frilly knickers.'

Meera's husband opened his eyes and looked at her with hostility. 'What kind of a mother are you to think such things of your daughter? You are disgusting. These things don't happen in good homes.'

'Yes,' said his wife so very quietly that he almost did not hear her. 'These things do happen in our homes.'

A woman three bungalows down had spoken to Meera of her trauma. Her husband's male friend had sexually abused their own daughter. They would send their child to play with the daughter of the friend, over to their house, and the man had been using his fingers. He had also exposed himself to the little girl often and tried to get her to hold him as he masturbated. We are playing a game, he kept telling her, Vasco da Gama took off his pyjama and pulled out his banana.

'Vasco da Gama,' said the little girl at the dinner table one day and completely out-of-the-blue as the mother served banana custard to their guests as dessert, 'took off his pyjama and pulled out his banana.'

There was a small silence at the dinner table and then the father asked, very loudly, 'Who taught you that?'

The child would not answer.

'Tell me who taught you that or I will slap you hard!' said the father.

214

The child raised her finger and pointed to the father's friend.

The friend quickly laughed, he looked at his own wife at the dinner table who looked stunned, and said, 'Can you believe this? I was telling you about the terrible poems the children pick up and she memorized it!'

The man then, as quickly, turned to the child's father and laughed a lot as he said, 'You better watch it my friend, your daughter is growing up to be quite a chutputtee.'

Chutputtee. Chaalu. Cheez. All the words men use in ostensible derision but always with that gleam of desire in their eyes.

The man, owner of an advertising agency, continues to be the father's friend.

Meera's husband said their daughter need not go.

Meera has not told her husband about her own experience because she does not think he is man enough to truly understand. She says this without any bitterness or rancour. She is currently visiting a child counsellor because she truly wants to understand how she can give her daughter the intrinsic freedom a son automatically attains. She muses, 'We talk a lot about women's empowerment these days. But financial strength is not emotional strength, is it? And how would we, ourselves as women, react if our daughter says she wants an Aids-free certificate from the boy who has chosen to marry her through an arranged match?'

Meera had been sexually abused as a child by her male cousin. He had systematically abused several girls in their extended family, fondling them heavily whenever he could. When Meera said she would tell her mother, the cousin laughed, 'Rape toh nahin kiya na? Did not rape any of you, did I?' To the girls the women of the family said, 'Hush, do not tell anyone and don't go near him in the future.'

The cousin mocked the girls by undressing them with his eyes at family functions.

Mummy brought them a mockingbird.

The girls were duly married off.

Daddy got them wedding rings.

Two of these girls could not bear to let their husbands touch them, eventually their marriages broke down. 'It's all your fault,' said their husbands and parents.

The girls had to get themselves a looking glass.

•   siddharth

Siddharth	Twelve years	Pune

Will Siddharth grow to be able to heal on his own? Or does Siddharth need counselling? And is he likely to turn into a perpetrator himself? Right now he is in Pune, attending school and playing cricket like any other boy; but on some days something bad creeps into his mind and he can be found alternating between bewilderment and dread.

Siddharth comes during the summer holidays from Pune to Mumbaii to visit his grandparents. It is summer holidays now and the school near his grandparents' house has organized a one-week personality development course by Otto Sir who comes every year to teach the six to fourteen-year-old boys. This year Siddharth's parents have enrolled him for it, after checking with the other Bandra and nearby Khar schools where Otto Sir runs similar classes.

It feels strange to come to such a quiet school, and even a little exciting. All the classrooms are empty, the long hallways deserted, the bell completely silent. Otto Sir is conducting the personality development course in the classroom at the back, near the staff room. There are forty-two children in his personality development class, Siddharth knows some of them, they all stand up when Otto Sir comes into the class.

Otto Sir talks to them about the importance of meditation and he shows them how to do it. On the second day Otto Sir asks them to begin the class with the meditation techniques he taught them yesterday.

'Take off your sandals, shoes and socks. Leave them by the side of your desks.' The children are only too happy to oblige. 'Close your eyes,' says Otto Sir, 'and relax. Relax. Put your head on the desk if you want. Does not matter if you fall asleep. Relax. Take a deep breath and relax. Does not matter if you shout during your meditation. Some times children see lovely flowers and birds when meditating, they shout happily. Sometimes children see dragons, they also shout. Shout if you want, Otto Sir will not scold you, it is an important part of your personality development.'

Siddharth screws his eyes tight and tries to meditate. He thinks of a bright bird he can bring to his mind, the bird refuses to come. Siddharth screws his eyes tighter.

He starts, gets frightened when he feels a hand on his shoulder.

'Shh, it is me, son,' says Otto Sir. 'You are having trouble meditating, I see. Come with me, shh, do not disturb the other children, walk softly, no, no, do not wear your shoes.'

Siddharth goes with Otto Sir to the staffroom where sheets of newspapers have been spread on the big table.

'Here son,' whispers Otto Sir, 'you can lie down on the table and concentrate on your meditation.'

Siddharth is helped onto the table by Otto Sir and lies down, screwing his eyes tight once again, trying to bring the bird to his mind. Otto Sir goes to the classroom, closes that door and comes back.

'Take off your shirt and pant, son. It will help you meditate. Here, turn around, sleep on your stomach, it is the best way to meditate.'

Siddharth feels hands on his buttocks, separating the cheeks, he moves.

'Shh. You will disturb the other children. They are already meditating, you can ask them afterwards how easily they are developing their personalities. But you have to work harder. Now relax. Just relax.'

Siddharth feels something hot, hard, pressing into him; it is like, like, it's like the handle of his cricket bat. But why is Otto Sir putting the cricket bat-handle . . .

Siddharth feels pain. Like an avalanche of poison-tipped arrows.

Siddharth shouts.

'Shh. Over, over, over.'

Siddharth feels something sticky, squishy, through his haze of pain and semi-consciousness.

Siddharth feels Otto Sir wiping him with the paper, it scrapes.

'Now you lie down here for some time while I see to the other children.'

Siddharth does not remember anything after that, why he came home early, when he slipped off the table, quietly put on his clothes, how he got home. His memory is one of feeling more secure, curled up on his grandfather's knee and putting his nose right into his grandfather's kurta so that he could feel comforted by the familiar, warm, loving smell.

Then everybody took him to his grandfather's doctor-friend's hospital where they put medicine in his bum because it was burning very badly.

Now it is not burning so much.

But everyone is still coming home to talk in whispers and grandfather and father are whispering back. Mummy is suddenly crying and suddenly hugging Siddharth and on the phone when she is talking to her friends, she is cursing Otto Sir and saying, 'Why my son? Were there no other children to pick on?'

One lady has come, with a video cameraman. Grandfather's tone has become loud, Siddharth has been sent away into the bedroom and he can hear him from there.

'No I do not wish to say anything and you cannot take pictures of a minor . . . Please ask your cameraman to leave my house . . . We are deeply disturbed by what has happened, we want to be left alone . . . No we will not be filing a police complaint because our child will be harassed in court and he will be doubly wounded . . . Why should you insist on only speaking to me, go and talk to the parents of the fifty other boys he has been doing this to since the last six years, they are all in Bandra and Khar schools, why have those parents not complained, it is not possible that they do not know . . . Why should I mind if the parents beat him up black and blue . . . Do you know that the principals of the schools are saying since we are not filing a police complaint, they cannot stop him from coming to the schools . . . Why don't you ask the principals of these schools why they have not done anything till now? No, you cannot meet my grandchild, please leave my house right now.'

Siddharth's summer vacation is over, he has come back to Pune, school has long since begun. His best friends in Pune are asking him all the time what happened to him in Mumbaii, but Siddharth is not telling them because his grandfather and mother have made him promise that he will not say anything.

When he comes to Mumbaii for a weekend for a religious function in the family, his best friend in Mumbaii tells him, 'My daddy was telling my mummy that they went again and beat up Otto Sir in his house. His daughter was crying like anything and Otto Sir's wife was also crying because she had many marks on her face and hands.'

Why are they beating up Otto Sir all the time?

Siddharth's grandfather says, 'Because he is not a good man.'

Why is he not a good man?

Siddharth's mother says, 'Because he used to beat his wife and do horrible things to his own brother also.'

What horrible things?

'Hush. Just horrible things.'

Will they beat him more and lots and lots?

Siddharth's father says, giving him a hug, 'Now they won't need to beat him because we have made sure he leaves Mumbaii. He has sold his house and shifted with his family to Bangalore.'

We will also go to Bangalore?

'Hush!'

Bombay High Court advocate Raju Zunzarrao Moray hears of the incident, he lives in Bandra, he knows Siddharth's family, he knows the parents and guardians who have bashed up Otto Sir; he speaks with everyone concerned, those who thrashed him say they had to do something to stop the man since the boy's parents and grandparents were not willing to do anything about it. Privately, Raju Moray agrees, this would certainly be one effective way of dealing with such a swine; but it is not the final solution and so he phones Siddharth's uncle.

'You must,' urges advocate Raju Moray of Siddharth's

uncle, 'go to the police. It is imperative. I will be there with you, as a concerned parent it is my duty to help you. Come, let us go to the police together.'

No, says Siddharth's family, never.

Here Raju Moray perforce lets the matter rest; until his own son comes home and tells him and his wife Shweta something that makes his blood run cold. Their son tells them that his school is organizing a one-week personality development course by one Otto Sir.

Raju Moray speaks to the principal of his son's school and puts his foot down as a parent, no Otto Sir in this school, not for one week, not for a minute.

The principal replies, 'On what grounds do I stop it? On allegations from parents of another school which they refuse to act on?'

Advocate Moray thinks quickly. 'You stop it,' he tells the principal, 'or else there might be a picket by some concerned parents right outside the school's gate. These parents will inform the Press about their picket which will surely come to cover such a protest. I don't think a picket of this kind has been organized anywhere in the country, by parents and outside schools, for such a reason before. Think about it, the national Press will cover it with great enthusiasm.'

The principal does not need time to think, 'Okay,' he says very quickly, 'consider the personality development course by Otto Sir as withdrawn. But what do I tell him?'

'Tell him he is a bastard,' says Raju Zunzarrao Moray firmly. 'Yes, tell him that he is a bastard of the highest order to be doing this to defenceless children, that too in the name of something sacred like teaching. And yes, tell him this as well, that I am writing to the police commissioner about him.'

He does, on 8 June 1999, detailing the entire incident which took place with Siddharth on 25 May 1999.

The letter is hand delivered. The receiving clerk at the police commissioner's office says that such a letter must be made to 'the proper authority'.

'So you are telling me that the police commissioner, as the highest police officer of any city, is not the proper authority for all criminal matters?'

The sarcasm is lost, as is the letter in the haze of time.

In September 1999 the Supreme Court of India judges in another case that all complaints to any police station or police official have to be addressed by those officials. In other words, all of you in the police are meant to work for the good of the citizens of India, if any one citizen approaches you with a problem, you are henceforth deemed as the proper authority to deal with it.

On 25 October 1999, Raju Zunzarrao Moray gets a visitor from the police station near his residence.

The police officer tells him, 'Your complaint to the police commissioner has come to us. We were well aware of the incident but no one came forward to register it as a case. This is the first written complaint on the matter, so you are our First Informant. Therefore, we will have to start our investigations with you first.'

All right, is Raju Moray's reaction, but then what.

'After investigating you, we will investigate everyone else.'

'Okay,' says Raju Moray, 'but just remember that I was not an eyewitness to even the boy who came home hurt. You need to speak with the boy's family.'

'We will.'

A doubt flicks in Raju Moray's mind. 'By now the boy has gone back to Pune. Suppose his family here says nothing of the sort happened.'

'Then it will be assumed that you have made a false complaint.'

'What absolute nonsense!'

'Not nonsense; it is a serious matter to make a false complaint.'

'But it is not a false complaint.'

'If you cannot prove it, it is; also, then you have no business to unnecessarily clutter up our files and cause us unnecessary hardship.'

Raju Moray re-starts the conversation, 'Listen, let us assume—correctly, since I know what they have decided—that the boy's grandfather says that there was no incident. Then what?'

'Then we will call you to the police station to question you on why you filed a false complaint.'

'But it is not . . . oh all right, then what happens?'

'Then we will call you, and we will call you again for questioning, as and when the need arises.'

'I have to go to court you know, I have to be available for my clients and my practise. You should at least tell me when you would call me, I cannot come in the mornings, I can after court during the evenings. And, obviously, I see no reason to come every day to simply sit in the police station.'

'Then it is better you write a letter saying you are withdrawing your complaint so that we can close the file.'

'But you have not even opened a case file till now because no case has been filed. Where is the question of closing an un-opened file?'

'These are technical matters; better you just say in a letter you are withdrawing your complaint.'

The complaint is withdrawn, a letter to this effect delivered to the police station who accept it as the proper authority to do so; as proof they even stamp a copy of the letter as 'received'.

The receiving clerk firmly presses the rectangular

wooden block into the padded ink box, he lifts it, he brings it down on the copy of the letter; he stamps it with finality.

Thup!

Otto Sir is now free to teach the male children of India anything, anywhere in the country.

There is another African saying, a proverb this time: to raise a child it takes a village.

An entire village was ready this time to support a child called Siddharth.

But the centre of a child's life is its parents.

And the centre of a parent's life has to be the natural laws, and the laws of the land.

Siddharth's centre could not hold because the laws of the land did not hold; the legal process would not truly assist his distraught parents.

And when no centre holds, things begin to fall apart: villages too.

Innocent Siddharth. Alternating between bewilderment and dread.

Frightened Siddharth. Future perpetrator, perpetuator?

That little boy in Pune, playing cricket, going to school, is he okay? Can he, ever, be okay?

So many little boys like Siddharth in India. Are they identifying with their aggressor to the extent that they think all teachers are 'like that', will they grow and be a teacher 'like that' themselves? Will they grow with sexual identity confusion and become homosexual; or will they grow, marry and do it to their children? Are they getting nightmares right now; do they need counselling? Will they—as they grow—do things to the little boys in their school? Their neighbouring children who visit their home to play with them? Will they lie in wait to also do things to their little girl cousins when they meet them at weddings and other family functions? Or will they go to their homes and do it?

Is that why Razia's cousin sexually abused her in her own home, because he too had once been in Siddharth's place?

Or did he just do it to Razia, and her sister, because no parent stopped him?

●   **r a z i a**

Razia   **Thirteen years**   **Hyderabad**

She insists she is being continuously sexually molested by her male cousin when he visits their home.

Her ammee says, 'He is my very own sister's son. You should be ashamed of yourself for saying this.'

Razia comes to her ammee again and insists.

'Keep quiet or I shall tell your abba who will beat you up for talking such rubbish, then he will stop you from going to your painting classes on Sundays.'

Razia comes to her ammee once again and says the same thing. Her male cousin sexually abuses her each time he visits their home; she threatens to tell her parents and he laughs to her face.

'Look at you,' says her ammee, 'just look at you. All skin and bone, why would he even want to touch you? Your elder sister was beautiful before we got her married last year, if he was so bad, would he have not done something to her instead?'

'He has,' replies Razia.

'You are so shameless, first you want to spoil your cousin brother's name and now you want to ruin your sister's marriage.'

'He has, she told me on her wedding day.'

'Why did she tell you?'

'She wanted me to know that now that she was not in the house anymore, he would do all those dirty things with me.'

'Have you told her anything after that?'

'No.'

'Good girl, at least you have some sense to keep the family's izzat.'

Razia asks of her ammee, 'Don't you want to know why she did not tell you?'

'Hush.'

'I want to tell you, she said she did not tell you because you would not believe it since he is your sister's son.'

'Hush, I said.'

Razia begins menstruating. Razia's ammee visits her sister in Secunderabad and tells her what has been happening to her daughters.

'Hush,' says Razia's ammee's sister to her, looking around quickly to see if her mother-in-law has heard. She lowers her voice to a whisper, 'Men are men, what can we tell them? And even if we tell them, can they control themselves? You know, and I know, what every girl goes through. So it is better you keep an eye on Razia in the house and tell her not to excite him.'

Razia's ammee tells Razia that she should make sure he does not put his thing into her thing otherwise a baby will be born.

Razia laughs, she laughs so much that her bony body doubles over with the convulsions, 'Will you,' she asks, gasping for breath between the shouts of laughter, 'stand there and make sure it does not happen? I don't see how I can. If I do, there will be commotion and if there is noise abba will beat me up and stop my painting classes.'

Razia's ammee tells Razia's abba that their daugher now runs the risk of getting pregnant.

'Pregnant? Pregnant! Where have you been all this time? What have you been doing? Why have you let matters get till here? What kind of third-rate family do you come from where the men don't know how to respect their own sisters? Why did you not tell me earlier? So that you could protect your third-rate sister and her family? What kind of blood runs in your family's veins, this is disgusting! Now I will have to sort out this matter which has been started by your family.'

Razia's abba sends for the male cousin and confronts him. 'Tumney hamarey khandaan key izzat pey haath dala hain.'

No, denies the cousin, he has never done anything to spoil the khandaan's izzat.

'How dare you suggest that my daughter is lying?'

'She is your family,' says the cousin, 'I do not wish to comment on how she has been brought up. But I will say this, even at the risk of incurring your wrath for which I beg your forgiveness. If I were such a horrible man should there not have been a similar complaint from your elder, beautiful, daughter?'

'Are you daring to suggest that my daughter is imagining all this because she is plain?'

'It is not for me to comment on your family. But, again, I risk your wrath. I can give you some instances of when I have visited your home and your younger daughter has stuck to me like a leech, crying all the while that she wants me to marry her.'

'You liar!'

'I swear that she has said I must marry her.'

'You swear?'

'I swear.'

Razia's abba is silent for a while and then he sighs. 'I have to beg of you not to come here again.'

'It will be as you wish,' says the cousin. 'And again, at the risk of incurring your wrath I must say this, there are other male cousins who come into this house as well. Perhaps they too should be stopped so that they do not suffer the humiliation I just did.'

Razia's ammee asks her the next morning as she breakfasts before leaving for her painting class, 'Tell me the truth. Did he ever do those things to you?'

'Yes, he did.'

'But he has sworn that he has done nothing, it is you who has flung herself on him.'

Razia turns hard-as-stone eyes on her mother. 'You only listen to what you want to.'

'Razia! Swear that you are not lying.'

'I swear it.'

'Say swear, say I swear on all that we hold holy.'

'I swear on Allah that it is all true.'

Razia's ammee breaks down and sobs, she holds her crumpled, cotton dupatta in her left palm and covers her wet eyes, 'Who am I to believe when they both swear that they are telling the truth? Please help me, oh God, please help me.'

Razia watches her mother weep for a while. Then she walks away. When she returns from her painting class, she has an as-yet damp sheet of thick white paper on which something has been painted in rough brush strokes. She gives it to her mother in the kitchen and walks away once again.

The mother looks at it, she can make no sense of the painting at all, it looks like some bizarre kind of modern art. Razia's ammee sets it aside, mentally counting the years left before they can legally marry off Razia.

'Did you like my painting?' asks Razia of her ammee at lunch.

'Oh yes, it was very nice. You must spend more time painting than imagining things.'

Razia looks at her abba and asks of him, 'Did you like my painting?'

'Your ammee did not show it to me.'

'Where is it ammee, I want to show it to abba.'

'Later, later, child, let him have his lunch in peace. As it is he gets only one day of rest on Sundays at home and God knows there has been enough tension in the house lately.'

During dusk, Razia approaches her father, 'Abba, did you see my painting?'

'No.'

'Can I show it to you now?'

'Oh, all right.' He is feeling expansive.

Razia's abba holds the large white sheet with both his hands and stares at it.

'What is it, beta, I cannot understand what you have drawn. Surely it would make more sense for you to draw landscapes, or people, and show us your talent?'

'But it is people I have drawn.'

'It is? I cannot see them, beta.'

'Can I explain my painting to you?'

'Okay, but don't take too long, I have to watch the news on television in another five minutes.'

'Painting-teacher said to draw any scene from real-life which has people in it. So I drew from the Hindi picture ammee and I saw long time back in the theatre. The hero marries the heroine because another man has spoilt her. This is their wedding scene, and this is my sister with her husband and they are clapping for the hero and heroine but I am not there.'

'Hush, what are you saying?' hisses Razia's ammee.

'Do you like it abba?' asks Razia, she has not even heard her mother.

'Yes, yes, it is very nice. Next time you must do a landscape. Now go to bed.'

Five months later Razia commits suicide. She throws herself from the top of a neighbouring tall building. She lands with hardly a sound among people going about their business on the road. The post-mortem reveals a three-month old foetus in her broken body.

Children can have two kinds of deaths.

The real one.

And the one later, when they grow up, which people see.

- Ellen Bass and Laura Davis. *The Courage to Heal: A Guide for Women Survivors of Child Sexual Abuse.* HarperCollins, 1994.

The authors weave personal experience with professional knowledge to show the reader how she can come to terms with her past while moving powerfully into the future.

- Ellen Bass and Louise Thornton. *I Never Told Anyone.* Harper & Row, 1983.

Writings by women survivors of Child Sexual Abuse.

- Alice Miller. *Thou Shalt Not Be Aware.* Farrar, Straus, Giroux, 1984.

Society's betrayal of the child.

- Sandra Butler. *Conspiracy of Silence: The Trauma of Incest.* Bantam, 1985.

Feminist analysis of Child Sexual Abuse.

- John Crewsdon. *By Silence Betrayed: Sexual Abuse of Children in America.* Little Brown, 1988.

An award-winning journalist's look at Child Sexual Abuse in America.

- Beatrix Campbell. *Unofficial Secrets: Child Sexual Abuse and the Cleveland Case*. Virago Press, London, 1988.

A British journalist's examination of the 165 cases of Child Sexual Abuse which were diagnosed in the first half of 1987 in Cleveland, Great Britain.

- Allan Levy (ed.), *Focus on Child Abuse: Medical, Legal and Social Work Perspectives in Great Britain*. Hawksmere Ltd, England, 1989

Contributions from a High Court judge, doctors, lawyers, social workers and the police. Includes the recommendations of the Cleveland Report in full.

- Louise De Salvo. *Virginia Woolf: The Impact of Child Sexual Abuse on Her Life and Work*. Ballantine, 1989

Scholarly study of the impact of Woolf's sexual abuse on her living and creativity.

- Louise Armstrong. *Kiss Daddy Goodnight*. Pocket Books, 1987.

The speakout on father-daughter incest which challenges society on its continual.

- Sylvia Fraser. *My Father's House*. Virago, Press, London, 1989.

A beautifully written memoir by this Canadian journalist who for the better part of her life had no recollection of her father's sexual relationship with her as a child. Yet some connection always remained—pain, terror, and guilt were never far beneath the surface. A heart-wrenching and ultimately healing story.

- Ellen Bass and Laura Davis. *Beginning to Heal: A First Book for Survivors of Child Sexual Abuse.* HarperCollins, New York, 1993.

Easy-to-read introduction to the healing process based on their *The Courage to Heal.*

- Sue Blume. *Secret Survivors: Uncovering Incest and Its After Effects in Women.* John Wiley, New York, 1990.

Clearly describes the long-term effects of incest to help survivors discover that their experiences and reactions make sense.

- Patrick Gannon. *Soul Survivors: A New Beginning for Adults Abused as Children.* Prentice Hall, 1989.

A guide which deals with all types of abuse for both women and men. Includes sections for partners and one on parenting.

- Patricia Love. *The Emotional Incest Syndrome.* Bantam, 1990.

What to do when a parent's love rules your life.

- Kathy Evert and Inie Bijerk. *When You're Ready: Sexual Abuse by a Mother.* Launch Press, California, 1988.

A woman's story as she is molested by her mother.

- Kathryn Harrison. *Thicker Than Water.* Random House, 1991.

An account of a girl molested by her mother and raped by her father. Disturbing details.

- Linda Gray Sexton. *Mirror Image.* Doubleday, 1985.

Centres on the healing of a teenage victim of mother-daughter incest.

- Kathleen Fleming. *Lovers in the Present Afternoon.* Naiad Press, Florida, 1984.

Lesbian book deals with incest by a brother.

- Vernon Wiehe. *Sibling Abuse: Hidden Physical, Emotional and Sexual Trauma.* Free Press, New York, 1990.

Addresses this often overlooked and minimized abuse.

- The Troops for Truddi Chase. *When Rabbit Howls.* Dutton, 1987.

Truddi Chase first developed multiple personalities when her stepfather raped her at age two. Written by her numerous selves during therapy, this book shows how the mind copes with the horror of sexual abuse.

- Richard Berendzen. *Come Here: A Man Overcomes the Tragic Aftermath of Childhood Sexual Abuse.* Villard Books, 1993.

This astronomer—who repressed memory of abuse for fifty years—tells his story at the hands of his mother.

- Mic Hunter. *Abused Boys: The Neglected Victims of Sexual Abuse.* Fawcett Books, 1990.

Healing for the man molested as a child.

- Rik Isensee. *Growing up Gay in a Dysfunctional Family.* Prentice Hall, 1991.

Guide for gay men reclaiming their lives after being abused at home as children. Offers specific suggestions for working through problems involved.

- Mike Lew. *Victims No Longer*. Harper & Row, 1988.

For men recovering from incest in childhood. Talks about male survivors as survivors and not potential perpetrators.

- Laura Davis. *Allies in Healing: When the Person You Love Was Sexually Abused as a Child*. HarperCollins, USA, 1991.

A guide for partners who are taking care of themselves and the survivors they love.

- Eliana Gil. *Outgrowing The Pain*. Launch Press, California, 1984.

A book for and about adults abused as children.

- Eliana Gil. *Outgrowing The Pain Together*. Dell Bantam Doubleday, 1992.

For partners and spouses of adults abused as children.

- Geneen Roth. *When Food Is Love: Relationship Between Eating and Intimacy*. Dutton, 1991.

A look at the relationship between compulsive eating, childhood pain and every person's struggle to achieve intimacy.

- Maya Angelou. *I Know Why The Caged Bird Sings*. Bantam, 1980.

A moving portrayal of incest and its effects within a novel which celebrates life.

- Margaret Dickson. *Maddy's Song*. Houghton Mifflin, 1985.

Fiction, beautifully written novel about a girl's struggle to break free from a physically abusive father.

- Toni Morrison. *The Bluest Eye*. Pocket Books, 1970.

Fiction, novel about a young survivor.

- Anna C. Salter. *Transforming Trauma*. Sage Publications, Delhi, 1995.

A Guide to Understanding and Treating Adult Survivors of Child Sexual Abuse

- Bill Gillham. *The Facts About Child Sexual Abuse*. Cassell Educational Ltd., London, 1991.

Basic, and now a trifle outdated, but deft handbook using studies conducted in Great Britain.

- Lorraine Waterhouse (ed.), *Child Abuse and Child Abusers: Protection and Prevention*. Jessica Kingsley Publishers, London, 1996.

- Anne Bannister (ed.), *From Hearing to Healing: Working with the Aftermath of Child Sexual Abuse*. John Wiley & Sons, England, 1998.

- Wattam, Hughes & Blagg (ed.), *Child Sexual Abuse: Listening, Hearing and Validating the Experiences of Children*. John Wiley & Sons, England.

- Parton & Wattam (ed.), *Child Sexual Abuse: Responding to the Experiences of Children*. John Wiley & Sons, England.

- C.B. Drauker. *Counselling Survivors of Child Sexual Abuse*. Sage, Delhi, 1996.

- David Finkelhor. *A Source Book on Child Abuse*. Sage, Delhi, 1986.

- David Finkelhor (ed.), *The Dark Side of Families: Current Family Violence Research*. Sage, Delhi, 1983.

As is evident, the listing below is by no means exhaustive. It lists a select number—among the very few existing ones in the country—of professionals who specialize in the emotional and legal aspects of Child Sexual Abuse in India. The listing also includes professionals—doctors and other mental health workers—who counsel college students and adults who have been sexually abused as children, though this might not be their only area of work. Counselling adults who were victims of Child Sexual Abuse is both, taxing and time-consuming for both, the professional and the patient. Therefore, additional care has been taken to ensure that the professionals recommended are caring and concerned individuals; equally important, these doctors listed say they do not prescribe drugs unless very necessary.

A word of warning here for those who have been sexually abused in childhood and as adults would consider approaching any of those listed for counselling. Since these are specialists, they tend to be overwhelmed with the work load; please do not feel betrayed or any less strong if they put you on a kind of waiting list.

Parents whose children have been sexually abused must also see what they can achieve at home instead of simply rushing the child off to a counsellor. As Anita Ratnam explains it, 'Unless it is a tough or complex case, why should parents not be dealing with it themselves and at home? The problem is in the house, surely the most sensible resolution must also arise from within on what is best for the child?' She gives the example of a persistent flasher. 'Supposing there is a man constantly exposing his genitals to the child outside the school or building. There should be an environment within the house that the child can speak about if it disturbs her or him. Then, the parents while appearing to be natural, should carefully choose words to explain the situation, after which they should take adequate measures against the persistent flasher. Why should it even come to a point where the child is so distraught by this sexual abuser that she, or he, needs professional counselling?'

These are all paid services, each has its own fee structure. They have been listed in alphabetical order according to the city where they are located. All, and more, care has been taken to ensure that only absolutely reliable professionals are mentioned; readers are nevertheless advised to use their own discretion. Neither the Author nor her publishers, Penguin Books India, can be held responsible for any outcome with these professionals.

bangalore

- Dr Shekhar Seshadri, National Institute of Mental Health and Neuro Science, Post Bag Number 2900, Bangalore 560 029. Phone: (area std code: 080) 6642121 e-mail: shekhar@nimhans.kar.nic.in
  Psychiatrist for both, children who have been sexually abused and adults who were sexually abused in childhood, female and male. Also designs preventive programmes, trains in Child Sexual Abuse counselling, conducts workshops for schools, colleges, youth groups and child care agencies on the awareness and preventive aspects of Child Sexual Abuse. Is now also working on gender sensitization programmes like the masculinities

project which helps young men understand what it is to be genuinely male; can be held as workshops for male college students and other interested groups of males in corporations and community clubs.

- Ms Anita Ratnam, Samvada, 303 Rams Infantry Manor, 70 Infantry Road, Bangalore 560 001. Telefax: 5587493 e-mail: samvada@mahiti.org
  Counsels college students who have been sexually abused in childhood. Conducts counselling training for organizations and groups which want to learn how to counsel teenagers who have been—or are being—sexually abused. They travel all over India as also Nepal, Bhutan, Sri Lanka and Pakistan.

calcutta

- Dr Sujit Ghosh, Flat 17, Saptarag, 11/3 Old Ballygunge 2nd Lane, Calcutta 700 019. Telefax: (area std code: 033) 2404145 e-mail: sujitinc@vsnl.com
- Psychiatrist for both adults and children. Female clients are given the choice of professionally consulting his female colleagues who are therapists and counsellors for issues around child sexual abuse.
- Ms Jolly Laha & Ms Rotraut Roychowdhury, Samikshani, 37 Southend Park, Calcutta 700 029. Phone: 466 3504.
  Counsel both adults and children.
- Ms Veena Lakhumalani, Manager—Governance, Social Justice & Health, The British Council, 5 Shakespeare Sarani, Calcutta 700 071. Phone: 282 5370. Fax: 282 4804 e-mail: veena.lakhumalani@in.britishcouncil.org
  Conducts workshops of three-day duration to sensitize teachers and principals of schools and colleges about Child Sexual Abuse. Since so often the child is being abused at home and therefore cannot speak about it in

the house, school and college are where teachers and principals can detect Child Sexual Abuse and quickly intervene to assist the child. Several such workshops have been held in Calcutta schools and colleges. They cover eastern India and North-east too, and are open to travelling in the country for sensitization programmes with principals and teachers. All costs outside Calcutta are to be borne by the hosts.

• Ms Baitali Ganguly, Secretary, Jabala, 9, Bank Colony, Ground Floor, Dhakuria, Calcutta 700 031. Phone: 483 3408.

Works in middle-class areas and schools with the dual-language facility of Bengali. Conducts sensitization sessions with schoolteachers and awareness campaigns in schools.

chennai

• Dr Vijay Nagaswami, C-8, Alsa Towers, 186 Poonamallee High Road, Kilpauk, Chennai 600 010. Phone: (area std code: 044) 6412427. Fax: 6429749 e-mail: vnagaswami@vsnl.com

Works with adolescents and adults.

delhi

• Ms Naina Kapur, Director, Sakshi, B—67, South Extension One, First Floor, New Delhi 110 065. Phone: (area std code: 011) 4623295. Fax: 4643946 e-mail: s.sakshi@mailcity.com

Provides legal aid for sexually abused children as also counselling; women who are situated in such violence are also counselled. Sakshi's panel of lawyers assist on the police, medical and judicial process of a Child Sexual Abuse case.

- Ms Jasjit Purewal or Ms Javita Narang, Ifsha (Interventions for Support, Healing and Awareness), C-52 South Extension Two, New Delhi 110 049. Phone: 011- 6253289. Fax: 011- 6253298
e-mail: ifsha@vsnl.com
Counsels cases of Child Sexual Abuse as also adults who have been sexually abused in childhood. Ifsha also conducts awareness-raising interactive workshops for school children. In three Delhi schools they have worked with the same group of students over a period of nine months and divided the workshop into three phases each addressing issues like gender stereotypes, socialisation, body, self-esteem, imagery, sexual abuse and exploitation. Schools outside Delhi are being covered by workshops in similar same-group batches for five days at a time, a fixed two-hours a day, with a gap of around three months between each five-day phase. However, the number of days and hours for schools outside Delhi are flexible. Ifsha also conducts workshops all over the country on several aspects of Child Sexual Abuse and its healing in both adults and children.

goa

- Dr Nandita de Souza, Sangath Centre for Child Development and Family Guidance, 841/1, Alto Porvorim, Goa 403 521. Phone: (area std code: 0832) 414916 e-mail: sangath@goa1.dot.net.in
Dr de Souza's phone: 417458,
her e-mail: ndesouza@goa1.dot.net.in
She counsels children. Sangath works in the area of child development and the behavioural and mental health of families. Sangath also conducts workshops on childhood and sexuality for parents, teachers and other

carers of children. The multidisciplinary team of professionals which works with victims of sexual abuse at Sangath includes the developmental and behavioural paediatrician Dr de Souza, psychiatrist Dr Vikram Patel, psychologist Gracy Andrew and social worker Fiona Dias Saxena whose phone number is 413556. Her e-mail: fiona_dias@usa.net

She counsels children and young adults of both sexes as part of her work at Sangath. Uses a therapeutic approach which covers at least five sessions not just with the victim but in participation with a significant other; in the case of children who are sexually abused, it is mostly the mother who enters the counselling as the significant other. Works extensively on conflict resolution in the child.

- Ms Nishtha Desai, Campaign Against Paedophilia, F-2 Anandi Apartments, Bablo Naik Colony, Opposite St Inez Church, Panaji, Goa 403 001. Phones: 222397, 420141, 421082. e-mail: crg@goa1.dot.net.in

Specifically liaises between local police and people to stem the rising number of paedophiles entering Goa.

hyderabad

- Dr Madhusudan Joshi, Padmavati Health Centre, Basheerbagh, Hyderabad 500 029. Phone: (area std code: 040) 3220997 (residence), 3227649 (office) e-mail: msjoshi@hd2.dot.net.in

Counsels children, adolescents and adults.

lucknow

- Ms Tulika Srivastava, Association for Advocacy and Legal Initiatives (Aali), C-33A, Sector A, Mahanagar, Lucknow 226 006. Phone: (area std code: 0522) 326936 e-mail: aali@lw1.vsnl.net.in

Provides legal assistance for women and children.

mumbaii

- Dr Amit Desai, 41 Sunder Mahal, Third Floor, 141 Marine Drive, Mumbaii 400 020. Phone: (area code: 022) 2046715. Also attends a clinic for the suburbanites at Rajaveer Clinic, 303 Kannaiya, Third Floor, 250-B Linking Road, Bandra West, Mumbaii 400 050. Phones: 6400580, 6557439. Residence: 2815240, 2816636 e-mail: shaista@bol.net.in
Counsels children, teenagers and adults; refers severely distressed child cases to the specialist Dr Manek Bharucha.

- Dr Manoj Bhatwadekar, 5, Sahar Tower, Parsiwadi, Sahar Road, Andheri East, Mumbaii 400 099. Phone: 8214353.
Counsels children, teenagers and adults.

- Ms Kalindi Muzumdar, Roxana, Third Floor, 109 Maharishi Karve Road, Next to the Income Tax office, Mumbaii 400 020. Phone: 2063322.
Counsels both sexes, male and female, and all ages, children to teenagers to adults.

- Advocate Flavia Agnes, Majlis, A-2/4 Golden Valley, Kalina-Kurla Road, Kalina, Santa Cruz East, Mumbaii 400 098. Phones: 6180394, 6160252. Fax: 6148539 e-mail: majlis@vsnl.com
Provides legal services for women and children.

One man picks up a finger, a part of his body, a bottle and violates a child.

One man. One child.

Then more men. Many more children.

Thus, now, a situation which has turned so serious in the country that multi-disciplinary and multi-agency approaches need to be urgently undertaken to prevent Child Sexual Abuse in India as also protect the child.

If you agree that the laws need to be urgently put in place to protect the child, please write to the Union Law Minister at 401, C Wing, Shastri Bhawan, New Delhi 110 001. Fax: 3384241.

If you agree that Child Protection Courts (CPCs) need to be set up, please write to the Union Law Minister at the address and fax number given above.

If you agree that Child Protection Units (CPUs) need to be an important part of policing, please write to the Union Home Minister at 104, North Block, New Delhi 110 001. Fax: 3014221.

If you think the two key political parties—the Congress and the Bharatiya Janata Party—need to be equally concerned about the issues around Child Sexual Abuse please write to them at Congress, 10 Janpath, New Delhi 110 011. Bharatiya Janata Party, 7, Race Course Road, New Delhi 110 011.

Please send a copy of all your letters to the Prime Minister of India, 152, South Block, New Delhi 110 011. Fax: 3016857

And please play your role, the most important one, to protect the child. Remember it begins in, and around, a child's house. Only parents can stop it. After them, the principals and teachers of the child.

There is no final way of arriving at a statistic which would indicate whether Child Sexual Abuse is increasing or not. What is clear, however, is that it is not a static crime. Therefore working with the percentages mentioned in this book—25 per cent of boys and 40 per cent of girls under sixteen years of age—and applying them to population projections provided by government, here are some figures. The central statistical office categorizes children from 15 to 19 in a separate sub-group. Therefore the calculations here are totaled for children up to 14 years of age. This perforce omits children who are 15 and 16 years of age. This also means that the figures you read below are actually an under-representation of the numbers of children who would have been sexually abused in India by the year 2002.

If their parents and guardians do not step in to stop it.

- 4,15,94,735 young boys.
- 6,28,53,160 young girls.

•